Contemporary Approaches
to Public Budgeting

Contemporary Approaches
to Public Budgeting

Edited by

Fred A. Kramer
University of Massachusetts

Winthrop Publishers, Inc.
Cambridge, Massachusetts

Library of Congress Cataloging in Publication Data

Main entry under title:
    Contemporary approaches to public budgeting.

    Includes bibliographical references.
    1. Budget—United States.   2. Program budgeting—United
States.   3. Management by objectives.   4. Zero-base budgeting—
United States.   I. Kramer, Fred A.
HJ2052.C65   353.007'22   79-1101
ISBN 0-87626-168-3

Cover design by David Ford

© 1979 by Winthrop Publishers, Inc.
17 Dunster Street, Cambridge, Massachusetts 02138

10   9   8   7   6   5   4   3   2

To Margaret B. Kramer, my mother.
May her optimism become contagious.

Contents

Preface

Contemporary Approaches to Public Budgeting seeks to serve two purposes. First, it can be used to cover the mandatory budgeting section in introductory public administration courses where the instructor uses a series of paperbacks rather than a single textbook. Second, it can serve as a supplement in more specialized public budgeting courses. This reader should also be useful in those policy-oriented courses that integrate program analysis and evaluation with decision making in the public sector.

The volume is organized to encourage discussion. First the question of politics versus analysis is raised. Then each section presents one of the major budgetary reforms of the past fifteen or twenty years from the viewpoints of advocates of the techniques, describes the use of each technique at either the local, state, or national level, and provides theoretical criticism of the technique. The concluding section deals with implementing budget reforms.

Students in my seminars in public budgeting and systematic analysis and introduction to public administration courses at the University of Massachusetts are familiar with these selections from their visits to the reserve room at the library. Their response—and the encouragement of Winthrop's Jim Murray—led me to make these selections available to other students and instructors of public budgeting.

Alison Mills copyedited the manuscript and designed the book. I thank her for improving my prose and making the production of this volume progress smoothly.

I acknowledge my debt to the authors of these articles. I think they share my desire to make public budgetary analysis and politics comprehensible and maybe even fun.

F.A.K.

ix

Contemporary Approaches
to Public Budgeting

Traditional Simplification Versus Systematic Analysis

1

In the early seventies, the Council of State Governments published a text called *Changing State Budgeting*. The text's author, Kenneth Howard, noted that the title was chosen to reflect two meanings of changing. First, state budgeting was in the process of changing. And second, people should actively try to change state budgeting. Howard's reasons for choosing such a title are valid today for budgeting at all levels of American government. Public budgeting is changing. A new breed of public manager is making it change more.

Budgetary behavior reflects the continuum of decision theories. At one end, as figure 1 shows, are rational-comprehensive, or systems, theories that emphasize economic rationality in decision making. At the other end are incremental theories that emphasize political criteria and limit the scope of individual decisions.[1] Rarely are administrative decisions based solely on either economic or political rationality. Instead, as I have argued in another forum, "the basic polar positions . . . have not changed in theory, but, in practice, a *modus vivendi* has been achieved."[2]

Tension still exists between political/incremental budgetary decision making and decision making based on systematic analysis

1

Figure 1
Decision Theory Continuum

Systems Analysis   Incremental
                              Mixed

Economic Rationality   Political Rationality

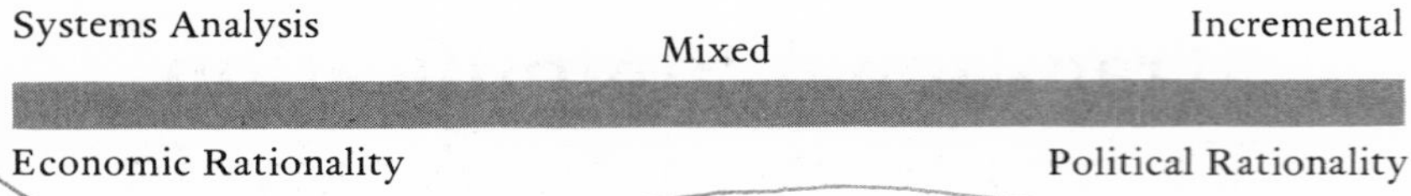

and planning. In some cases, analytic work has altered the style of argument if not the outcome.[3] Most decisions made in government are based on a mixed decision model in which certain analytic techniques clarify the issues but values and political power determine who wins and loses.

Modern budgetary techniques claim to move budgetary decisions more toward the economic rationality end of the decision theory continuum, but all of the techniques discussed in this volume can be used for political purposes. Indeed, I argue in the following selection that these techniques are a centralizing tool that is not politically neutral. Gene Fisher, in the second article, presents systematic planning and analysis as a tool that helps us make better decisions.

Notes

1. Charles Lindblom, "The Science of 'Muddling Through,' " *Public Administration Review* vol. 19 (Spring 1959), pp. 79–88. Also see his *Intelligence of Democracy* (New York: The Free Press, 1965).

2. Fred A. Kramer, "Policy Analysis as Ideology," *Public Administration Review* vol. 35, no. 5 (September–October 1975), p. 509. Both the Lindblom and the Kramer articles are reprinted in Kramer, ed., *Perspectives on Public Bureaucracy*, 2nd ed. (Cambridge, Mass.: Winthrop Publishers, 1977).

3. Such predictions were made during the sixties. See William M. Capron, "The Impact of Analysis on Bargaining in Government," paper delivered before the American Political Science Association Annual Meeting, New York City, September 1966. Reprinted in Louis C. Gawthrop, *The Administrative Process and Democratic Theory* (Boston: Houghton Mifflin, 1970), pp. 354–71.

An Introduction to
Contemporary Public Budgeting

Fred A. Kramer

Ever since V. O. Key bemoaned the lack of budgetary theory in the forties, public managers and public policy scholars have sought to develop ways .to answer his question: "On what basis shall it be decided to allocate X dollars to Activity A instead of Activity B?"[1] The managers and scholars have suggested a number of answers—many of them touted as panaceas.

Performance budgeting—tying workload measures to various governmental activities—was supposed to be the answer in the fifties. Planning-programming-budgeting systems devised by economists were to be the way of the sixties. Management by objectives was to pick up the pieces of earlier budget reform failures in the early seventies. Zero-base budgeting is today's answer, and a variant of all these reforms, mission budgeting, is on the horizon.

All these answers to the Key question have failed to deliver what their most zealous supporters had promised.

The public budgeting techniques have failed to live up to the expansive expectations of their advocates because, as Aaron Wildavsky has pointed out, they failed to recognize that politics is a legitimate way to answer Key's question.[2] Some decision makers, borrowing from business experience and welfare economics theory, have tried to substitute rationality in the form of dollars-and-cents analysis for political judgments. Although only a handful of the most ardent supporters of these techniques would argue that economic

A different version of this essay appeared in Kramer, *Dynamics of Public Bureaucracy* (Cambridge, Mass.: Winthrop Publishers, 1977), chapter 8.

standards must be substituted for political ones, the forms and processes of governmental budgeting in many jurisdictions have been affected by these new techniques. Public budgeting is still political, but the techniques of political accommodation in the budgetary process in the United States have been changing in the past two decades.

Contemporary public budgeting at all levels still operates in a political milieu. Increasingly, however, strong executives have used modern techniques to accomplish two purposes: (1) to develop meaningful alternatives to enhance the role of centralized decision makers, and (2) to demand program results through program analysis and evaluation. These dual purposes of modern budgeting techniques appear at all levels of government although the more sophisticated techniques are more often employed in larger jurisdictions, which have the resources to support them.

Each of the three techniques discussed in the selections that follow—program budgeting, management by objectives (MBO), and zero-base budgeting (ZBB)—seeks to enable governments to deal with program information in a systematic way. Although acceptance of each of these techniques has been mixed, apparently each has succeeded under certain conditions. Program budgeting, although discarded at the national level in 1971, has received support in Pennsylvania and the city of San Diego. Management by objectives is being used in New Mexico and in many other jurisdictions. Zero-base budgeting is being tried in the federal government and has been used in Georgia, Texas, and at the local level in other states. The varying degrees of success of these techniques suggest that there are many ways to reach the goals of management control through centralization of budgetary decision making and use of program evaluation.

This introduction emphasizes the political aspects of traditional budgeting, which still are a major part of the governmental budgeting process. The other selections in this volume show the possibilities and difficulties of the three main budgetary reforms of the past twenty years: program budgeting, MBO, and ZBB. Examples of how the techniques have been used at the state, federal, and local levels are included. In addition, since all of these techniques have a common source in program analysis and share similar implementation problems, articles dealing with these subjects have been chosen.

Public Budgeting Defined

Simply stated, a budget is a plan. A budget document is a reflection of what we expect to do in the future. Not all plans are budgets, however. We may have a plan to retrain highly specialized aerospace scientists to solve urban problems. We may know what courses and methods of training we would like to use. We may know what organizations we plan to use as consultants on the project, and we may even know what universities or training institutes we want to do the retraining. But even a highly detailed plan is not a budget until we specify how much money we are willing to commit to the project. A budget, therefore, is special kind of plan in that it is concerned with money. It deals with how much a government plans to spend and how that expenditure is to be financed.

A budget deals with expenditure and revenue questions for a specific future time period, usually a *fiscal year*. A fiscal year is any consecutive twelve-month period a jurisdiction has chosen to define as its budget year. In some jurisdictions the fiscal year is concurrent with the calendar year. For most state governments the fiscal year runs from July 1 through June 30. The United States government used to operate on that timetable but shifted the fiscal year to October 1 through September 30 as part of congressional reforms of the budget process that were passed in 1974.

When passed by the legislature and signed by the chief executive of a particular jurisdiction, a budget becomes law. The amounts of money specified in the budget document are legally binding during that fiscal year. Agencies cannot spend more than is specified unless they are able to get supplemental or deficiency appropriations through the same legal channels as the original budget. Although a formal budget is legally binding only for the fiscal year for which it was designed, some budget documents show the implications of current budget decisions for spending in future years.

A budget is more than simply a legally binding financial plan. It is also a multipurpose document that reflects and seeks to serve the information needs of the participants in the budgetary process. Allen Schick, one of the foremost authorities on both the politics and techniques of budgeting, has suggested that the budget has three main uses: (1) control, (2) management, and (3) planning.[3] A budget controls administrators by tying them to the stated policies of their superiors and legislative overseers. Control through a budget is obtained through accounting practices and reporting procedures that restrict the transfer of funds from one account to another, limit the number of positions available to an agency, and create mountains of paperwork. Such procedures are thought necessary to keep lower-level bureaucrats accountable to their superiors and to discourage affronts to fiscal integrity—i.e., stealing public funds.

The management function of a budget involves efforts to carry out the approved plans and policies efficiently and effectively. The management function is one of the principal roles of central budgeting offices at all levels of government in the United States. In part, renaming the Bureau of the Budget (BOB) the Office of Management and Budget (OMB) in 1970 was recognition of the potential management role that a budgeting office can play in designing and coordinating organization units. Some budget documents include information on costs and workloads that is helpful to program managers and higher-level decision makers in both the executive and legislative branches.

Managerial information needs often influence the planning aspects of budgeting. In the budgetary context, as Schick has pointed out, "planning involves the determination of objectives, the evaluation of alternative courses of action, and the authorization of select programs."[4] Planning in this sense is closely linked to broad policy choices. Because of the incremental nature of much policy decision making, planning in the budget process reflects political pressures as well as financial analysis.

Traditional Budgeting

None of the budgeting reforms has had a revolutionary impact on public budgeting. Traditional budgeting has been changing through the gradual acceptance of reforms rather than dramatic breakthroughs. Many aspects of traditional budgeting survive because of the complexity and uncertainty of the budgetary process. In many jurisdictions the key institutional actors in budgetary decision making continue to play the roles they have played in the past. As Wildavsky has suggested, the agencies decide how much money to ask for, the central budget office decides how much to recommend, and the legislative appropriations committees have the final say on how much to give. Often these participants agree on ways to simplify the process to make it manageable.[5]

Wildavsky has suggested two concepts—*base* and *fair share*—that have enabled participants to handle budgeting in the real world:

> The base is the general expectation among the participants that programs will be carried on at close to the going level of expenditures but it does not necessarily include all activities. Having a project included in the agency's base thus means establishing the expectation that the expenditure will continue, that it is accepted as part of

what will be done, and, therefore, that it will not normally be subjected to intensive scrutiny.[6]

The base, in other words, represents those programs that all participants agree are a legitimate part of an agency's responsibility and should not be seriously questioned.

Fair share differs from the base. According to Wildavsky, "Fair share means not only the base an agency has established but also the expectation that it will receive some proportion of funds, if any, which are to be increased over or decreased below the base of the various governmental agencies."[7] The agencies, the central budget office, and the appropriations committees agree that budgeting should be incremental; that is, changes in agency budgets should be relatively small and in proportion to overall budget changes.

The notions of fair share and base support a picture of the budgetary process that is not grounded in rational-comprehensive analysis. Instead of having to justify all programs every year as would be the case in a true "zero-base" budget, the agency, which always has a key role in defining how much money it wants, concentrates on making marginal increases for so-called quality improvements and trying to get new programs accepted as part of the base. Figure 1 presents the budgeting activities that go on at the agency level.

Of course, there are constraints upon an agency's actions. In the federal government, directives from either the president or the director of the Office of Management and Budget (OMB) indicate what the budget request ceilings should be. Under normal conditions these ceilings will be in line with the base and fair-share concepts. In some cases, however, OMB or the White House may force an evaluation of some agency programs. If an agency or bureau is singled out for an in-depth evaluation, it is forced into a defensive posture of trying to justify its program without the luxury of an accepted base.

In the traditional incremental budgeting process, agencies in all jurisdictions must justify their programs. But many of these programs have become accepted parts of the business of government, and other participants do not expect, or want to see, detailed cost-benefit justifications for them. Budget reviewers choose to concentrate on newer programs or areas marked for drastic increases. This means that some programs that have outlived their usefulness will continue to claim their "fair share" for years. Perhaps this is a price that society can afford to pay. Given limited time and expertise, concentrating on new programs or exceptional increases in old ones might be a sensible control strategy for budget reviewers.

Figure 1
The Real Agency Budget Process

- Last year's appropriation
- Automatic increases for existing personnel
- Cost of inflation to continue existing level of services
- Cost of additional service by unit
- New program costs—"quality" improvements

Agency Budget Strategies

Wildavsky's seminal work catalogued agency budget strategies, which confirmed the symbiotic relationships between agency, clientele, and legislative committee. Wildavsky found several people active in the budget process who emphasized that success in the budget game was not based on how good the budget estimates were but how good a politician the administrator was. "Being a good politician . . . requires essentially three things: cultivation of an active clientele, the development of confidence among other government officials, and skill in following strategies that exploit one's opportunities. . . ."[8]

Cultivation of clientele involves identifying the groups that benefit from an agency's service, encouraging them to demand more of the service, and accommodating them. Depending upon the clientele's political power, agencies can successfully lean on them for support at points in the budget process. Wildavsky notes that it makes good political sense to encourage advisory groups, to mobilize favorable opinion, and to link a faltering program to a more popular one (the Weather Bureau linked itself to a Polaris submarine program during the 1960s). Wildavsky cautions that agencies should not become captives of their clientele, however.

Since the budgetary process takes place in an uncertain atmosphere, the participants find it beneficial to trust one another. Wildavsky views this as a key element for agencies because they perceive that other participants in the process can hurt them if the agencies prove untrustworthy. Gaining the confidence of others depends on informal contact between agency people and legislative committee members and staff. Such informal contact, especially with members of the legislature, furthers agency success and strengthens the relationships.

Strategies to increase an agency's chances of getting an acceptable budget take many forms. Wildavsky notes that administrators can prepare for hostile questions during legislative appropriation hearings by staging mock hearings in advance. Using informal relationships with legislators, agencies can "plant" favorable questions, or they can comply with requests for information from hostile participants by deluging them with paper. Sympathetic participants can be given information that will help the agency. Although Wildavsky notes that there is no substitute for an administrator's being familiar with his or her budget, an aggressive defense of an agency's request clearly requires much more than accounting expertise.

Agency administrators play the role of advocate for their programs, but this should not surprise us. Agencies are vitally concerned with the programs that they can develop, operate, and expand. As John Wanat points out:

> Agencies prosper—and their personnel prosper—when clients are pleased, and clients are pleased when favorable programs are operational or forthcoming. Since agency personnel do not have any responsibility for collecting money, they do not worry about balanced budgets or fiscal probity but leave such worries to others. Agencies, however, are in constant contact with substantive problems needing solutions and clients desiring service.[9]

Agencies see the budget process from a programmatic perspective that is influenced by the professional needs of their own personnel and the desires of their interest group constituencies.

Thomas Anton, who studied state budgetary behavior, sees a related reason for the agency advocacy role. He suggests that agency administrators seek larger budgets every year to show agency personnel that they are engaged in worthwhile activities that should command a larger share of the public purse each year. Asking for more—even more than the administrators expect to receive—also shows that the administrators are aggressive and competent. By asking for more than they expect to receive, agency administrators allow the central budget officers to play their role of cutting agency requests and deciding how much to recommend.[10]

The Central Budget Office

In all but the smallest jurisdictions, central budget offices coordinate the executive budget-making process and perform other management functions for the chief executive. In addition to performing the obvious budget estimation, preparation, and execution functions, well-developed central budgeting offices review legislative proposals from the agencies to ensure that they conform to the chief executive's program. They also assess the impact such legislation may have on future budgets. This central clearance of legislation is important since many legislative proposals are developed by the administrative agencies themselves. Central budgeting offices are often involved in standardizing forms, statistical measures, and data processing procedures to aid in governmental management. They also may have responsibilities with personnel, which in many jurisdictions involves a large proportion of governmental expenditures.

The central budgeting office can routinely provide the chief executive with the information it gathers to support budget requests. Information sharing is a two-way street, however. Not only can the central budget office serve as a channel to let the chief executive know what is happening at the agency levels, but it can also let the agencies know what the chief executive's priorities are. Since the central budget office has frequent contact with the agencies, perhaps this dual educational role is its most important function. Figure 2 summarizes these functions, all of which are performed at the national level by the Office of Management and Budget (OMB).[11]

Today it is hard to imagine large-scale governments operating without the guidance and coordination of central budgeting offices, but the development of such offices is relatively recent. Even at the national level there was no central budgeting office until 1921. Until then each agency prepared and submitted its budget to the relevant appropriations subcommittees in Congress. The result was chaos and what appeared to be uncontrolled increases in the federal budget. The Budget and Accounting Act of 1920 established a central budgeting office, the Bureau of the Budget, as part of the Treasury Department. The BOB was moved to the Executive Office of the President when that office was established as a result of the Brownlow Committee reforms in 1939. In 1970, acting on recommendations of the Ash Council, President Richard Nixon implemented a reorganization plan that recognized the management role of the BOB by renaming it the Office of Management and Budget.

Although formal organizational arrangements differ, central budgeting offices at all levels in American government provide needed staff services to the chief executive and usually attract people who consider themselves the elite of public bureaucracy. Since one of the principal problems of chief executives is to find out what the bureaucracy is doing, they have a strong tendency to rely on central budget offices to provide that information. These offices have responded by attempting to develop reporting systems that can provide

Figure 2
Central Budget Office Functions

- Budget estimation and preparation
- Budget execution
- Legislative clearance
- Standardization of administrative procedures
- Educational role between chief executive and agencies and vice versa

information on agency programs. In the federal government, the Office of Management and Budget and its predecessor agency, the Bureau of the Budget, sought to implement such systems as planning-programming-budgeting (PPB) and management by objectives (MBO), which were later discarded in favor of zero-base budgeting (ZBB). OMB officials may pay lip service to the needs of individual agencies in implementing budget reforms, but their key role in developing and operating the budget machinery gives them additional power in relation to the other participants in the budgetary process. Even though central budgeting staffers might see themselves as philosopher-kings capable of acting in the public interest, they can become the subject of political controversy.[12]

There is potential for ill feelings between central budget officials and legislators. Legislators jealously protect their prerogatives, especially their powers of the purse. Sometimes they feel that the central budgeting office intends to operate the government as it wishes. Since the central budgeting office is usually identified with the chief executive, legislative criticism of that office is often a way of criticizing the chief executive without appearing to do so. Central budget officials sometimes react arrogantly to legislative efforts to initiate or control programs. This attitude is summed up by the statement of a former OMB official who said, only partly in jest, that he never saw a good idea come out of Congress.[13]

The Legislative Role

Although legislatures at most levels in the United States are laboring under a cloud of public doubt about their competence, they play a key role in the budget process. In most American jurisdictions the executive branch, through the chief executive and the central budgeting office, drafts the budget. The legislators have the power to approve or deny the budget proposals. Historically, control of the public purse by legislatures has been the main control on executive action.

Perhaps, however, the role of legislatures in budgeting is primarily symbolic rather than real.[14] Nevertheless, we can reasonably make several assumptions about legislative intentions concerning budgeting:

> First, legislatures review budget proposals with the intent of making decisions about policies, programs, and the allocation of resources. Second, they aim to make these decisions in a more or less rational manner, and rationality, as tempered by the political realities of the time, is deemed a desirable goal. Third, procedures, practices, and organization machinery play an important role in determining the rationality of decision making and the effectiveness of controls over spending.[15]

How close legislatures come to reaching these goals is related to the skill of the legislators and their staff support. Many jurisdictions in the United States lack skilled legislators and staff support of any kind.

At the national level, the appropriations subcommittees of Congress used to view themselves as guardians of the public treasury.[16] In the late 1960s and early 1970s the appropriations committees gave up this role and supported larger budgets for the agencies they were to control. The seemingly uncontrolled rise in the federal budget combined with delays in funding—rarely during the 1960s did Congress complete action on all appropriations bills before the start of the fiscal year—renewed the criticism that the congressional budget review procedure was too fragmented to allow Congress a meaningful role in the budget process.

In an effort to reassert legislative prerogatives in the budgetary process, Congress passed the Congressional Budget Reform and Impoundment Act of 1974. The act set up a Congressional Budget Office (CBO) and changed the fiscal year. Figure 3 presents the new budget timetable for congressional action. The president's current services budget spells out the figure needed to keep government programs operating at the same level during the next fiscal year. Presenting the current services budget in November is supposed to give the Congressional Budget Office time to identify ongoing programs Congress might want to prune. In addition to a current services budget, the Office of Management and Budget must present Congress with a complete list of tax expenditures, which are tax breaks or subsidies to those who qualify. An example of a tax expenditure is the liberal

Figure 3
Congressional Budget Timetable

On or before:	*Action to be completed:*
November 10	President submits current services budget.
15th day after Congress convenes	President submits his budget.
March 15	Committees submit reports to budget committees.
April 1	Congressional Budget Office submits report to budget committees.
April 15	Budget committees report first concurrent resolution on the budget to their Houses.
May 15	Committees report bills authorizing new budget authority.
May 15	Congress adopts first concurrent resolution on the budget.
7th day after Labor Day	Congress completes action on bills providing budget authority.
September 15	Congress completes actions on second required concurrent resolution on the budget.
September 25	Congress completes action reconciliation process implementing second concurrent resolution.
October 1	Fiscal year begins.

Source: *The United States Budget in Brief, Fiscal Year 1977* (Washington, D.C.: U.S. Government Printing Office, 1976), p. 51.

allowance for depreciation of rental property available to real estate owners before they compute their taxes. Tax expenditures used to bypass the entire budget process because they represented revenue that was never collected and so never appeared in agency programs as a subsidy. Still, such tax expenditures constitute federal aid to the beneficiaries in the same way direct payments to airlines or welfare recipients do. The budget reforms of 1974 have enhanced Congress's ability to act in a reasonable fashion in the budget process, although the congressional role is not as strong as the executive role in budgetary matters.

Legislative Budget Politics

Aaron Wildavsky and others who perceive the politics of the budgetary process as primarily an exercise in incrementalism have denigrated the legislature's policy-making role in the budget process. Studies of dollar amounts allocated to agencies and departments have shown that the changes from year to year are slight—that is, incremental.[17] There is, however, a developing body of scholarship that suggests a more positive role for the legislature, at least for Congress. Arnold Kanter has shown that Congress has favored some weapons systems over others and has put up the money to support its preferences.[18] Peter Natchez and Irving Bupp have reported similar findings with regard to the Atomic Energy Commission.[19] In these studies, certain agency programs experienced great growth and others survived cutbacks although the overall budget for the agency showed incremental change. The simple incremental model which assumes that legislatures seek to maintain stability in funding levels may hold at the agency level but not for specific programs.

Clearly, Congress does have some impact on programs and policies through the budget process. Perhaps as the reforms take hold they will have even greater impact. We can assume, therefore, that most programs are funded with congressional approval if not congressional blessing. Many programs benefit special interests. These remain on the books and are funded because Congress lacks the will to break up the symbiotic relationships between agency, clientele, and the relevant legislative committees (see figure 4). The political pressures that support ongoing programs are real. Policy subsystems based on specialized knowledge and interests do make policy in virtual seclusion unless other political pressures raise the level of conflict to a more visible arena. These policy decisions are reflected in the budget. For legislators to deal effectively with the complexity of budget problems, they must specialize. By specializing, they may become part of the symbiotic triangle. This inhibits the legislature from dealing with the budget as a whole, although the 1974 reforms have established machinery to do so.

Controlling the overall budget of any government jurisdictions means more than reviewing which special interests get what level of subsidy each year. At the state and national levels, a large proportion of each year's budget consists of expenditures that do not go through

Figure 4
Symbiotic Relationships of Political Bureaucracy

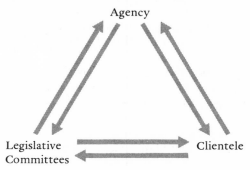

the appropriations process at all. At the national level such expenditures are in the form of permanent appropriations like revenue-sharing funds or *entitlement programs,* such as welfare, unemployment, and veterans' benefits. In these programs people who fall into a specific category are entitled by law to certain benefits. If unemployment is widespread because of a sluggish national economy, each unemployed person is entitled to benefits under existing laws. The government must make good on its legal commitment. Congress has no choice but to give money under these conditions. Funds must automatically be allocated to such programs, unless Congress decides to change the law regarding the particular entitlement program. State governments have many similar programs, which make a substantial portion of the budget virtually uncontrollable in any given year.

Legislative control through the budget process depends on many things. Legislatures must have the will to reassess old programs that benefit certain interests. They must understand the implications of entitlement programs before such programs become law. To do so, legislatures need increased budgetary staff. But even with larger staffs, there is only a limited amount of time and energy that a legislator can devote to budgetary problems. Political visibility, therefore, determines which elements in the budget come in for the closest scrutiny.

The Executive Branch and Budget Reform

The impetus for management and budgetary reform, however, has not come from legislatures but from executive branches. Pressed by revenue squeezes often caused by entitlement programs that force executives to recommend unpopular tax increases to meet demands for new programs, chief executives at all levels have sought to exert more control over the budget process. They have tried to force meaningful decision making at higher level in the executive branch by focusing on improved performance and better results from the various programs.[20]

But the values implied in this new executive concern for program results may run counter to the values of the traditional budget process. Peter F. Drucker, the father of management by objectives, has argued:

> The importance of a traditional budget-based institution is measured essentially by the size of its budget and the size of its staff. To achieve results with a smaller budget or a smaller staff is, therefore, not "performance." It might actually endanger the institution. Not to spend the budget to the hilt will only convince the budget maker—whether a legislature or a budget committee—that the budget for the next fiscal period can safely be cut.[21]

Under these conditions, Drucker adds, " 'Results' . . . means a larger budget. . . . And the budget is, by definition, related not to the achievement of any goals, but to the *intention* of achieving those goals."[22]

Program budgeting, management by objectives, and zero-base budgeting all aim to change these definitions of performance and results in government activities. Each of these techniques seeks to allow or even force government to set priorities and concentrate efforts. Implicit in each of these techniques is the view that executive leadership, backed by information developed through systematic planning and analysis, will be able to break the symbiotic political subsystems that have been nurtured through the budget-politics-as-usual traditional budget-making process.

While it is doubtful that these techniques will meet fully the management needs of public executives, they have provided a mechanism by which executive attention can be focused on programs in a systematic way through the budgetary process. These techniques, despite any claims to the contrary, enhance executive control through greater centralization of the budgetary process. They have the potential to improve budgetary decision making by systematically evaluating programs. There will continue to be tension between pure politics and pure analysis in the budgetary process. Political considerations will, and should, continue to play a major role in these decisions. But the development of modern budgetary techniques, which have gained limited acceptance in the past, probably will affect future budgetary decisions more and more.

Notes

1. V. O. Key, Jr., "The Lack of a Budgetary Theory," *American Political Science Review* vol. 34, no. 4 (December 1940), p. 1137.

2. Aaron Wildavsky, *The Politics of the Budgetary Process*, 2nd ed. (Boston: Little, Brown and Co., 1974), chapter 4.

3. Allen Schick, "Road to PPB: The Stages of Budget Reform," *Public Administration Review* vol. 26, no. 4 (December 1966), pp. 243–44.

4. *Ibid.*, p. 244.

5. Wildavsky, *Politics of the Budgetary Process*, chapter 2.

6. *Ibid.*, p. 17.

7. *Ibid.*

8. *Ibid.*, p. 64. Also see his chapter 3.

9. John Wanat, *Introduction to Budgeting* (North Scituate, Mass.: Duxbury Press, 1978), p. 51. Wanat suggests several additional actors in the budgetary process. See his chapter 4.

10. Thomas J. Anton, "Roles and Symbols in the Determination of State Expenditures," *Midwest Journal of Political Science* vol. 11 (1967), pp. 27–43.

11. James W. Davis and Randall B. Ripley, "The Bureau of the Budget and Executive Branch Agencies: Notes on Their Interaction," *Journal of Politics* vol. 29 (1967), pp. 749–69.

12. Joel Havemann, "Zero-Base Budgeting," *National Journal* vol. 9, no. 14 (April 2, 1977), p. 517.

13. Joel Havemann, "Executive Report/OMB's New Faces Retain Power, Structure Under Ford," *National Journal Reports* vol. 7, no. 30 (July 26, 1975), p. 1072.

14. Thomas J. Anton found the state legislature to be practically irrelevant to spending decisions in *The Politics of State Expenditure in Illinois* (Urbana, Ill.: University of Illinois Press, 1966), p. 246.

15. S. Kenneth Howard, *Changing State Budgeting* (Lexington, Ky.: Council of State Governments, 1973), p. 309.

16. Richard F. Fenno, Jr., "The House Appropriations Committee as a

Political System: The Problem of Integration," *American Political Science Review* vol. 60, no. 3 (September 1966), pp. 310–24; also Wildavsky, *op. cit.*

17. Wildavsky, *op. cit.*; and Otto A. Davis, M. A. H. Dempster, and Aaron Wildavsky, "A Theory of the Budgetary Process," *American Political Science Review* vol. 60, no. 3 (September 1966) pp. 529–30.

18. Arnold Kanter, "Congress and the Defense Budget: 1960–70," *American Political Science Review* vol. 66, no. 1 (March 1972), pp. 129–43.

19. Peter B. Natchez and Irving C. Bupp, "Policy and Priority in the Budgetary Process," *American Political Science Review* vol. 67, no. 3 (September 1973), pp. 951–63.

20. Anton, "Roles and Symbols in the Determination of State Expenditures," pp. 32–34.

21. Peter F. Drucker, "Managing the Public Service Institution," *Public Interest* no. 33 (Fall 1973) pp. 49–50.

22. *Ibid.*, p. 50.

The Role of
Cost-Utility Analysis
in Program Budgeting

Gene H. Fisher

. . . [P]rogram budgeting as envisioned in this [article] involves several essential considerations. The primary ones may be summarized under three main headings: structural (or format) aspects, analytical process considerations, and data or information system considerations to support the first two items.

The *structural* aspects of program budgeting are concerned with establishing a set of categories oriented primarily toward "end-product" or "end-objective" activities that are meaningful from a long-range-planning point of view.[1] In such a context emphasis is placed on provision for an extended time horizon—some five, even ten or more, years into the future. These characteristics are in marked contrast with conventional governmental budgeting, which stresses functional and/or object class categories and a very short time horizon.

Analytical process considerations pertain to various study activities conducted as an integral part of the program budgeting process. The primary objective of this type of analytical effort is to systematically examine alternative courses of action in terms of utility and cost, with a view to clarifying the relevant choices (and their implications) open to the decision-makers in a certain problem area.

Information system considerations are aimed at support of the first two items. There are several senses in which this is important, the primary ones being (1) progress reporting and control and (2) providing data and information to serve as a basis for the analytical process—especially to facilitate the development of estimating relationships that will permit making estimates of benefits and costs of alternative future courses of action.

The present [article] is concerned primarily with the second of the items listed above: analytical process considerations. That an analytical effort is an important part of program budgeting (at least as practiced in the Department of Defense) is made clear in a recent statement by Secretary of Defense McNamara:

> As I have pointed out in previous appearances before this Committee, in adding to a Defense program as large as the one we now have, we soon encounter the law of diminishing returns, where each additional increment of resources used produces a proportionately smaller increment of overall defense capability. While the benefits to be gained from each additional increment cannot be measured with precision, careful cost/effectiveness analyses can greatly assist in eliminating those program proposals which clearly contribute little to our military strength in terms of the costs involved.
>
> This principle is just as applicable to qualitative improvements in weapons systems as it is to quantitative increases in our forces. The relevant question is not only "Do we want the very best for our military force?", but also, "Is the additional capability truly required and, if so, is this the least costly way of attaining it?"
>
> Let me give you one hypothetical example to illustrate the point. Suppose we have two tactical fighter aircraft which are identical in every important measure of performance, except one—Aircraft A can fly ten miles per hour faster than Aircraft B. However, Aircraft A costs $10,000 more per unit than Aircraft B. Thus, if we need about 1,000 aircraft, the total additional cost would be $10 million.
>
> If we approach this problem from the viewpoint of a given amount of resources, the additional combat effectiveness represented by the greater speed of Aircraft A would have to be weighed against the additional combat effectiveness which the same $10 million could produce if applied to other defense purposes—more Aircraft B, more or better aircraft munitions, or more ships, or even more military family housing. And if we approach the problem from the point of view of a given amount of combat capability, we would have to determine whether that given amount could be achieved at less cost by buying, for example, more of Aircraft B or more aircraft munitions or better munitions, or perhaps surface-to-surface missiles. Thus, the fact that Aircraft A flies ten miles per hour faster than Aircraft B is not conclusive. We still have to determine whether the greater speed is worth the greater cost. *This kind of*

determination is the heart of the planning-programming-budgeting or resources allocation problem within the Defense Department [italics supplied].[2]

Numerous analytical approaches may be used to support the total program budgeting process. Here we shall focus on one of them: cost-utility analysis. Before turning to this subject, however, a few of the other types of analysis should be noted briefly.

In terms of the types of problems encountered in the total program budgeting process, one might think of a wide spectrum going all the way from major allocative decisions on the one hand to progress reporting and control on the other. Major allocative decisions involve such questions as: should more resources be employed in national security in the future, or in national health programs, or in preservation and development of natural resources, etc.?[3] Ideally, the decision-makers would like to plan to allocate resources in the future so that for a given budget, for example, the estimated marginal return (or utility) in each major area of application would be equal. But this is more easily said than done; and at the current state of analytical art, no one really knows with any precision how the "grand optimum" might be attained. In the main, the analytical tools now available (particularly the quantitative ones) are just not very helpful in dealing directly with such problems. Intuition and judgment are paramount.

At the other end of the spectrum—progress reporting and control—the main problem is to keep track of programs where the major decisions have *already been made*, to try to detect impending difficulties as programs are being implemented, and to initiate remedial actions through a feedback mechanism when programs are deemed likely to get out of control in the future. Numerous techniques are available for dealing with these types of program-management problems. Examples are the following: financial and management accounting techniques;[4] network-type systems for planning, scheduling, progress reporting, and control;[5] critical-path methods (within the framework of a network-type system);[6] Gantt chart techniques for program planning and control;[7] and various program management reporting and control schemes developed in recent years in the Department of Defense to help program managers in the management of complex weapon system development and production programs.[8]

The area between the ends of the spectrum is a broad and varied one, offering the oppotunity for applying a variety of analytical techniques. These techniques are focused primarily toward problem areas short of dealing with determination of the "grand optimum," although they can be of real assistance in sharpening the intuition and judgment of decision-makers in grappling with the very broad allocative questions. Technically, this is called "suboptimization," and it is here that the analytical efforts are likely to have the highest payoff.[9]

In cases where a wide range of alternative future courses of action needs to be examined in a broad suboptimization context, the main subject of this chapter, cost-utility analysis,[10] may well be the most useful analytical tool. However, in other cases where the suboptimization context is much narrower and a wide range of alternatives is not available, the problem may be one of examining relatively minor variations *within* an essentially prescribed future course of action. The suboptimization context may be relatively narrow for numerous reasons—severe political constraints, lack of new technology to provide the basis for a wide range of alternatives, etc. Here, something akin to capital budgeting[11] techniques may be most appropriate.

In many instances the above-mentioned techniques may have to be supplemented by other methods. For example, in numerous major decision problems it is not sufficient to deal only with the *direct* economic consequences of proposed alternative future courses of action, ignoring their possible indirect or spillover effects. In such instances it may well be vitally important to consider indirect economic effects either on the economy as a whole or on specified regions or sectors of the total economic system. Certain transportation problems involve considerations of this type.[12] Also, in the case of certain national security and space decisions, especially in the higher echelons of the decision hierarchy, it is often necessary to consider possible regional or industry sector economic impacts associated with alternative weapon system development and procurement choices.[13] One way to deal with such problems is through the use of macroeconomic models that attempt to take into account key interactions among important components of the economic system: for example, interindustry (input-output) models for the economy as a whole[14] and various types of regional models dealing with parts of the total national economy.[15]

Thus it is clear that numerous analytical methods and techniques exist that may be used to support various facets of the total program budgeting process. We have dealt with this point at some length to emphasize that the subject of this chapter, cost-utility analysis, is not the only analytical tool that might be used in program budgeting.

Let us now turn to our central theme. In the following paragraphs cost-utility analysis is discussed in somewhat general and abstract terms. . . .

What is Cost-Utility Analysis?

Attempting to define cost-utility analysis poses somewhat of a semantics problem. Numerous terms in current use convey the same general meaning but have important different meanings to different people: "cost-benefit analysis," "cost-effectiveness analysis," "systems analysis," "operations research," "operations analysis," etc. Because of such terminological confusion, in this [article] all these terms are rejected and "cost-utility analysis" is employed instead.

Cost-utility analysis, as envisioned here, may be distinguished by the following major characteristics:

1. A fundamental characteristic is the systematic examination and comparison of alternative courses of action that might be taken to achieve specified objectives for some future time period. It is important not only to systematically examine all the relevant alternatives that can be identified initially but also to *design additional ones* if those examined are found wanting.[16] Finally, the analysis, particularly if thoroughly and imaginatively done, may at times result in modifications of the initially specified objectives.

2. Critical examination of alternatives typically involves numerous considerations, but the two main ones are: assessment of the cost (in the sense of economic resource cost) and the utility (the benefits or gains) pertaining to each of the alternatives being compared to attain the stipulated objectives.

3. The time context is the future—often the distant future (five, ten, or more years).

4. Because of the extended time horizon, the environment is one of uncertainty—very often great uncertainty. Since uncertainty is an important facet of the problem, it should be faced and treated explicitly in the analysis. This means, among other things, that wherever possible the analyst should avoid the use of simple expected value models.

5. Usually the context in which the analysis takes place is broad (often very broad) and the environment very complex, with numerous interactions among the key variables in the problem. This means that simple, straightforward solutions are the exception rather than the rule.

6. While quantitative methods of analysis should be used as much as possible because of items 4 and 5 above,[17] purely quantitative work must often be heavily supplemented by qualitative analysis.

In fact, we stress the importance of *good* qualitative work and of using an appropriate combination of quantitative and qualitative methods.

7. Usually the focus is on research and development and/or investment-type decision problems, although operational decisions are sometimes encountered. This does not mean, of course, that operational considerations are ignored in dealing with R&D and investment-type problems.

8. Timeliness is important. A careful, thorough analysis that comes six months after the critical time of decision may be worth essentially zero, while a less thorough (but thoughtfully done) analysis completed on time may be worth a great deal.

The Primary Purpose of Cost-Utility Analysis

In the context being considered in this [article] let us be very clear about what is the main purpose of analysis in general, and cost-utility analysis in particular. Contrary to what some of the more enthusiastic advocates of quantitative analysis may think, we visualize cost-utility analysis as playing a somewhat modest, though very significant, role in the overall decision-making process. In reality, most major long-range-planning decision problems must ultimately be resolved primarily on the basis of intuition and judgment. We suggest that the main role of analysis should be to try to *sharpen* this intuition and judgment. In practically no case should it be assumed that the results of the analysis will *make* the decision. The really interesting problems are just too difficult, and there are too many intangible (e.g., political, psychological, and sociological) considerations that cannot be taken into account in the analytical process, especially in a quantitative sense. In sum, the analytical process should be directed toward assisting the decision-maker in such a way that (hopefully!) his intuition and judgment are better than they would be without the results of the analysis.[18]

Viewing the objective of cost-utility analysis in this way is likely to put the analyst in a frame of mine that will permit him to be much more useful to the decision-maker than if he takes a more hard-core view. There are two extremes here. On the one hand, it might be argued that the types of long-range-planning decision problems considered in this [article] are just too complex for the current state of analytical art to handle. Therefore, decisions must be made purely on the basis of intuition, judgment, and experience—i.e., the zero analysis position. At the other extreme are those who (naïvely) think that all problems should be tackled in a purely quantitative fashion, with a view essentially to making the decision. Such a view implies explicit (usually meaning quantitative) calculations of cost and utility for all the alternatives under consideration. This may be possible, at times, for very narrowly defined, low-level suboptimization problems; but even this is questionable.

More generally, in dealing with major decision problems of choice, if the analyst approaches his task in an inflexible hard-core frame of mind, he is likely to be in for trouble. For example, he may soon give up in complete frustration; or he may wind up with such a simplified model that the resulting calculations are essentially meaningless; or his conclusions may not be ready for presentation until two years after the critical decision time and would therefore be useless to the decision-maker.

The viewpoint taken here is that in most cases the relevant range is between the extremes mentioned above, and that in such a context there is a wide scope of analytical effort that can be useful. Furthermore, even when only a relatively incomplete set of quantitative calculations of cost and utility can be made (probably the general situation), much can be done to assist the decision-maker in the sense that the term "assistance" is used in this chapter. To repeat: the objective is to *sharpen* intuition and judgment. It is conceivable that even a small amount of sharpening may on occasion have a high payoff.

One other point seems relevant. In that rare circumstance when a fairly complete set of calculations of cost and utility is possible and a resulting conclusion about a preferred alternative is reached, it may well be that the conclusion itself is not the most useful thing to the decision-maker. For one thing, as pointed out earlier, the analysis usually cannot take everything into account—particularly some of the nebulous nonquantitative considerations. The decision-maker has to allow for these himself. But more important, most high-level decision-makers are very busy men who do not have time to structure a particular problem, think up the relevant alternatives (especially the *subtle* ones), trace out the key interactions among variables in the problem, etc. This the analyst, if he is competent, can do, and should do. And it is precisely this sort of contribution that may be most useful to the decision-maker. The fact that the analysis reaches a firm conclusion about a preferred alternative may in many instances be of secondary importance.

Some Major Considerations Involved in Cost-Utility Analysis

At this point, one might logically expect the title to be "How To Do Cost-Utility Analysis"—a cookbook, so to speak. We avoid this for two main reasons: (1) If such a treatise were attempted it would take an entire book; and more important, (2) it is doubtful that even a book on the subject is possible. At the current stage of development of analytical methods, cost-utility analysis is an art rather than a science. The really significant problems to be tackled are each in a sense unique, with the result that it is not possible to give a definitive set of rules on how to do an appropriate analysis. All that can be done is to give some guidelines, principles, and illustrative examples. But books, or major parts of books, have been written on this subject.[19] Here the treatment must of necessity be more limited.

Some important guidelines to be followed in carrying out a cost-utility analysis (not necessarily in order of relative importance) are discussed in the following paragraphs.[20]

Proper Structuring of the Problem and Design of the Analysis

This is by far the most important of the guidelines. Given an incredibly complex environment, that which is relevant to the problem at hand must be included, and that which is irrelevant excluded. There are no formal rules to guide us. The experience, skill, imagination, and intuition of the analyst are paramount. It is at this point—the *design* of the analysis—that most cost-utility studies either flounder hopelessly or move ahead toward success. In sum, if we can structure the problem so that the *right questions* are being asked, we shall be well on the way toward a good analysis. This sounds trite, but it really is not. The author has seen all too many instances of large amounts of effort being expended on an analytical exercise addressed to the wrong questions.[21]

Another point is that typically the problem and the design of the analysis may well have to be restructured several times. Considerations that were initially thought to be important may, after some preliminary work, turn out to be relatively unimportant, and vice versa. Finally, in the process of doing some of the analytical work new questions and new alternatives may come to mind.

The Conceptual Framework

In general there are two principal conceptual approaches:[22]

1. *Fixed utility approach.* For a specified level of utility to be attained in the accomplishment of some given objective, the analysis attempts to determine that alternative (or feasible combination of alternatives) likely to achieve the specified level of utility at the lowest economic cost.

2. *Fixed budget approach.* For a specified budget level to be used in the attainment of some given objective, the analysis attempts to determine that alternative (or feasible combination of alternatives) likely to produce the highest utility for the given budget level.

Either (or both) of these approaches may be used, depending on the context of the problem at hand. In any event, the objective is to permit *comparisons* to be made among alternatives, and for this purpose something has to be made fixed.

At this point a comment on the use of ratios (e.g., utility to cost ratios) seems in order. Very often such ratios are used to evaluate alternatives. The use of ratios usually poses no problem as long as the analysis is conducted in the framework outlined above (i.e., with the level of either utility or cost fixed). However, the author has on occasion seen studies where this was not done, with the result that the comparisons were essentially meaningless. For example, consider the following hypothetical illustration:

Alternatives	Utility (U)	Cost (C)	U/C
A	20	10	2
B	200	100	2

If the analysis is preoccupied with ratios, the implication of the above example is a state of indifference regarding the choice between A and B. But *should* the analyst be indifferent? Most probably not, because of the wide difference in scale between A and B. In fact, with such a great difference in scale, the analyst might not even be comparing relevant alternatives at all.[23]

Building the Model

Here the term "model" is used in a broad sense. Depending on the nature of the problem at hand, the model used in the analysis may

27

be formal or informal, very mathematical or not so mathematical, heavily computerized or only moderately so, etc. However, the main point is that the model need not be highly formal and mathematical to be useful. In any event, the following are some important points to keep in mind:

1. Model building is an art, not a science. It is often an experimental process.

2. The main thing is to try to include and highlight those factors that are relevant to the problem at hand, and to suppress (judiciously!) those that are relatively unimportant. Unless the latter is done, the model is likely to be unmanageable.

3. The main purpose in designing the model is to develop a meaningful *set of relationships* among objectives, the relevant alternatives available for attaining the objectives, the estimated cost of the alternatives, and the estimated utility for each of the alternatives.

4. Provision must be made for explicit treatment of uncertainty. (There will be more on this later.)

5. Since by definition a model is an abstraction from reality, the model must be built on a set of assumptions. These assumptions must be made *explicit*. If they are not, this is to be regarded as a defect on the model design.

Treatment of Uncertainty

Because most really interesting and important decision problems involve major elements of uncertainty, a cost-utility analysis of such problems must provide for explicit treatment of uncertainty. This may be done in numerous ways.

For purposes of discussion, two main types of uncertainty may be distinguished:

1. Uncertainty about the state of the world in the future. In a national security context, major factors are technological uncertainty, strategic uncertainty,[24] and uncertainty about the enemy and his reactions.

2. Statistical uncertainty. This type of uncertainty stems from chance elements in the real world. It would exist even if uncertainties of the first step were zero.

Type 2 uncertainties are usually the least troublesome to handle in cost-utility studies. When necessary, Monte Carlo[25] and/or other techniques may be used to deal with statistical fluctuations; but these perturbations are usually swamped by Type 1 uncertainties, which are dominant in most long-range planning problems. The use of elaborate techniques to treat statistical uncertainties in such problems is likely to be expensive window dressing.[26]

Type 1 uncertainties are typically present in most long-range decision problems, and they are most difficult to take into account in a cost-utility analysis. Techniques that are often used are sensitivity analysis, contingency analysis, and a fortiori analysis.[27]

Sensitivity Analysis Suppose in a given analysis there are a few key parameters about which the analyst is very uncertain. Instead of using "expected values" for these parameters, the analyst may use several values (say, high, medium, and low) in an attempt to see how sensitive the results (the ranking of the alternatives being considered) are to variations in the uncertain parameters.[28]

Contingency Analysis This type of analysis investigates how the ranking of the alternatives under consideration holds up when a relevant change in criteria for evaluating the alternatives is postulated, or a major change in the general environment is assumed. (For example, in a military context, the enemy is assumed to be countries A and B. We might then want to investigate what would happen if C joins the A and B coalition.)

A Fortiori Analysis Suppose that in a particular planning decision problem the generally accepted intuitive judgment strongly favors alternative X. However, the analyst feels that X might be a poor choice and that alternative Y might be preferred. In performing an analysis of X versus Y, the analyst may choose deliberately to resolve the major uncertainties in favor of X and see how Y compares under these adverse conditions. If Y still looks good, the analyst has a very strong case in favor of Y.

Creation of a New Alternative Although the three techniques listed above may be useful in a direct analytical sense, they may also contribute indirectly. For example, through sensitivity and contingency analyses the analyst may gain a good understanding of the really critical uncertainties in a given problem area. On the basis of this knowledge he might then be able to come up with a newly designed alternative that will provide a reasonably good hedge against a *range* of the more significant uncertainties. This is often difficult to do; but when it can be accomplished, it may offer one of the best ways to compensate for uncertainty.

Treatment of Problems Associated with Time

More likely than not, the particular problem at hand will be posed in a dynamic context; or at least the problem will have some dynamic aspects to it. While a "static"-type analysis can go a long way toward providing the decision-maker with useful information, very often this has to be supplemented by analytical work that takes time into account explicitly.

A case in point is with respect to the treatment of the estimated *costs* of the alternatives for a fixed level of utility.[29] The nature of the problem may be such that the costs have to be time-phased, resulting in cost streams through time for each of the alternatives. The question then arises whether the decision-maker is or is not indifferent with respect to the time impact of the costs. If he is not indifferent concerning time preference, then the cost streams have to be "discounted" through time, using an appropriate rate of discount.[30] Determining specifically what rate to use can be a problem; but it is usually manageable.[31] If it is not, an upper bound rate and a lower bound rate may be used to see whether it really makes any difference in the final conclusions of the problem.

It should be pointed out that the analyst pays a price for introducing time explicitly into an analysis:[32]

1. It complicates the analysis by increasing the number of variables and hence the number of calculations. If we put time in, we may have to take something else out.

2. As implied above, it complicates the selection of a criterion for evaluating alternatives: solution X may be better for 1966 and worse for 1970; solution Y may be just the reverse.

Validity Checking

In the preceding paragraphs we have discussed building the analytical model, "exercising" the model (sensitivity and contingency analysis), etc. Another important consideration (often relatively neglected) is checking the validity of the model. Because the model is only a representation of reality, it is desirable to do some sort of checking to see if the analytical procedure used is a reasonably good representation, within the context of the problem at hand. This is difficult to do, especially in dealing with problems having a time horizon five, ten, or more years into the future.

In general, we cannot test models of this type by methods of "controlled experiment." However, the analyst might try to answer the following questions:[33]

1. Can the model describe known facts and situations reasonably well?

2. When the principal parameters involved are varied, do the results remain consistent and plausible?

3. Can it handle special cases in which we already have some indication as to what the outcome should be?

4. Can it assign causes to known effects?

Qualitative Supplementation

We have already stressed the importance of qualitative considerations in cost-utility analysis—particularly qualitative *supplementation* of the quantitative work. Introduction of qualitative considerations may take several forms:

1. Qualitative analysis per se as an integral part of the total analytical effort.

2. Interpretation of the quantitative work.

3. Discussion of relevant nonquantitative considerations that could not be taken into account in the "formal" analysis.

The latter item can be particularly important in presenting the results of a study to the decision-maker. The idea is to present the results of the formal quantitative work, interpret these results, and then say that this is as far as the formal quantitative analysis per se will permit us to go. However, there are important *qualitative* considerations that you (the decision-maker) should try to take into account; and here they are (list them). Finally, relevant questions about each of the qualitative items can be raised and important interrelations among them discussed.

Summary Comments

We stress again that the discussion above pertains to a long-range-planning context, with emphasis on specifying, clarifying, and comparing the relevant alternatives. Because comparative analysis is the prime focus, it is vitally important continually to emphasize *consistency* in the analytical concepts, methods, and techniques used. That is, instead of trying for a high degree of accuracy in an *absolute* sense (which is usually unattainable anyway), the analyst should stress development and use of procedures that will treat the alternatives being considered in an unbiased, consistent manner.

The main points presented in this [article] may be summarized as follows:

1. An analytical activity is an important part of the total program budgeting process.

2. Cost-utility analysis pertains to the systematic examination and comparison of alternative courses of action that might be taken to achieve specified objectives for some future time period. Not only is it important to examine all relevant alternatives that can be identified initially but it is also important to design additional ones if those examined are found wanting.

3. The primary purpose of cost-utility analysis is usually not to *make* the decision but rather to sharpen the intuition and judgment of the decision-makers. Identification of the relevant alternatives and clarification of their respective implications are of prime importance.

4. In a long-range-planning context, the following are some of the major considerations involved in doing a cost-utility analysis:

a. Proper structuring of the problem is all-important. The analysis must be addressed to the right questions.

b. In making comparisons, an appropriate analytical framework must be used. For example, for a specified level of utility to be attained in the accomplishment of some given objective, the alternatives may be compared on the basis of their estimated economic resource impact; or vice versa, for a given budget level the alternatives may be compared on the basis of their estimated utility.

c. It is usually necessary to construct a model (either formal or informal) to be used in the analytical process. Here the main purpose is to develop a set of relationships among objectives, the relevant alternatives available for attaining the objectives, the estimated cost of the alternatives, and the estimated utility for each of the alternatives.

d. Uncertainty must be faced explicitly in the analysis. Sensitivity analysis, contingency analysis, and a fortiori analysis are three possible techniques that may be used in dealing with the problem of uncertainty.

e. Although it complicates the analysis because of an increase in the number of variables, very often *time-phasing* of the impacts of the various alternatives is a requirement. If the decision-makers are not indifferent with respect to time preference, the estimates of time-phased impacts must be "equalized" over time through the use of a "discounting" procedure.

f. Since the model is only a representation of reality, it is desirable to do some validity checking of the analytical procedure; e.g., can the model describe known facts and situations reasonably well?

g. Although cost-utility analysis stresses the use of quantitative methods, the analyst should not hesitate to supplement his quantitative work with appropriate *qualitative* analyses.

Notes

1. In many instances end products may in fact be *intermediate* products, especially from the point of view of the next higher level in the decision hierarchy.

2. From the introduction of the Statement of Secretary of Defense Robert S. McNamara before the committee on Armed Services on the Fiscal Year 1965–1969 Defense Program and 1965 Defense Budget, January 27, 1964, *Hearings on Military Posture* and H.R. 9637, House of Representatives, 88th Congress, 2d sess. (Washington, D.C.: U.S. Government Printing Office, 1964).

3. For example, see Arthur Smithies, *Government Decision-Making and the Theory of Choice*, P-2960 (Santa Monica, Calif.: The RAND Corporation, October 1964).

4. See Robert N. Anthony, *Management Accounting* (Homewood, Ill.: Richard D. Irwin, Inc., 1960), chaps. 13–15.

5. One example is the so-called PERT system. For a description, see *USAF PERT, Volume I, PERT Time System Description Manual*, September 1963, and *USAF PERT, Volume III, PERT Cost System Description Manual*, December 1963 (Washington, D.C.: Headquarters, Air Force Systems Command, Andrews Air Force Base, 1963).

6. See James E. Kelley and Morgan R. Walker, "Critical-Path Planning and Scheduling," *Proceedings of the Eastern Joint Computer Conference* (Ft. Washington, Pa.: Manchly Associates, Inc., 1959), pp. 160–173; and F. K. Levey, G. L. Thompson, and J. D. Wiest, *Mathematical Basis of the Critical Path Method*, Office of Naval Research, Research Memorandum No. 86 (Pittsburgh, Pa.: Carnegie Institute of Technology, May 30, 1962).

7. L. P. Alford and John R. Bangs, *Production Handbook* (New York: Ronald Press, 1947), pp. 216–229.

8. For a good example, see *Systems Data Presentation and Reporting Procedures (Rainbow Report)*, November 1, 1961 (with revisions as of March 9, 1962), Program Management Instruction 1–5 (Washington, D.C.: Headquarters, Air Force Systems Command, Andrews Air Force Base, 1962).

9. For a discussion of suboptimization, see Charles Hitch, "Suboptimization in Operations Problems," *Journal of the Operations Research Society of America*, vol. 1, no. 3, May 1953, 87–99; and Charles J. Hitch and Roland N.

McKean, *The Economics of Defense in the Nuclear Age* (Cambridge, Mass.: Harvard University Press, 1960), pp. 396–402.

10. Sometimes called "systems analysis"; e.g., see Roland N. McKean, *Efficiency in Government Through Systems Analysis* (New York: Wiley, 1958).

11. For example, see Joel Dean, *Capital Budgeting* (New York: Columbia University Press, 1951); Harold Bierman, Jr., and Seymour Smidt, *The Capital Budgeting Decision* (New York: Macmillan, 1960); and Elwood S. Buffa, *Models for Production* and Operations Management (New York: Wiley, 1963), chaps. 13 and 14.

12. For example, see Brian V. Martin and Charles B. Warden, "Transportation Planning in Developing Countries," *Traffic Quarterly* (January 1965), pp. 59–75.

13. See *Convertibility of Space and Defence Resources to Civilian Needs: A Search for New Employment Potentials*, compiled for the Subcommittee on Employment and Manpower of the Committee on Labor and Public Welfare, Senate, 88th Cong., 2d Sess. (Washington, D.C.: U.S. Government Printing Office, 1964). Note especially Part III, "National Adjustments to Shifts in Defense Planning," and Part IV, "Studies in Regional Adjustment to Shifts in Defense Spending."

14. W. W. Leontief *et al.*, *Studies in the Structure of the American Economy* (New York: Oxford University Press, 1953).

15. For example, See Walter Isard *et al.*, *Methods of Regional Analysis: An Introduction to Regional Science* (Boston and New York: Technology Press of Massachusetts Institute of Technology and John Wiley & Sons, Inc., 1960).

16. E. S. Quade, *Military Systems Analysis*, RM-3452-PR (Santa Monica, Calif.: The RAND Corporation, January 1963), p. 1.

17. Also because of inadequate data and information sources.

18. Apparently this view is held by Alain C. Enthoven, Deputy Assistant Secretary for Systems Analysis, Department of Defense. He writes: "Where does this leave us? What is operations research or systems analysis at the Defense policy level all about? I think that it can best be described as a continuing dialogue between the policy-maker and the systems analyst, in which the policy-maker asks for alternative solutions to his problems, makes decisions to exclude some, and makes value judgments and policy decisions, while the analyst attempts to clarify the conceptual framework in which decisions must be made, to define alternative possible objectives and criteria, and to explore in as clear terms as possible (and quantitatively) the cost and effectiveness of alternative courses of action.

"The analyst at this level is not computing optimum solutions or making decisions. In fact, computation is not his most important contribution. And he is helping someone else to make decisions. His job is to ask and find answers to the questions: 'What are we trying to do?' 'What are the alternative ways of achieving it?' 'What would they cost, and how effective would they be?' 'What does the decision-maker need to know in order to make a choice?' And to collect and organize this information for those who are responsible for deciding what the Defense program ought to be." See Alain C. Enthoven, "Decision Theory and Systems Analysis," *The Armed Forces Comptroller*, vol. IX, no. I (March 1964), p. 39.

19. For example, see Hitch and McKean, *The Economics of Defense*, especially Part II; and McKean, *Efficiency in Government*.

20. Observance of these guidelines will not in itself produce a good analysis, but it will most surely help. Many of the points listed are based on Quade, *Military Systems Analysis*, pp. 8–24.

21. Incredible as it may seem, there have been studies that started out by asking questions about which alternative would maximize gain and at the same time minimize cost—clearly an impossible situation.

22. The fixed level of utility or budget is usually specified by someone "outside the analysis"; i.e., it is usually a datum given to the analyst. Very often, the analyst will use several levels (e.g., high, medium, and low) to investigate the sensitivity of the ranking of the alternatives to the utility or budget level.

23. For a further discussion of the possible pitfalls of using ratios, see McKean, *Efficiency in Government*, pp. 34–37, 107–113.

24. For example: Will there be a war in the future? If so, when? General or local? With what political constraints? Who will be our enemies? Our allies? See C. J. Hitch, *An Appreciation of Systems Analysis*, P-699 (Santa Monica, Calif.: The RAND Corporation, August 18, 1955), p. 6.

25. For a discussion of Monte Carlo techniques, see Herman Kahn and Irwin Mann, *Monte Carlo*, P-1165 (Santa Monica, Calif.: The RAND Corporation, July 30, 1957); and E. S. Quade, *Analysis for Military Decisions*, R-387-PR (Santa Monica, Calif.: The RAND Corporation, November 1964), pp. 407–414.

26. Hitch, *Appreciation of Systems Analysis*, p. 7.

27. Quade, *Military Systems Analysis*, pp. 23–24.

28. Enthoven, in "Decision Theory and Systems Analysis," pp. 16–17, talks about sensitivity analysis in the following way: "If it is a question of uncertainties about quantitative matters such as operational factors, it is generally useful to examine the available evidence and determine the bounds of the uncertainty. In many of our analyses for the Secretary of Defense we carry three estimates through the calculations: an 'optimistic,' a 'pessimistic,' and a 'best' or single most likely estimate. Although it is usually sensible to design the defense posture primarily on the basis of the best estimates, the prudent decision-maker will keep asking himself, 'Would the outcome be acceptable if the worst possible happened, i.e., if all the pessimistic estimates were borne

out?' Carrying three numbers through all of the calculations can increase the workload greatly. For this reason, a certain amount of judgment has to be used as to when the best guesses are satisfactory and when the full range of uncertainty needs to be explored. If there are uncertainties about context, at least one can run the calculations on the basis of several alternative assumptions so that the decision-maker can see how the outcome varies with the assumptions.''

29. Maintaining a fixed level of utility *through time* is often a tricky problem in itself. We cannot go into this matter in the present limited discussion.

30. One may raise the question regarding under what conditions the decisionmaker *would* be indifferent. Economic theorists might argue that there probably should not be any such condition. However, in practice, decision-makers often find themselves in an institutional setting (the Department of Defense, for example) where it is customary to be indifferent regarding time preference; hence, discounting of cost streams through time is not done. This is not to say that the decision-makers are correct in principle.

It should be emphasized that the type of discounting under discussion here is purely to equalize cost streams through time with respect to time preference—not to compensate for risk.

31. For example, see E. B. Berman, *The Normative Interest Rate*, P-1796 (Santa Monica, Calif.: The RAND Corporation, September 15, 1959).

32. Hitch, *Appreciation of Systems Analysis*, pp. 11–12.

33. Quade, *Military Systems Analysis*, p. 20.

Program Budgeting
and the Planning-Programming-
Budgeting System

2

Some have traced the beginnings of program budgeting to the ways used to allocate scarce materials during World War II,[1] but program budgeting was not widely used in government until Charles Hitch and Robert McNamara employed a variation of the technique, the Planning-Programming-Budgeting System (PPBS), in the Department of Defense (DOD) in 1961. In 1965, President Lyndon B. Johnson announced that the system, which had achieved apparent success in the DOD, would be used in all agencies of the federal government. The "success" in DOD included a role in the selection of such weapons systems as the TFX fighter plane, a highly sophisticated plane that was to be used by the Air Force and the Navy with great cost savings to the DOD. There was a bit of a problem when this plane, later called the F-111, was flown in Vietnam. The highly sophisticated aircraft had difficulty staying in the air, even when enemy missiles and anti-aircraft artillery were silent.

But in 1965 it looked as if PPB had worked, and worked well, in the Pentagon. It did not work nearly as well in the other agencies of the federal government. Frederick C. Mosher and John E. Harr, in a study of the failure to implement a programming system in foreign affairs, compared the Defense Department with other agencies.[2] They noted that the Rand Corporation had been at work on defense programming questions for years and had developed a "bag of rather sophisticated tools and a trained body of carpenters skilled in the use of these tools."[3] They noted that there were relatively few overlaps with other organizations and that DOD's mission was clearly defined.

They attributed a great deal of importance to the secretary of defense, Robert McNamara, whom they characterized as "a strong executive and an able administrative politician possessing amazing capabilities of intellectual grasp, analytical ability, and memory."[4] This emphasis on the unique characteristics of McNamara was reflected in the "Rouse report," a Bureau of the Budget study that sounded the death knell for PPBS in 1969. The Rouse report found that PPBS-like analysis was useful in domestic agencies when agency heads demanded systematic planning and analysis. Few domestic agency heads wanted analysis, let alone understood it as well as McNamara did.[5]

Mosher and Harr suggested that the Defense Department had additional advantages. It had a relatively simple organizational structure and reported only to one appropriations subcommittee and one substantive committee in each house of Congress. But few other agencies have this luxury of organizational and legislative simplicity. DOD had a unified accounting system that was especially useful in assessing the cost of hardware items, the principal expenditure focus of the department. Although DOD cost estimates for weapons procurement programs were significantly lower than the real costs, determining the costs of hardware programs is much easier than assessing the costs and benefits of social programs.

The Planning-Programming-Budgeting System was based on a rationalized, integrated program structure. In theory, all programs in the federal government were to be broken down into distinct elements and put together so those elements contributed to larger programs. The program structure consisted of the division of each agency's mission into several *program categories*. These were divided into sub-missions called *program subcategories*, which were made up of *program elements.* At each level the mission of each program was to be specifically defined. The article by Tory Tjersland included in this volume presents a model program structure for a PPB-like system developed and tried in the state of Washington. The Washington state program structure was based on the same logic as that used in the federal government.

PPBS in the federal government called for three new documents to accompany the budget presentation. These documents were the program memorandum (PM), the program and financial plan (PFP), and special analytic studies (SAS). The program memorandums were supposed to be analytic justifications that would set out the alternatives and recommendations for each program element. The program and financial plan was to show future implications of programs advocated in the PM by projecting budget figures five years into the future. Special analytic studies were to be full-scale analytic efforts on issues identified by the central budgeting office and agency heads.

In practice, the federal PPB operation specialized in creating paper, much of it demanded but never used by the Bureau of the Budget in its policy-making deliberations. The program memorandum emphasized the justification of existing practices over poorly constructed alternative proposals. The program and financial plan contained suspect data for which the agencies were not held accountable since the real decisions involved only the budget year under consideration.

In some cases, however, particularly when the agency head wanted to use analytic work, the PPB exercise was moderately successful. When agency personnel saw that the PPB materials were being used in agency decision making rather than for the BOB, they developed better materials, which did prove to be marginally useful.[6]

But generally, PPB in the federal government failed to live up to the expectations of its advocates. Several reasons were offered for the failure. William Niskanen, formerly a high official in the Office of Management and Budget, declared that the multiple objectives of many government programs meant that a clean program structure was impossible to develop. Niskanen was amused by the planning orientation of PPB, since the pressure of the budget process forces participants in the process to look only one year ahead. Most of the participants did not have the time or the inclination to deal with five-year projections. The phony figures developed for the PFP undercut the credibility of the whole effort. The heart of PPBS—analysis—also came in for severe criticism from

Niskanen. Most of the analytic efforts were based on a national income economic model and failed to identify all the beneficiaries of the various programs.[7]

Perhaps the most important factor that Niskanen brought out, however, related to the political implications of PPB. Although PPB was sold as if it had no political impact, Niskanen pointed out that any system designed to help administrators keep track of how subordinate agencies are performing their work will have a centralizing effect.[8] There is a strong tendency in any large organization for incomplete information to flow from top to bottom and vice versa. In government agencies much of the information that flows upward is forced through a filter that permits only self-serving information to pass on up. Through this control of information, policy subsystems can continue to make symbiotic accommodations at a low level of visibility.

This action, however, leads to overall inefficiency and ineffectiveness, which is exactly why the higher levels of government administration are trying to develop reliable reporting systems. Even though PPB was not as successful as its advocates had hoped, it did contribute to the greater acceptance of systematic planning and analysis in governmental budgeting.

In the selections that follow, David Novick, the father of program budgeting, ties program budgeting to traditional budgetary activity and provides a strong defense of the technique. Tory N. Tjersland shows how a program budgeting system can be incorporated into budgetary decision making at the state level. There may be some irony here, however. A budget analyst for the Washington state legislature claimed that the system presented by Tjersland was never implemented.[9] Leonard Merewitz and Stephen H. Sosnick question whether program budgeting can ever work because of certain theoretical problems.

Notes

1. For a brief history of program budgeting, see David Novick, "Introduction: The Origin and History of Program Budgeting," in Novick, ed., *Program Budgeting: Program Analysis and the Federal Budget*, 2nd ed. (New York: Holt, Rinehart and Winston, 1969), pp. xix–xxviii.

2. Frederick C. Mosher and John E. Harr, *Programming Systems and Foreign Affairs Leadership: An Attempted Innovation* (New York: Oxford University Press, 1970), pp. 9–11.

3. *Ibid.*, p. 9.

4. *Ibid.*, p. 10.

5. For a shortened version of the Rouse report, see Edwin L. Harper, Fred A. Kramer, and Andrew M. Rouse, "Implementation of PPB in 16 Domestic Agencies," *Public Administration Review* vol. 29, no. 6 (November–December, 1969), pp. 623–32.

6. *Ibid.*, pp. 630–31.

7. William A. Niskanen, "Improving U.S. Budget Choices," *Tax Foundation's Tax Review* vol. 32, no. 11 (November, 1971), pp. 41–44.

8. *Ibid.*

9. Donald F. Peterson, discussant, Panel on Legislative Review and Oversight Function, National Meeting of the American Society for Public Administration, Washington, D.C., April 21, 1976.

What Program Budgeting
Is and Is Not

David Novick

During the 1960s the concept of program budgeting generated substantial interest, speculation, experimentation, and literature in business and at all levels of government throughout the western world. With the widespread introduction of this new management idea after the middle of the decade, a great variety of activities were undertaken in its name. Some of the proposals, however, bore little resemblance to it other than the use of the words *program budgeting* as part of an argument for changes in management that were not at all program budgeting or the planning-programming-budgeting system (PPBS).[1]

What Program Budgeting Is

Program budgeting is a management system that has ten distinctive major features. These are:

1. Definition of an organization's objectives in terms as specific as possible.

2. Determination of programs, including possible alternatives, to achieve the stated objectives.

3. Identification of major issues to be resolved in the formulation of objectives and/or the development of programs.

4. An annual cycle with appropriate subdivisions for the planning, programming, and budgeting steps to ensure an ordered ap-

Reprinted by permission of the publishers and The Rand Corporation from *Current Practice in Program Budgeting (PPBS)*, David Novick, editor, New York: Crane, Russak & Company, Inc., copyright © 1973 by The Rand Corporation.

proach and to make appropriate amounts of time available for analysis and decision-making at all levels of management.

5. Continuous reexamination of program results in relationship to anticipated costs and outcomes to determine need for changes in stated programs and objectives as originally established.

6. Recognition of issues and other problems that require more time than is available in the annual cycle so that they can be explicitly identified and set apart from the current period for completion in two or more years, as the subject matter and availability of personnel require.

7. Analysis of programs and their alternatives in terms of probable outcomes and both direct and indirect costs.

8. Development of analytical tools necessary for measuring costs and benefits.

9. Development each year of a multi-year program and financial plan with full recognition of the fact that in many areas resource allocations in the early years (e.g., years one through five) require projections of plans and programs and their resource demands for ten or more years into the future.

10. Adaptation of existing accounting and statistical-reporting systems to provide inputs into planning and programming, as well as continuing information on resources used in and actions taken to implement programs.

The General Approach

Traditional budgeting is aimed largely at efficiency in carrying out specific tasks. It is an appropriation rather than a policy-making approach. Program budgeting sets its sights on larger purposes, the objectives of an organization. These are stated in terms of available alternatives, which in turn are appraised in cost-benefit considerations. Once the issues involved in establishing policy are illuminated, the decision-makers can better make the overall decisions. When these are placed in a context of available resources, the next steps to efficiency in operation or performance can be taken as they usually are. That is, in the terms of the traditional budget.

To carry out the major objectives of program budgeting, three general areas of administrative and operational activities are involved. These are program format, analysis, and information and reporting.

1. *Program format* concerns the organization's objectives and the

programs established to meet them. Program budgeting begins with an effort to identify and define objectives and to group the organization's activities into programs that can be related to each objective. This aspect of the system is revolutionary, since it requires groupings by end product or output rather than, as in traditional budget practice, by line items of input arranged in terms of object classes, administrative organizations, or activities. The new method allows us to look at *what* is produced—output—in addition to *how* it is produced—which *inputs* we consume.

One of the strengths of program budgeting is that it cuts across organizational boundaries, drawing together the information needed by decision-makers without regard to divisions in operating authority among jurisdictions. Examining a program as a whole has its obvious advantages. Contradictions are more likely to be recognized, and a context is supplied for consideration of changes made possible only by cutting across existing agency line barriers.

The purpose of program budgeting is to identify and understand relationships and interdependencies. That is, to consider individual items in terms of related activities and the totality. For example, in planning for a local government, the program budget considers not only the customary issues of land utilization, aesthetics, and architectural design, but goes beyond them into the economic and social consequences of the physical changes in structures, streets, and neighborhoods. Once such effects are identified, decisions can be reached on whether or not the output is worthwhile, and if it is, how much of the organization's limited resources should be appropriated to it.

The program budgeting summary document presents resources and costs categorized according to the program or end product to which they apply. This contrasts with traditional budgets that assemble costs by type of input—line item—and by organizational or object categories. The point of this restructuring of budget information is that it focuses attention on competition for resources among programs and on the effectiveness of resource use within programs. The entire process by which objectives are identified, programs are defined and quantitatively described, and the budget is recast into a program-budget format is called the format or structural phase of program budgeting.

An outstanding feature of program budgeting is an emphasis on analysis at all stages of activity. Although it is sometimes not recognized, the developments of the appropriate format or structure in and of itself requires analysis. The examination of an organization's objectives and the identifying of its programs and program elements can constitute a major contribution to improvement of management even when the more complete analytical capability contemplated in the program budget is not fully developed.

One product of the structural phase is a conversion matrix or crosswalk from the budget in program terms to the traditional line-item, organization, and object-class budget. In program budgeting, organization gives way to program, and line-item detail is aggregated into summary figures more appropriate to policy-making decisions.

For example, the wages and salaries figure for the environment program in Figure 1 is not only the sum of personnel service payments in the program elements which constitute environment-oriented activities in water, air, land, pollution, etc., but also an aggregation of pieces of the wages and salaries data in each operating department whose activities contribute to environmental control. If Figure 1 were not abbreviated, the illustration would include the contributions from other departments and supporting services such as central electronic data processing. Detail is not the purpose, however, and such activities are instead grouped into a general support program.

Program structures rarely conform to the appropriation pattern or to the organizational structure. Therefore, the program presentation of activities and resource requirements cannot be interrelated with budget data on appropriation and/or organization except by the crosswalk. As indicated earlier, the program structure provides insight into the objectives of the organization; and the allocation of budget authority to programs provides a measure of the organization's priorities. The selected agency budgets grouped by program categories in the U.S. federal budget documents are an example of the crosswalk at a very high level of aggregation.[2]

The crosswalk prepared for the members of the Pennsylvania Legislature as part of their program budget for 1971–1972 may be the most useful illustration available. It is set out in terms of organizations, appropriations, Commonwealth (of Pennsylvania) major programs, and program subcategories.[3]

To aggregate the multitude of line items of the traditional budget or even the summaries of its operating departments into their program-element contributions or costs, it is necessary to make allocations, and some of them may be rather arbitrary ones. The important features of the crosswalk are (1) to have the two documents balance no matter what the dimensions of the classifications, and (2) to ensure that decision-makers and reviewing entities can identify next year's traditional budget in program terms, and vice versa.

By use of the crosswalk we also are able to convert data in existing

Figure 1
Crosswalk: Traditional Line-Item Budget to New Program Budget

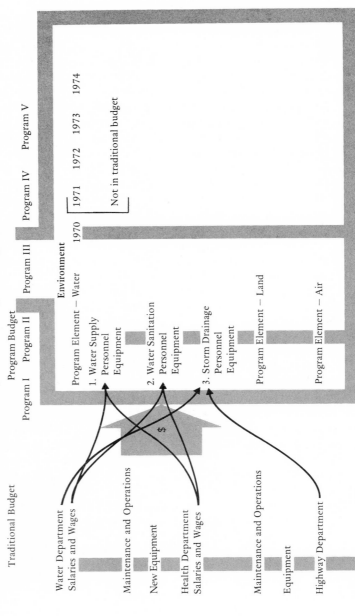

Figure 1 reproduced from *Management: A Book of Readings* by H. Koonz and C. O'Donnell, 3rd ed., copyright 1972 by McGraw-Hill Inc. Used with permission of McGraw-Hill Book Company.

46

records and reports into that needed for program planning. It permits program decisions to be translated into methods already in use for directing, authorizing, controlling, recording and reporting operations. If the management methods currently being used in any of these areas are inadequate or unsatisfactory, they should be improved, whether or not the organization has a program budgeting system. In any case, the program budget must derive its information and relationships from existing management records and practices and must rely on them for the implementation of the programs.[4]

2. The second area of the general approach is *analysis*. The program-budgeting method of decision-making subsumes a systems-analysis capability with which the resource and cost implications of program alternatives and their expected "outputs" or accomplishments may be estimated, examined, and compared. When a systems-analysis capability does not exist or is inadequate, it should be created or upgraded, since analysis is the most important part of this approach to management decisions. A wide range of techniques is employed in these program analyses, including statistical analysis, modeling, gaming, simulation, operations analysis, and econometrics. Both the resource-cost side and the benefit-effectiveness side of program consequences are analyzed.

Quantification is sought wherever possible, but many matters do not readily lend themselves to quantitative measurement. In these instances, qualitative analysis is required. In every case, whether the analysis is quantitative, qualitative, or an appropriate mixture of the two, there is to be explicit identification of the problem, the alternative ways of resolving it, and an attempt to measure the cost and effectiveness of each possibility.

Program analysis is not confined to predetermined alternatives; development of new and better alternatives is part of the process. It is likely that analysis of possibilities A, B, and C will lead to the invention of alternatives D and E, which may be preferable (more cost-effective) to the original candidates. Therefore, the analysis part of program budgeting cannot be viewed merely as the application of a collection of well-defined analytical techniques to a problem. The process is much more flexible and subtle, and calls for creativity by the managers and the analysts and interaction between analysts and decision-makers during the process.

3. The third part of the program budgeting system deals with *information and reporting*. The accounting and related statistical-reporting systems identify information for all activities of the organization. Neither new accounting nor new statistical-reporting systems are called for. Instead, reidentification or restructuring in the existing

systems is required for utilization of information in the planning and programming parts of the new activity. When program determinations are made, the reporting requirement imposes on existing systems the need to provide continuing information (usually monthly and/or quarterly) on the use of resources and the operational steps taken in the implementation of the programs.[5]

Although the accounting and statistical reports of necessity are carried on in terms of actions in the current calendar, the reporting provision must require and provide specific identification of today's activities in terms of impact in both the balance of the current year and the future years of the multiyear plan.

Information and reporting is an important part of the total system since (a) accounting for appropriated funds is a requirement in any government or business, (b) knowing and measuring progress towards stated objectives is important, (c) analysis for the future can only be based on measurements derived from past experience, (d) much of the mystery of traditional budgeting derives from the esoteric nature of the reports, and (e) a huge mass of data is now produced by modern record-keeping practice, office machines, and the computer in the name of information and reporting. (Instructions for preparing documents and forms used to collect, store, and report information are procedures and are not included here. Any good program structure can readily be converted to the coding of any accounting, statistical, or reporting system.)

All of the ideas in program budgeting are best developed when they are adapted to the special requirements of the organization introducing the new methodology. This is even more true of the information and reporting activities, since here it is definitely a matter of adapting an ongoing accounting, statistical, or reporting system to meet the program budgeting requirements.

A brief summary that relates the areas of operation to the major features of program budgeting and to the kinds of documents the system produces is sketched in Figure 2.

Reasons for Program Budgeting

The primary reason for program budgeting is that it provides a formal, systematic method to improve decisions concerning the allocation of resources. Obviously, these allocation problems arise because available resource supplies are limited in relation to the demands for them. This leads to a need for making choices among demands in terms of what to do, how much to do, and when to do it.

Figure 2
Sketch of Program Budgeting

Major Features	Operation Areas	Representative Documents

Define objectives
Determine programs
Assign activities to programs
Establish plan-program-
   budget cycle
	Structural
	aspect
		Multi-year program
		  and financial plan

Develop cost/benefit
  measurement methods
Identify and evaluate alternatives
Develop and apply criteria
	Analytical
	aspect
		Program memoranda
		  including alternatives
		Issue analysis
		Special studies

Use existing reporting system
Update programs
	Data and
	information
	aspect
		Accounting and
		  statistical reports
		Program change
		  proposals

Figure 2 reproduced from *Management: A Book of Readings* by H. Koonz and C. O'Donnell, 3rd ed., copyright 1972 by McGraw-Hill Inc. Used with permission of McGraw-Hill Book Company.

Program budgeting is designed to open up debate on these questions and put the discussion on a new basis. It does this by requiring explicit identification of all actions—ongoing or new proposals—in terms of programs related to stated objectives. This enables the top decision-makers to act in terms of the total organization rather than on the basis of ideas limited by individuals or operating units. The orientation of this new method is to plan the future in both short-term and long-range aspects, and to make decisions on what is to be done.

A second reason for program budgeting is that planning should be carried on with adequate recognition of what costs are. When an organization's plans call for more resources than it has or is likely to have available to it, planning becomes a game not played for "keeps." An organization that is unable to carry the costs of its objectives should revise its objectives; otherwise it will be wasting some of its substance. Resource considerations introduce realism into planning.

Since as many alternative plans as possible should be examined at the planning level, resource considerations should be in highly aggregated terms. We should use "in the ball park" estimates of costs to facilitate examining a large number of possibilities in a reasonably short period of time. In program budgeting the name of the game is "alternatives" and we seek a menu of the most relevant ones.

When we have selected the most promising plans from that list, we analyze them in a less aggregative but still not completely detailed form. This is programming. Here activities are identified and feasibility is established in terms of capability, resource requirements, and timing of each one of the alternatives. The selection is linked to a budgetlike process because the final budget decisions determine the allocation of resources not only for the next year but in many cases make commitments for many years into the future.

To formulate a single program requires that we make decisions on feasibility, resource demands, and timing. Even so, data used for programming are still not as detailed as next year's budget. The budget is an operating and financial document and, as such, must give great detail for inputs like personnel, supplies, and equipment, and assignment of such resources to administrative units. That kind of detail overwhelms decision-making and makes unmanageable a process designed for choosing among alternatives.

The third basic reason for program budgeting is that it provides for a basis of choosing between available and feasible alternatives, a choice that takes place at the conclusion of programming. At that point the issues involved have been illuminated. The decision-makers can exercise their judgment and experience in an appropriate and informed context, as they determine "what to do."

Given these decisions, the details of "how to do it" can then be laid out. This is the point at which performance budgeting, management by objectives, work measurement, and other methods of improving efficiency take over. In program budgeting the focus at this point is on annual allotment of funds for the next step to be taken along a path that has been thoughtfully set by policy-makers at all levels. Probably more important, the direction of the path and the distance to be covered in the next year will have been established after the consideration of a number of possible futures for the entire government or business organization.

This means that program budgeting is not designed to increase efficiency in the performance of day-to-day tasks, nor is it designed to improve administrative control over the expenditure of funds. It is instead a recognition of the fact that more money is wasted by doing the wrong thing efficiently than can be wasted by doing the right thing inefficiently. In short, program budgeting aims at the decision-making process; that is, top-level determination of what to do, how much to do, and when to do it, rather than deciding on how to carry on day-to-day operations, decisions which are best made by those who are closest to the activity.

What Program Budgeting Is Not

Some systems that have been called program-budgeting systems may be useful improvements, but they do not deal with choosing objectives, developing plans through systematic analysis of costs and effectiveness, resource allocation, and the other major decision areas which are its essentials. These include:

1. Reorganization plans justified on the basis that the organization must fit the program structure.

2. New accounting or statistical system that identify program elements.

3. Management-information systems undertaken as a substitute for major PB features.

4. Elaborate new personnel recruiting, education, or training undertaken without developing the PB organization and procedures which will utilize them effectively.

5. Extensive use of the words *program* and *program budgeting* in existing documents and procedures in lieu of developing and introducing the PB concepts and required changes.

6. Treating performance budgeting and other methods for improving administration of specific tasks as a substitute for PB treatment of major decision-making problems.

The General Disclaimer

In both government and business, responsibility for the work required to accomplish a coherent set of objectives is divided among a number of organizations. In government, for example, programs with objectives for health and education are distributed among a dozen bureaus and independent agencies as well as levels of government. The activities of each are sometimes complementary, sometimes in conflict. As a result there is no overall coordination of the resource allocations relevant to program objectives.

Since program budgeting cuts across organization and administrative lines, there are cases where this has been translated to mean that the activity is limited to the structural phase and resultant reorganization to fit the new identification or programs. This is not only an incomplete view of what is involved but also a most undesirable one.

It should be recognized that the PB management concept calls for continuous reexamination of program results and for reidentifying and restructuring programs and objectives. Normally, this would be done on an annual basis. One can readily visualize the chaos that could result in administration and operations if organizational changes were required for every change in program format.

> The program budgeting system is not a reorganization plan nor does it seek or require changes in organization to fit the program structure.[6]

In the same way, the information and reporting requirement of program budgeting, with its emphasis on accounting and recurring statistics, has sometimes been translated into the need for the development of a new accounting system or a major change in the existing one. As indicated in the preceding discussion of organization, programs can be expected to change or, at a minimum, be modified on a recurring basis. This makes it not only unnecessary but undesirable to change the accounting or the reporting systems to conform to the currently identified program structure.

The emphasis on maintaining existing accounting and reporting systems derives from the recognition of two major factors. First, temporary change is always undesirable and since programs and objectives are both subject to change, molding them to fit the format developed at any one point in time provides only limited advantage and has all the disadvantages that will be encountered when they must be changed to fit the next development of the format. The second reason is that both the operators and the decision-makers are knowledgeable about the existing system and therefore find it more comfortable to do their work in a situation in which changes have been kept to a minimum and are of a kind that are made essentially once and for all time.

Another reason for not making frequent changes is that in providing information for the inputs into the planning and programming process, and in reporting on actions taken in the execution of programs, the emphasis on detail is different from that in traditional line-item budgets. As we move through the process from the lowest level of operation and decision up through the higher levels of executive decision-making, there is a steadily increasing need to present aggregated instead of detailed information. The important new development for accounting and statistical reporting is to ensure that, as we move up the ladder and aggregate the data, the units of record do not lose integrity through the continuing introduction of judgment or "fudge factors."

> Program budgeting is not a new accounting system nor does it necessarily require changes in the existing accounting and statistical reporting systems to fit the program structure.[7]

What is needed is an examination of both the accounting records and the basic records from which statistical reports are drawn to ensure that these can in fact be translated into the required inputs in planning, programming, and budgeting activities as well as in recording and reporting. This means an emphasis on units of account that are "pure." That is, units that can be carried upward in the account or statistical-reporting system as is and do not require the introduction of adjustments when accumulated into more aggregative units of information.

> Program budgeting is not a management-information system, even though a good MIS is very useful to its operations.

Management-information systems have come into fashion recently. As a result, in many cases the development of program budgeting has been regarded as synonymous with the installation of a new computer system and the related techniques for making management data more readily available—and nothing more. Although a good MIS is always desirable and can be used to very good advantage in the working of a program budgeting system, it lacks the planning emphasis and surely does not include the appropriate recognition of the development of programs, the analysis of alternatives, and the development of all of the related analytical activities and tools that are so important in the concept of program budgeting.

Although program budgeting, because of its emphasis on analysis, frequently calls for individuals with an analytical approach and/or training, program budgeting requirements are not met just by introducing elaborate new personnel recruiting, education, or training efforts. For the most part, what is needed is some redirection of existing personnel and the kind of education and training essential for this purpose. But the program requirements will not be met just by new personnel policies and activities.

The word *budget* in program budgeting, or the planning-programming-budgeting system, sometimes leads to the assumption that, if the title *program* is introduced into the existing budget documents, the result is in fact a program budget. Obviously, the word *program* is available for anyone to use in any manner that he sees fit.

The emphasis on program in this new system is on output, or end-product measurement, rather than on the inputs as they are emphasized in traditional budget-making. Therefore, whether the existing budget is the straight line-item type, performance-oriented, or based on organization and object class, adding the word *program* in selected places or in the title does not make it a program budget and in no way accomplishes the purpose of program budgeting.

It is especially worth noting that program budgeting is not performance budgeting. Performance budgeting developed mainly in the [1950s] and has had a major impact at the state and local government levels. It has also been used extensively in business. The performance budget is a way of choosing between a series of alternative ways of "how to do" a specific task. It does not provide for evaluation of the importance of the task in terms of either the total program or individual programs designed to meet a set of goals. In short, it is a way of choosing among alternative means available for doing a task rather than a way of determining whether the task should be performed at all or, if it is to be undertaken, the amount of it that is required.

Program budgeting recognizes the need for administrative and organizational budgets as well as performance budgeting and does not contemplate that they be abandoned or relabelled. Instead, it requires that they be used in conjunction with the PB by means of the crosswalk.

The program budget has a time element that extends beyond the typical next-year's budget. The multiyear program and financial plan lays out not only next-year's financing but also the estimates of funding that would be required for future years on the basis of decisions already made when the final action is taken. In this sense, next-year's budget is an important first step in the operation on the multiyear program, and the five and ten year projections represent the "spend-out" implications of decisions made to date.

This does not mean making fundamental changes in existing budget practice. In the traditional line-item, object-class, performance, or organization and activity budget, there is a need for detailed identification by object or activity classes which requires, as we have seen, more detail than is either necessary or possible to use as we move up to the policy level in the decision process. For this reason, the primary change is in adding program budgeting to the traditional annual-budgeting process. This permits the development of the multiyear program and financial plan at a high level of aggregation from which a "crosswalk" can be made to the traditional one-year, line-item budget by object class.

The Contrast in Brief

In short, program budgeting is characterized by an emphasis on objectives, programs, and program elements, all stated in output terms. Cost, or the line-items of the traditional budget, is treated at an appropriate level of aggregation which ensures that plans and programs are developed with adequate recognition of their resource implications.

Analysis and the use of a large variety of analytical techniques are the backbone of this new system of management. PB requires explicit identification of assumptions, the development of all relevant options and alternative outcomes to the extent that time and personnel permit. PB's process of analysis forces recognition of the organization and operation line-cutting features of programs. In the same way, the analytic process forces translation of a broad goal, like better education, into operational terms like courses, students, teachers, libraries, etc., that identify both the purposes of the education process and the resources that can reasonably be made available for it. Analysis takes many forms and places substantial emphasis on the use of such tools as computers and mathematical models. However, the computer and the model are simply part of the kit of tools for analysis; they are not the decision-makers.

Program budgeting also places a new emphasis on continuous reporting of both the accounting and statistical type, including ad hoc data-collection methods when appropriate. These serve the purpose of providing the inputs into the next planning and programming cycle, as well as of measuring how the determinations on resources and program are being carried out (progress reporting).

New organization charts, accounting systems, personnel recruitment and training systems, management-information systems, or the generous use of the word *program* in traditional budgets are not in themselves program budgeting. They cannot promise the improvement in decision-making that is the primary goal of the program budgeting process.

Notes

1. PPBS is the more common usage in the United States and many other countries. Programme budgeting is widely used in England. In France, it is "Rationalization des Choix Budgetaires" (RCB). Program budgeting (PB) will be the preferred usage herein.

2. *Special Analyses,* Budget of the U.S. Government, pp. 289–317, U.S. Government Printing Office, Washington, D.C. 1971.

3. *Commonwealth of Pennsylvania,* Program Budget Vol. 1, July 1971–June 1972, pp. 261–314.

4. For a different point of view see "The Use and Abuse of Program Structure" by Allen Schick, International Federation of Operational Research Societies, Washington, D.C., 1967.

5. Complete enumeration on a periodic basis is not always required. For example, sample surveys might be used.

6. Change in organization may be desirable, but it is not one of the general principles of program budgeting. For a discussion of the organization implications of program budgeting see R. J. Mowitz, *The Design and Implementation of Pennsylvania's Planning, Programming, Budgeting System.* The Pennsylvania State University, 1970, pp. 39–41. Also for the impact in terms of President Nixon's reorganization proposals in 1971, see Chapter 26 [of *Current Practice in Program Budgeting (PPBS)*].

7. Changes in the accounting or reporting systems may be desirable and in fact may be suggested by the program-budgeting analyses, but they are not required by this management system.

PDS Is a Better Way

Tory N. Tjersland

. . . Perhaps most devastating to the professional development of public management today is the typical exclusion of managers from the decision-making process that formulates and approves the budget, that shapes how much shall be spent for what and by whom. Many governmental budget documents contain thousands of line items for which money is to be spent—and that's about all. The question of what results are to be achieved, or even the work plans for accomplishing any specific results, often are left to pure assumption or inference.

In many cases, the budget is used solely as a static control device to prevent spending beyond appropriated amounts. Previous budget figures are used as the baseline for projection and justification of proposed funding because—"the previous figures were thoroughly justified the last time final choices were made." Accordingly, the decision framework customarily keys only on new money requests.

It is all too easy for us to be weary of the struggle and conclude that nothing much can be done to turn the decision-making process around, but there is promise for those willing to try to reshape government by reshaping the planning and budgeting decision system.

The Office of Program Planning and Fiscal Management, which is the central state planning and budgeting agency for Washington's Governor Daniel J. Evans, conducts periodic reviews of the state's budget document to improve it as a management and policy making aid. Governor Evans has established four criteria which an improved planning and budgeting process must meet: (1) make state govern-

From *Governmental Finance*, vol. 4, no. 1 (February 1975), pp. 10–19. Used with permission.

ment more economical in its operation; (2) improve the utility of state programs and increase the quality of public services; (3) improve the informational basis for making public fiscal decisions; and (4) improve communications to citizens so that they will be more fully aware of the quantity and quality of public services which their taxes are supporting.

Washington state's traditional budget document is the culmination of sixty years of efforts to standardize the state's budgeting procedures. It is essentially an agency-oriented budget which displays planning and budgeting information by programs within an agency format broken down by objects of expenditure and source of funds on a two year basis.

Our traditional agency budget document opens with a budget message from the governor, outlining highlights of proposed goals for state government expenditures for the ensuing biennium. Succeeding sections answer key questions about current and future economic conditions, population projections, employment and unemployment trends, personal income, and the U.S. Consumer Price Index. From these sources, revenue estimates are made. Special statewide programs are also explained and analyzed separately in this manner.

The remaining sections contain information on specific state agencies arranged by broad functions: general government; human resources; education; natural resources and recreation; and transportation. Legislative and judicial branch functions are displayed separately as these funds cannot be changed or modified by the Governor. Altogether, the above five functional areas comprise more than 100 state agencies, boards, and commissions.

Within these broad functional areas, each agency is introduced by a *Revised Code of Washington* number designating its basic statutory authority. Included, also, is a concise narrative description of the agency structure, its organization, and its overall responsibilities, followed by a brief description of its particular goals and objectives for the ensuing budget period. Next, an italicized budget justification follows, addressing the recommended agency budget for the proposed biennium.

Where changed funding is recommended, such factors as workload indicators, changes in agency program emphasis, and the effect on staffing and funding levels are specified. Objects of expenditure within each agency program, together with fund sources and staff levels, then appear in tabular form for the past year, current year, and proposed biennium. Most government budget documents, while they obviously do vary in format and content, come fairly close to the above convention.

There is value in the state's traditional budget document to policy makers. For instance, the narrative portions of the traditional budget identify current policy issues, significant budgetary or operational changes, and the reasons for these changes, but always within an agency structure and within each respective agency program. Often, however, more than one agency will have similar program goals and objectives, but their means for achieving these goals and objectives are rarely identified, much less coordinated, within the budget document.

It is in this area of overlapping interagency programs and goals that the limitations of a program within an agency budget become obvious. In our view, the traditional budget document can be improved substantially by:

• Giving greater emphasis to measuring the outputs of government, which are direct services to the public or changes to the environment;

• Increasing the emphasis given to planning beyond the ensuing budget period so that the absence of longer range projections need not obligate future policy makers to costs which were not considered or anticipated at the time of the initial appropriation;

• Providing additional data on the issues of public need and demand, rather than relying almost exclusively on the requirements of accounting, control, and reporting of the appropriation itself; and

• Redirecting the priority given to individual agencies and their organizational units to the functions or programs being performed by the government as a whole.

The State of Washington has developed the Program Decision System (PDS), which addresses itself directly to the major limitations of the traditional agency budget. This new system identifies desirable state government objectives which are to be accomplished through the coordinated efforts of state agencies, boards, and commissions. It transposes the priority of budgeting from one of programs within an agency structure to one of budgeting on the basis of what public services state government performs and how these services directly affect the behavior of state citizens or the environment in which they live.

PDS development actually began in 1970 with the publication of a booklet titled *Program Financial Planning.* All the major shortcomings of the traditional budget were listed, together with some ideas on how we could improve the state's overall planning and budgeting process. In 1971, legislation was enacted to initiate performance auditing as a new and ongoing review function of the Legislative Budget Committee. In 1972, agency workload indicators were added to the agency budget document as well as a new requirement that state agencies attain a 5% productivity increase during the 1973–75 biennium. However, at that time we did not have the capability to measure agency productivity, so what generally occurred was a forced 5% reductions in resource appropriations. No one really understood the consequences of such a widespread cutback.

During 1973 the Governor re-established five functional policy cabinets composed of the state's top-level executives. Long-range policy planning seminars were held and, under the direction of Dr. Robert J. Mowitz of the Pennsylvania State University, a five week performance/productivity criteria seminar was conducted, attended by representatives from major state agencies. The primary task was to define state government in terms of statewide program goals, policies, objectives, and work outputs. Based upon these preliminary efforts, the major values of state government were identified and a preliminary program structure was assembled.

In addition, two other related efforts were launched in 1974. The first was "Alternatives for Washington," an innovative citizen planning effort to develop alternative futures for the state's populace in the ensuing decade. Second, an "Advisory Council on State Government Productivity" was established, consisting of 28 members appointed to represent professional and clerical state employees, state legislators, employee associations and organized labor officials, private sector business leaders, public educators, as well as federal and local government executives. The purpose of the advisory council is to seek out ways to improve the effectiveness and efficiency of state government. Though organized separately from PDS, these two major undertakings are designed to further strengthen the state's planning and budgeting process.

Implicit in the concept of the Program Decision System is that one of the basic functions of any organization is to accomplish specific quantifiable objectives as effectively as possible through the efficient and economical use of all available resources.

To determine whether an organization is meeting these conditions and to assure that they will continue to be met in the future, two things must be done. First, a value system must be determined making it possible to know whether or not organizational accomplishments are satisfying state government goals and policies over time.

The PDS logic defines a goal as a value statement which specifies a desired state of affairs. Goals are subjective and clearly subject to shifting cultural and social values. Also, goals are necessarily broad in scope—such as improving public health—and conditioned by available science and technology.

For example, the purpose of a human services system is to minimize the probability that anyone will become dependent upon that system, and if dependency does occur, that the length of time will be held to a minimum. In applying this PDS logic, programs that detect and deal with health conditions at an early stage are valued highly since they help prevent the development of advanced disease, which may require extensive hospitalization and rehabilitation or even death if left unattended.

Having first identified the values for the system as a whole (such as good health), the PDS logic secondly requires that a program structure be developed. The substantive values of the system are defined into major **programs** and program **categories.** Program categories are in turn broken down into specific quantifiable objectives which will satisfy the values above them; this level of program structure is called program **subcategories.** Finally, agency work activities carried out to accomplish the objectives of the system are organized into program **elements.**

Figure 1 displays in summary form the program structure logic as developed by Washington state government for the 1975–77 biennium. This particular figure traces the Protection of Persons and Property Program components within the Personal Safety Protection Category. It also breaks down the Traffic Accident Prevention Subcategory into nine distinct elements. Altogether the Washington state government program structure for the 1975–77 biennium consists of 10 state programs, 29 categories, 113 subcategories, and 516 elements, all of which total in excess of $6.78 billion in planned expenditures and the full-time employment of over 56,800 people.

Program structure is the means to organize policy choices and budgetary decisions across the entire scope and magnitude of state government. It is simply a classification system which links major state goals, policies, objectives, and the elements of each organizational unit. The logic of any classification system is to group like things together in such a way that useful comparisons and major decisions can be made regarding them. The program structure thereby plays an important role in helping managers and policy makers determine what and how decisions should be made.

The structure represents, and must continue to highlight, the best possible statement of the functions and activities of state government, including the individual contributions of each organizational unit. Therefore, it must be revised from time to time to reflect modifications in state government priorities, program experience, and knowledge.

Figure 1
Sample Program Structure Logic, Washington State Government Protection of Persons and Property Program

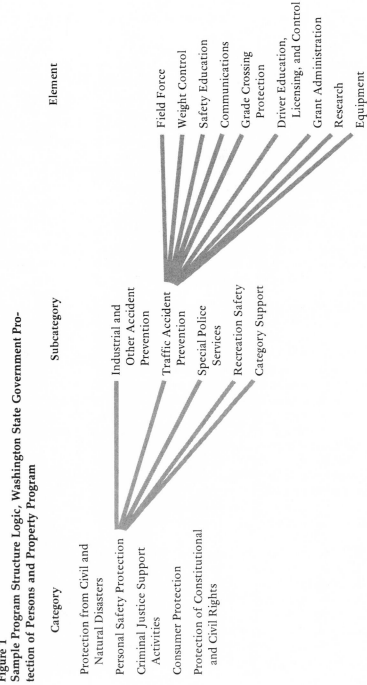

Category

Protection from Civil and Natural Disasters

Personal Safety Protection

Criminal Justice Support Activities

Consumer Protection

Protection of Constitutional and Civil Rights

Subcategory

Industrial and Other Accident Prevention

Traffic Accident Prevention

Special Police Services

Recreation Safety

Category Support

Element

Field Force

Weight Control

Safety Education

Communications

Grade Crossing Protection

Driver Education, Licensing, and Control

Grant Administration

Research

Equipment

PDS planning must be able to capture statewide trends and major issues that will tend to revise the value statements at the program and category levels of the program structure. To provide direction and remain responsive, policy guidance must be established to identify major shifts in values, new information, alternative program approaches, and other social and technological developments.

At the same time, there must be established an ongoing capability for reviewing the results of past decisions to assess the actual performance and productivity of state government. These periodic reviews, together with continuous program management research and policy analyses, serve as the basic planning blocks to keep policy makers informed of state government successes and failures, as well as of program conflicts, voids, and alternative approaches.

The Washington state government program structure for the 1975–77 biennium includes:

Program I—Legislative Branch Operations
Goal: To enact or reject legislation affecting public policy in the state, provide for the levy and collection of taxes and other revenue to support state and assist local government, and appropriate funds to implement public choices.

Program II—Judicial Branch Operations
Goal: To provide for the prompt and efficient administration of justice for all people within the state of Washington.

Program III—Economic Development and Regulation
Goal: To assure the efficient use of natural resources, labor, and capital of the state so as to provide optimum productivity and employment.

Program IV—Education and Cultural Resources
Goal: To provide opportunities for citizens of the state to satisfy their intellectual, cultural, and career needs and aspirations.

Program V—Environmental Resources and Recreation
Goal: To protect the physical environment of the state and to provide a variety of quality recreational activities.

Program VI—Health—Physical and Mental Well-Being
Goal: To provide for all citizens of the state an opportunity to achieve and maintain an adequate condition of physical and mental well-being.

Program VII—Social Services and Income Maintenance
Goal: To serve basic social needs and provide financial assistance to those citizens who are unable to provide their own means for survival.

Program VIII—Protection of Persons and Property
Goal: To provide an environment in which the citizens of the

state can live and work without danger to their health, safety, property, or general welfare.

Program IX—Transportation

Goal: To provide a system for the safe, convenient, and efficient movement of persons and goods throughout the state.

Program X—Administrative and Support Services

Goal: To provide an administrative system through which the goals and objectives of the state can be achieved.

Within each of the ten major state government programs, PDS seeks to identify, define, and quantify what happens to citizen behavior and the environment of Washington state as a result of state government efforts. PDS is basically a management by objectives approach to determine the difference between what state government *intends* to achieve and what it *actually* accomplishes for state citizens. This basic information, no matter what it is called, is essential for the Chief Executive, the Legislature, and interested citizens to qualify and quantify the performance and productivity of state government.

For instance, assume that a juvenile correctional institution demonstrates that it is extremely efficient in its operation by a comparison of its staff size related to the cost of housing, feeding, and rehabilitating juveniles. Also, assume that the institution uses recidivism as the measure of its effectiveness. Further, assume that the institution had a recidivism rate of 70% for the 1973–75 biennium; in other words, 70% of the juveniles who went through the institution's rehabilitation program ended up returning to the same or another similar institution. In this situation, we can say that, although the institution appears to be operated efficiently, the program for rehabilitating juveniles seems grossly ineffective—in our judgment, far too many juveniles return to a life of delinquency. Thus, either the program or the management of the institution requires some form of corrective action since the desired program purpose is not being accomplished satisfactorily. Traditional budget practices would not make this situation apparent, but PDS is designed to make these situations visible.

The PDS concept, when fully installed, reverses the planning and budgeting priority from one of making individual agencies more important than program activities to giving attention and emphasis first to the state program (what is to be done) and then to the individual agency (who is to do it). PDS is therefore another way of looking at state government. The decision point is focused on major state policy issues and performance trends. Rather than assume what will be accomplished if agency budget requests are approved, the discipline of

PDS stresses that this be made known prior to deciding budget recommendations and appropriations.

Given sufficient effort and active support, PDS can produce the following benefits:

• The ability to measure the performance and productivity of state government on a timely basis.

• Greater involvement of agency management in policy formulation and in those issues which affect program success.

• A logical framework for coordinating state agencies that have common objectives involving the same program.

• A far more meaningful display of program information for policy and budget decision making.

• The identification and definition of state goals, policies, and objectives to which state government aspires.

• A new capability for comprehensive state planning to better identify changing policy needs and priorities.

• A program information and reporting system that will provide a uniform basis for citizens and government officials to assess the quality and quantity of state government services.

• The ability to identify and define program voids and conflicts that affect state government effectiveness and efficiency.

• The accumulation of unmet public needs and demands through continuous program analyses and evaluation.

• The ability to project current decisions and resource commitments over at least four future years.

• The development and implementation of a common method for exploring alternative ways of accomplishing governmental objectives.

Obviously, the above will not be attained easily. Full installation of the Program Decision System will require persistent work and large scale investments over several biennia. The initial documentation of PDS for the 1975–77 biennium does contain many holes where program measures and data still have to be developed, but agency managers and state legislators are beginning to seriously question the state's traditional planning and budgeting practices in terms of finding a better balance between resources expended and results achieved. In addition, some organizational overlapping has been made obvious as a result of the initial documentation of the PDS structure.

To determine whether state government is effective and efficient in its operations, program measures must also be established. This necessitates that subjective values be transformed into factual statements that can be verified by numerical data over time. Thus, the accountability of state government to its citizens can be made explicit.

For instance, applying the program structure logic to a cancer detection center, the following traces the accountability of management for this service. The **program** would be health, with the goal of maintaining the physical and mental well-being of state citizens. The **category** might be public health, with the policy of identifying those citizens in need of services and referring them to existing treatment clinics. The **subcategory** might be community health improvement, with the objective of accurately finding and diagnosing conditions requiring treatment and referral to appropriate treatment clinics. One of several **elements** might be adult and child health.

Program **elements** produce **outputs,** and efficiency standards can be applied uniformly in the evaluation of these work outputs. Time and cost involved in processing patients through diagnostic clinics are variables that can be used as efficiency standards. Several other numerical counts might also be applied to establish the operating economy of the state's diagnostic clinics.

The effectiveness of the diagnostic clinic program, however, might best be determined by how many early first-detected cases of disease were found and how successful the state was in getting these patients to appropriate treatment centers. According to the program structure logic, this second measure, which is in effect a measure of the effectiveness of screening, is called an **impact indicator.** In other words, while elements produce outputs, **subcategories** produce **impacts.** By linking element outputs to subcategory impacts, the relative effectiveness/efficiency of state government can be determined. Also, by linking element outputs to subcategory impacts one can identify "make work" outputs—that is, those outputs that have no impact on the objective regardless of how efficiently they are produced—and eliminate them since they possess no material value to the program.

In addition, there is another program measure identified at the element level of the program structure that identifies the **workload** associated with each output. The extent to which state resources can be used effectively and efficiently by any single or cluster of program components must be sized carefully. The purpose of a workload statement is to identify the extent of public need or demand for any particular governmental service over time. Thus, workload statements are the means used for determining what service needs or demands exist over time and sizing the resources necessary to produce the outputs desired. These outputs, in turn, should achieve the subcategory impacts.

Figure 2, which corresponds to the sample program structure identified earlier in Figure 1, displays some typical PDS measurement data developed for the 1975–77 biennium. While Figure 2 illustrates only a small portion of the total program budget document display for the state's Protection of Persons and Property Program, it does summarize the PDS logic for making budgetary decisions governing how the state intends to stabilize the frequency and severity of motor vehicle accidents during the ensuing biennium.

All program measures appearing in the program budget document were developed by the agency managers responsible for achieving the subcategory objective. With the assistance of the central budget office, program measures were prepared on the basis of identifying the effectiveness and efficiency criteria with which agency managers will evaluate their activities and how these activities can be judged by others during the 1975–77 period. *Caution:* The selection and use of any given program measure requires that the agencies involved have the capability to routinely keep track of and produce on demand all of the program measurement information.

In several instances, better program measures were thought of by agency managers; however, the information base was either not available or was beyond the present capability of the agency involved. Therefore, the initial quality of program measures was less than desired because traditional agency program information is oriented more toward measuring work activity than toward measuring the achievement of predetermined objective targets. *Caution:* Agency managers needed considerable orientation and training to properly complete our PDS budget forms.

Figure 3 displays all of the state's resources requested for the 1975–77 biennium within the Traffic Accident Prevention Subcategory. Full-time equivalent staffing, dollar expenditures, and source of funds information are displayed also at each level of the program structure throughout the program budget document. In practice, these data are assembled at the element level, then aggregated upward throughout the entire program structure for budget display purposes.

There exist a number of major differences between the traditional agency budget document and the new program budget document, each of which was published as a separate volume and both of which are now before the Washington Legislature for final consideration. The most conspicuous difference is that the PDS approach employs a program structure built around state government goals, policies, and objectives for classifying various service functions and activities, and thus providing a uniform basis for statewide program planning, analysis, and most important, decision-making.

Figure 2
Washington State Government Sample PDS Measurement Data

Protection of Persons and Property Program
    Goal: To provide an environment in which the citizens of the state can live and work without danger of their health, safety, property, or general welfare.

Personal Safety Protection Category: Consists of the actions taken to protect the citizens of the state from accidents on the roads, at work, and at play, and to provide for situations requiring special police services.
    Policy: To protect the citizens of the state from injury and property loss by operating assistance and enforcement patrols, by conducting accident investigations, inspection, education, and by enforcing licensing regulations.

Traffic Accident Prevention Subcategory: Consists of the actions taken to reduce the occurrence and seriousness of motor vehicle accidents in the state.
    Objective: To stabilize the frequency and severity of motor vehicle accidents in the state.
    Impact indicators* are: 1) Number of Reported Accidents Per 100 Million Miles Traveled in the State; 2) Number of Accidents Investigated Per 100 Million Miles Traveled Caused by Driver Error or Defective Equipment; 3) Number of Fatal Accidents Investigated Per 100 Million Miles Traveled Caused by Driver Error Defective Equipment; 4) Number of Injury Accidents Investigated Per 100 Million Miles Traveled Caused by Driver Error or Defective Equipment; and 5) Number of Property Damage Accidents Investigated Per 100 Million Miles Traveled Caused by Driver Error or Defective Equipment.

Field Force Element: Consists of enforcement of state traffic regulations to insure the safe and orderly flow of traffic, and to render aid when needed.
    Workload/Output*: 1) Number of Miles Traveled—a) Number of Traffic Patrol Hours; 2) Number of Reported Traffic Accidents—a) Number of Traffic Accident Investigations; and 3) Number of Licensed Drivers—a) Number of Citations Issued for Driving While Under Influence of Alcohol and/or Drugs.

Weight Control Element: Consists of the enforcement of regulations concerning the size and weight of vehicles so as to protect the safety of the motoring public, and to prevent damage to roads, bridges, and other structures.
    Workload/Output*: 1) Number of Licensed Commercial Vehicles—a) Number of Commercial Vehicles Checked.

Safety Education Element: Consists of instructing the citizens of the state in safe and lawful motoring, cycling, and pedestrian practices.

Figure 2—*Continued*

Workload/Output*: 1) Number of Students Enrolled in Primary and Secondary Education—a) Number of Primary and Secondary Students Contacted; and 2) Number of Licensed Drivers—a) Number of Adults Contacted in Safety Education Programs.

Communications Element: Consists of communications support provided to the field force in enforcing traffic regulations, and in maintaining the orderly flow of traffic throughout the state.
Workload/Output*: 1) Number of Requests for Service—a) Number of Communication Responses.

Grade Crossing Protection Element: Consists of efforts to reduce traffic accidents at railroad-highway grade crossings through the installation of improved safety equipment.
Workload/Output*: 1) Number of Railroad Crossings Qualified for Signalization—a) Number of Railroad Crossing Signals Installed.

Driver Education, Licensing and Control Element: Consists of a system of education, licensing and control to insure that motorists of the state possess the knowledge, skill, and motivation necessary for safe and legal motoring.
Workload/Output*: 1) Number of Driver License Applications—a) Number of Driver Licenses Issued; and 2) Number of Licensed Drivers—a) Number of Drivers Participating in Driver Improvement Program; b) Number of Driver License Suspensions Processed.

Grant Administration Element: Consists of activities to monitor and financially assist state and local jurisdictions in the implementation of federal highway safety standards established by the National Highway Traffic Safety Administration and the Federal Highway Administration.
Workload/Output*: 1) Number of State and Local Requests for Roadway Improvement Projects—a) Number of Approved Roadway Projects; 2) Number of State and Local Requests for Vehicle Improvement projects—a) Number of Approved Vehicle Projects; and 3) Number of State and Local Requests for Driver Improvement Projects—a) Number of Approved Driver Projects.

Research Element: Consists of gathering and disseminating vehicle traffic accident data to conduct research to identify causes of traffic accidents and determine methods of prevention.
Workload/Output*: 1) Number of Traffic Accident Reports Received—a) Number of Traffic Accident Reports Processed; and 2) Number of Citations Issued by Washington State Patrol—a) Number of Traffic Citations Processed.

*Impact indicators and Workload/Output data are reflected in columnar fashion showing actual in FY74, estimated for FY75, and proposed for FY's 76 and 77.

Figure 3
Washington State Government Sample Program Budget Financial
and Manpower Data Display

Traffic Accident Prevention Subcategory
Subcategory Summary
Full-Time Equivalent Staff Years

Element	FY 74 Actual	FY 75 Estimated	FY 76 Proposed	FY 77 Proposed
Field Force	668.3	559.0	625.7	660.3
Weight Control	106.6	111.0	108.5	108.5
Safety Education	33.0	33.0	32.7	32.7
Communications	220.1	231.5	233.0	233.0
Grade Crossing Protection	0.0	0.0	0.0	0.0
Driver Education, Licensing, and Control	376.8	382.5	393.9	393.9
Grant Administration	0.0	0.0	0.0	0.0
Research	24.8	24.0	23.5	23.5
Equipment	0.0	0.0	0.0	0.0
Annual Total	1,429.6	1,341.0	1,417.3	1,451.9

Expenditure Detail

Element	FY 74 Actual	FY 75 Estimated	FY 76 Proposed	FY 77 Proposed
Field Force	12,332,753	13,974,135	14,769,626	14,822,483
Weight Control	1,576,604	1,877,859	1,883,171	1,891,399
Safety Education	606,565	667,395	705,546	717,308
Communications	2,859,243	3,561,021	4,117,175	3,766,321
Grade Crossing Protection	8,811	538,616	269,670	269,670

	FY 74 Actual	FY 75 Estimated	FY 76 Proposed	FY 77 Proposed
Driver Education, Licensing, and Control	5,289,092	5,698,728	6,521,571	6,638,076
Grant Administration	1,498,627	1,294,705	1,800,000	1,900,000
Research	241,041	256,745	260,323	265,851
Equipment	2,809	2,788	3,250	3,250
Annual Total	24,415,645	27,871,992	30,330,332	30,174,358
Biennium Total	52,287,637		50,504,690	

Subcategory Agency Expenditures

	FY 74 Actual	FY 75 Estimated	FY 76 Proposed	FY 77 Proposed
Subcategory Agencies				
Department of Motor Vehicles	5,289,092	5,698,728	6,521,571	6,638,076
Vehicle Safety Equipment Commission	2,809	2,788	3,250	3,250
Washington State Patrol	17,616,306	20,337,155	21,735,841	21,363,362
Washington Traffic Safety Commission	1,498,627	1,294,705	1,800,000	1,900,000
Washington Utilities and Transportation Commission	8,811	538,616	269,670	269,670
Annual Total	24,415,645	27,871,992	30,330,332	30,174,358
Biennium Total	52,287,637		60,504,690	

Source of Funds

Fund	FY 74 Actual	FY 75 Estimated	FY 76 Proposed	FY 77 Proposed
Motor Vehicle—State	17,066,481	19,420,521	20,239,091	19,866,612
Motor Vehicle—Federal	303,319	—	—	—
Grade Crossing Protection	8,811	538,616	269,670	269,670
Commercial Driver Training Schools	1,246	1,727	1,261	1,261
Salary Adjustment	62,741	137,140	—	—
Health Insurance	5,767	77,652	—	—
Unanticipated Recipts	18,507	—	—	—
Highway Safety—Federal	10,868,076	13,120,714	14,870,628	15,258,411
Highway Safety—Addition to Balance	(3,917,303)	(5,413,378)	(5,050,318)	(5,221,596)
Annual Total	24,415,645	27,871,992	30,330,332	30,174,358

While the traditional agency budget document uses organizational units as its structure for identifying various program activities within an agency and displays financial data broken down by objects of expenditure, the program budget document displays the state's activities according to individual program objectives, regardless of organizational responsibility, within a new decision making context.

As displayed in Figure 3, program activities to stabilize motor vehicle accidents are organizationally located in the Department of Motor Vehicles, the Vehicle Safety Equipment Commission, the Washington State Patrol, the Washington Traffic Safety Commission, and the Washington Utilities and Transportation Commission. In the traditional agency budget, these agencies are dispersed throughout the document. The PDS structure places them within the same decisional context of the Traffic Accident Prevention Subcategory. In selecting various policy alternatives and in making major decisions concerning motor vehicle safety, the program structure brings together all of the state's resources and functional activities currently devoted to that particular objective. Thus, PDS sets up a structural framework for concentrated program analyses to be conducted on a prioritized basis.

Even though program decisions and budget presentations under PDS are in terms of the program structure involving all of state government, activities are still carried out and management responsibilities are still executed through agency organizational units. Thus, the PDS budget display traces the effect of any given program decision on the appropriation items within each organizational unit. In this sense, the traditional agency budget and the new program budget documents can complement each other. They each contain necessary and useful information for decision-making purposes.

Two critical decision points emerge from the PDS logic. The first and most important decision is, what management objectives should be set to satisfy the state's goals? In effect, when the Governor recommends and the Legislature appropriates a given budget amount, the only substantive benefits being purchased for the state's citizens are the impacts associated with the specific objectives being funded.

Based upon the PDS logic, impacts are also the principal measures of state government effectiveness. Therefore, the selection and funding of impact indicators are critical policy decisions, since the choice of objectives expresses what the state is committed to achieve for its citizens at any particular point in time. Governmental performance should be judged accordingly.

The second most critical decision is in the selection of elements for accomplishing the impacts associated with each objective. Questioning and evaluating past program results, along with a constant search for better program alternatives that will efficiently produce the outputs necessary to realize more effective results, should be made paramount to the decision processes of manager and legislator alike.

The PDS structure is not an end in itself. It represents a beginning framework toward enhancing state government's decision-making capability. PDS is designed to be a dynamic process. As assembled and published, the PDS budget document for the 1975–77 biennium contains program, financial, and manpower information descriptive of the total program activities of state government within the context of the program structure. Our first publication of PDS is little more than a static file of information. It evolved within a climate that was heavily constrained by past commitments and practices, limited to projections for the 1975–77 biennium alone, and was pulled together without any attempt to undertake and complete program analyses on which to base current or future budget decisions.

Future PDS budget documents, beginning with the 1977–79 biennium, will display program, financial, and manpower information over four future years. Also, it is planned that the PDS cycle, as discussed below and diagrammed in Figure 4, be fully implemented before the 1977–79 biennium.

The PDS cycle begins with the Governor's Program Policy Guidelines document, which is to be issued during the early part of each even-numbered year. This new planning document is to be based upon statewide planning and program management analyses of the governor's budget office, the various state agencies and departments, and other appropriate sources. It will contain the results of selected performance reviews, the latest social and economic conditions of the state, together with policy issues and trend analyses of primary concern to the governor for the succeeding biennia. Further, the Governor's Program Policy Guidelines document will serve as the major vehicle for providing state agencies with uniform planning data to project their service priorities and resource requirements, such as economic, demographic, and social forecasts influencing future program decisions.

In response to the Governor's Program Policy Guidelines document, agencies will prepare Program Revision Requests. Program Revision requests will be required to contain at least five items of information: (1) A brief description of the proposed change and a statement of the purposes as they relate to the goals and objectives of the state; (2) Justification indicating the relationship of the proposed change to the Governor's Program Policy Guidelines, any significant changes in citizen behavior or the environment to which the agency is

Figure 4
Washington State Government Program Decision System Cycle

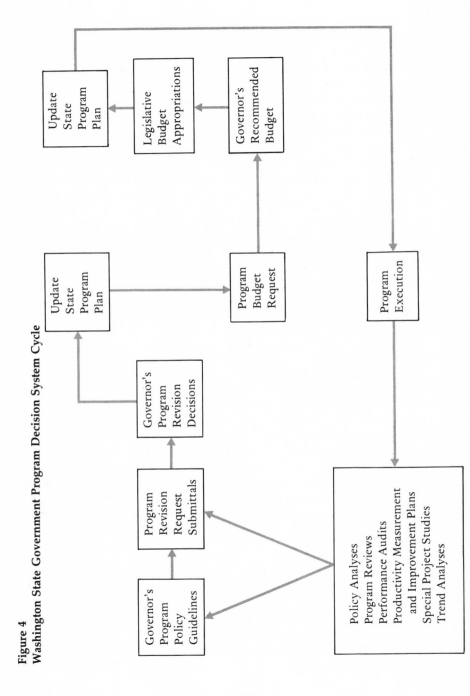

responding, special analytic studies, or other research data supporting the proposal; (3) Indication of program alternatives that were considered, including summary information about cost and benefits of other alternatives, if available; (4) Explanation of which programs, if any, will be phased down or eliminated should the Program Revision Request be approved, and the relationship of the proposed change to other elements, sub-categories, or categories if relevant; and (5) Any new legislative action required (other than appropriation) to carry out the program successfully. Also, the Program Revision Request will be the common vehicle for identifying ineffective and unnecessary program activities. Program Revision Requests will be analyzed by the governor's budget office, priorities will be reviewed by the governor's policy cabinets, and the governor will choose those program revisions which in his judgment meet the needs of the state within the financial limitations as he sees them.

After the governor has selected those Program Revision Requests to be implemented in the next biennium, the normal planning and budgeting requests from all agencies will be submitted to the governor's budget office and recommendations will be formulated. Next, program and agency budget proposals will be assembled and published as the governor's recommended budget for the ensuing biennium.

These decisions will be reviewed by the legislature in the same basic program context, but perhaps with differing opinions concerning program and agency priorities. The legislature's decisions will take the form of appropriation acts and statutory changes to provide funds and legal authority for operating the approved programs of state government.

Agencies will then proceed to implement approved program plans. Implementation will be reviewed by the agencies involved, the central budget office, and the Legislative Budget Committee to determine the relative effectiveness and efficiency of the resources expended toward accomplishing program goals and objectives in desired time periods. This review should lead to research into alternative ways to achieve the state's objectives at each subcategory level of the program structure. The results of these review and evaluation efforts will then be considered in preparing the next Governor's Program Policy Guidelines document, and the PDS cycle will begin anew.

An increasingly important aspect of this improved planning and budgeting process will be the review given to past program and agency activities to determine the extent to which the outputs of state government did in fact bring about the desired impacts. All future executive and legislative budget hearings should focus more attention on such performance and productivity reviews as well as give increased emphasis to improving the quality of program measures with which to make better judgments about the functions and activities of Washington state government. In this manner, PDS should become a basic tool to help Washington state government better achieve its ultimate objective—public service.

Glossary

Program Decision System   A logical system which identifies and defines the planning and budgeting decision-making processes in such a way so that the primary focus of choice is upon whether or not the goals, policies, and objectives of state government are being attained.

State Program Plan   A file of PDS information containing program, financial, and full-time equivalent staffing projected over a four-year period. It thus serves as the total input into all agency activity plans within the uniform framework of the Washington state government program structure.

Program Structure   The means employed to organize state government goals, policies, and objectives within a logical framework so that activities of different organizational units designed to accomplish similar results can be reviewed for decision purposes within the appropriate program context. Program structure also provides the means for determining what information is required to identify and define the public service needs and/or demands placed upon state government and what information is essential for the management and evaluation of program operations.

Program   The highest aggregation of public service functions and activities which defines the ultimate aims or aspirations of state government in terms of a desired state of affairs. Programs are necessarily broad and subjective.

Goal   A desired state of affairs based upon current knowledge and values. It is timeless in the sense that as achievement approaches, goals tend to be restated at a higher level of aspiration or entirely new goals are formulated. Goals reflect the basic values of society and are therefore always culture bound and subjective.

Category   The first major subdivision of the program structure which is defined in terms of agreed upon or established state government policy. Categories are also based upon subjective values.

Policy   A statement or plan of action which provides the principal direction and emphasis toward the achievement of a broad goal. A policy is derived from the state Constitution or from statutory law and is based upon the implied or expressed intent of the Legislature and/or the Chief Executive.

Subcategory The second major subdivision of the program structure which focuses upon objectives that can be measured in terms of quantifiable impacts. It is at this level of the structure that the substantive values of state government are transformed into factual statements that can be verified over time. Governmental accountability is made explicit at this level through the establishment of specific performance or effectiveness criteria.

Objective A desired quantifiable achievement within a specified time period that contributes to the implementation of particular policy.

Impact Indicator A measure which describes the effect objectives have upon individuals or the environment of the state. The accomplishment of subcategory objectives is measured in terms of impacts achieved.

Element The third and final major subdivision of the program structure which sets forth specific agency activities related directly to the production of a discrete output, or a group of related outputs, which in turn contribute to the accomplishment of subcategory impacts. It is at this level of the structure that visibility is gained into the work activities of state agencies as well as where all organizational units can be measured in terms of the productive or efficient use of their resources.

Workload The quantity which identifies how much of a given element's outputs are required. Workload is stated in terms of public need and/or demand for a particular output within a specific fiscal year.

Output Quantifiable units produced as a result of organizational activity carried out at the element level in response to a particular workload. Outputs contribute to the accomplishment of impact indicators.

Governor's Program Policy Guidelines A document which includes economic, demographic, and social trends of the state, identification of the governor's program priorities and specific problem concerns that require special management attention and emphasis in terms of preparing and submitting a Program Revision Request for implementation in the ensuing biennium.

Program Revision Request The means by which an agency proposes a new program activity or a significant change or modification to an existing program. Program Revision Requests are also the means for identifying outdated program functions and activities which can be eliminated from the structure. Program Revision Requests are normally prepared in response to the issuance of the Governor's Program Policy Guidelines document, but are not necessarily restricted by the presence or absence of the governor's leadership or direction.

Public Expenditure Analysis: Some Current Issues

Leonard Merewitz and Stephen H. Sosnick

Introduction

We have all heard recently of the struggle between the President and the Congress over who has the ultimate right to decide whether funds authorized and appropriated by Congress will be spent. In addition, we have come to understand that the aggregate level of federal spending has a major impact on the level of employment and the rate of price inflation. Less well known are the techniques by which either branch of government decides when a particular project should be funded, or whether a combination of programs is working effectively and efficiently. What, besides rhetoric, determines budgetary decisions at the federal and at the state level?

Public administrators now have some techniques other than simple budgets for organizing thinking about public spending. In the past decade the technique of planning-programming-budgeting has become popular for the systematic evaluation of the worth of public expenditures. This paper attempts to explain some basic concepts in nontechnical language. (For a more complete analysis, see Merewitz and Sosnick, *The Budget's New Clothes: A Critique of Planning-Programming-Budgeting and Benefit-Cost Analysis* [Chicago: Markham, 1971].)

From *Public Affairs Report* (Berkeley: Institute of Governmental Studies University of California), vol. 14, no. 5 (October 1973), pp. 1–7. Used with permission.

Planning-Programming-Budgeting

In the 1960s, planning-programming-budgeting (PPB), a way of describing, proposing, and defending expenditures, took the country by storm. The action began in 1961, when Charles J. Hitch became the Assistant Secretary of Defense. In 1965, President Lyndon Johnson ordered all agencies of the federal government to adopt PPB; in 1966 Governor Edmund G. (Pat) Brown did the same for California, and at least fourteen other states and uncounted numbers of counties, cities, and school districts have followed. The political party in power seems to have made no difference. Both Johnson and Brown were Democrats, but their Republican successors quickly reaffirmed the commitment to PPB. In 1971, however, President Richard Nixon's Bureau of the Budget, renamed the Office of Management and Budget (OMB), quietly ordered a retreat.[1] Director George Shultz and his staff had decided that PPB was expensive and was not accomplishing its objective, namely, to produce better decisions about the amount and composition of expenditures. Nevertheless, many federal agencies still use PPB for their internal management even though they do not submit the material formally to OMB.

PPB has five distinguishing operational features. They are (1) program accounting, (2) multi-year costing, (3) detailed description of activities, (4) zero-base budgeting, and (5) benefit-cost analysis. We shall describe and evaluate each of the five parts.

Program Accounting

Program accounting consists of grouping together expenditures having the same purpose, regardless of which subagencies spend the money or what types of goods are purchased. It means focusing on outputs rather than inputs.* A program budget shows a hierarchy of totals. It shows the total outlay proposed for each type of output, for various subgroups of outputs, for various groups of these subgroups. The Department of Health, Education and Welfare, for example, showed total expenditures for work on Heart Disease, for Increasing Knowledge, for Development of Health Resources, and for Health, the last being one of the department's four broad "program categories."

*Input: goods or services used in a production process.
Output: that which is produced, as in this case, a government service.

Program budgets are intended to supplement conventional government budgets, but not supplant them. Conventional budgets classify proposed expenditures by type of input and by administrative unit. They show, for example, total expenditures for each type of input, such as personnel or travel, acquired by each subagency, total expenditures for various groups of inputs or groups of subagencies, and total expenditures for various groups of these groups. Because elected officials authorize positions, salaries, capital outlays, and total expenditures separately, conventional budgets are also useful. They tell legislators, administrators, and auditors what expenditures are allowed for each input and each agency. Program accounting thus adds a third type of classification: expenditure by *program.*

It is doubtful that the benefits of program accounting outweigh the costs. Costs arise in delineating and redelineating programs and in producing an additional set of statements and reconciliations. The benefits of program accounting supposedly are better high-level decisions about spending, based on knowledge of the amount spent for each purpose. However, the additional information has limited value: it reflects discretionary groupings of activities and judgmental allocations of common costs, does not show how much money would be saved by scaling down an activity, and often is ignored by busy bureaucrats.

Multi-Year Costing

Multi-year costing is the second component of PPB. It consists of reporting, along with proposed first-year expenditures, the expenditures predicted for at least one future year. President Johnson's Bureau of the Budget instructed each agency to submit annually a "Program and Financial Plan" that showed outlays for every program element in the "fiscal year just past, the current year, and the budget year, plus at least four future years."[2]

Multi-year costing is useful in two circumstances. One relates to an investment whose payoff requires expenditures in future years. For example, multi-year costing was intended to help Secretary of Defense identify weapons systems whose ultimate cost would be prohibitive and reject them before the services got their foot in the door. The other use relates to a multi-year commitment, as with a new welfare program. In both cases multi-year costing can, by revealing future costs, facilitate rejection of exorbitantly costly activities.

With respect to ongoing activities, however, multi-year costing has little value. That future-year estimates for, say, law enforcement, seem excessive is not a good reason to curtail apparently worthwhile current expenditures. Future expenditures can be scaled down when they are proposed. For established activities, multi-year costing diverts attention, consumes time, paper, and storage space, produces numbers whose meaning is uncertain, and—because officials tend to hold themselves and their subordinates to whatever has been recorded—inhibits adjustment as more information becomes available.

Detailed Description

Detailed description of activities is the third component of PPB. It requires reporting for each program element (1) *objectives* (i.e., intended benefits) of the activity (e.g., the Department of Transportation listed safety and three other objectives); (2) *effectiveness* (i.e., a numerical indicator of actual or expected success) for the past year, the current year, the budget year, and at least four future years (e.g., the number of accidents prevented); (3) *output* (i.e., a numerical indicator of actual or intended results) for the past year, the current year, the budget year, and at least four future years (e.g., lane-miles of interstate highway completed); (4) *choices made* (i.e., courses of action selected) for the budget year (e.g., work on Interstate 80); (5) *alternatives considered* (i.e., courses of action deliberately rejected) for the budget year (e.g., work on Interstate 5); and (6) *reasons for the choices* (e.g., Interstate 80 is busier and cheaper than Interstate 5). Many will recognize this as a "systems approach."

It is important to contrast an activity level with an effect. If the objective is to get people to use libraries, then the number of libraries built or square feet constructed is a measure of activity level. A measure of effectiveness, however, might be the proportion of the population using a library once or more each year.

Detailed description of activities may be helpful to policy-makers. It may clarify what their subordinates are trying to accomplish, what the average cost will be, and where the subordinates exercised discretion. This information may help policy-makers both to compare benefits with costs and to review techniques. If so, the decisions that emerge after review will be more like those that would have been reached if every reviewer could have made his subordinates' decisions as well as his own. High-level officials presumably will view this result as beneficial. So do we—despite some reservations concerning overcentralization. Whether the gain outweighs the costs, however, is not clear.

Zero-Base Budgeting

Zero-base budgeting is the fourth component of PPB. It consists of defending the total expenditure proposed for a program. A program was to be defended by listing its objectives, the choices of subprograms within it, the alternatives considered but not appearing in the proposed program, and the reasons for the choices. The objective was to discourage administrators from taking it for granted that programs should be perpetuated and also to encourage policy-makers to reallocate funds.

While this objective is laudable, zero-base budgeting is not a promising way to accomplish it. Whether a discretionary program should be continued is a matter of judgment, not of demonstration. Furthermore, as the Secretary of Defense and others soon learned, it is hazardous to base this judgment on the reports of interested subordinates: they find something favorable to say about every program. To ignore the change from the previous appropriation, furthermore, simply makes evaluation more difficult.

Knowing what change is proposed enables policy-makers to use their impressions about the current state of the program, to see whether new policy or new commitments are at issue, and to apply whatever imperatives exist concerning total spending. Focusing on changes economizes both review time and political capital.

In 1963, Wildavsky and Hammann studied zero-base budgeting in the U.S. Department of Agriculture. They found that it had little effect on decisions. It did, however, consume over 180,000 administrative man-hours. Of 57 high officials interviewed, none favored repeating the experience annually.[3]

There are better ways to encourage officials to reallocate funds. One way is to give each department a devil's advocate, charged with presenting reasons why programs should be contracted or eliminated. The California Legislature has given a valued advisor this function: he is the Legislative Analyst. Another way is to require each administrator to disclose what would be gained or lost if his agency's appropriation were to be (1) the same amount as last time, (2) the amount that would be needed to hold his agency's output constant, and (3) the proposed amount. Given this kind of information about incremental gains and losses for various subagencies, higher officials would be able to redirect funds from seemingly less valuable to seemingly more valuable uses.

Benefit-Cost Analysis

Benefit-cost analysis consists of making a numerical estimate of at least one desired or undesired consequence of at least two alternative courses of action. President Johnson's Bureau of the Budget instructed federal agencies to "maintain a continuing program" of benefit-cost analyses, to start and finish them as seemed appropriate, and to make one "whenever a proposal for major new legislation is involved."

Benefit-cost analysis started in the 1930's with large public investments in water development. Planning and construction costs were heavily subsidized by the federal government.

Technical Considerations

The criterion implicit in benefit-cost analysis calls a change "good" if the sum of the gains (to whomever they accrue) exceeds the sum of the losses, i.e., if the benefits exceed the costs. There is no requirement that gainers compensate losers to make the latter (at a minimum) indifferent to the change. In *The Budget's New Clothes* we proceed from philosophical to analytical criteria of desirability: benefit-cost ratio (gross and net), the internal rate of return, and net benefits. No single criterion is without problems in some imaginable contexts, but the most reliable is to maximize the present value of net benefits (of the set of projects chosen) subject to budget constraints. For example, many analyses imply that the best project is one with the highest benefit-cost ratio. However, the scale of a project that maximizes the benefit-cost ratio is not necessarily the scale that maximizes net benefits. The benefit-cost ratio is misleading when not enough funds are available to do all "feasible" projects, i.e., those with a benefit-cost ratio greater than unity (1.0).

There are two reasons to discount future accruals. First, people are impatient, preferring benefits sooner rather than later. Second, capital can be used in many ways to increase welfare. If one opportunity is exploited, the gains on another must be foregone. Low discount rates favor school buildings over teachers; letter-sorting machines over clerks and mail handlers; dams over flood-plain zoning; and guided missiles, helicopters, and automatic weapons over soldiers.

Water development agencies have used discount rates near and below 3%. The President's Water Resources Council, which has been enforcing higher rates, suggested in a recent proposed policy statement that "the full cost . . . of long-term borrowing . . . is at least 7% and can be as high as 10%." These rates were imposed by President Nixon's OMB. All non-water agencies were directed to use 10%, while water agencies were allowed 7%—considerably higher than the 4⅞% they were using in 1970. The effect of a higher discount rate is to make future net benefits seem smaller, and consequently the project seem less desirable.

Uncertainty is a problem that affects public investments as well as private, and indeed affects any planning that is oriented toward the future. The scenario for the St. Lawrence Seaway did not include the existence of "supertankers"—large ships that do not use the Seaway. Although many outsiders criticize them, planning agencies have not always been overly optimistic. In some cases whole classes of benefits that were ignored in planning now yield the bulk of benefits from projects. An example is outdoor recreation, which was not considered until recently in the planning of water resources projects. Now water-based recreation often contributes over half of the benefits at reservoirs. Some suggest that since the government combines so many investments, it need pay less attention to uncertainty than the private sector. The law of large numbers assures that the actual value of the government's entire portfolio will be "very" close to its expectation. This observation leads to the conclusion that the government should employ a riskless discount rate. Others counsel using discount rates that include a risk premium.

Project Benefit Forecasts

Benefits have been attributed for the outputs of water, transportation, urban renewal projects and for "human capital improvements" obtained through health and education. Calculating benefits typically involves estimating the demand for particular public services. Demand estimation is a difficult forecasting problem. Often the demand for public services is more difficult to predict than the demand for private goods or services.

Project benefits have been estimated in four ways: (1) the willingness of beneficiaries to pay in the form of actual or imputed user charges; (2) the increase in capital values, if any; (3) cost savings, whether actual or potential; (4) increase in national income. Examples of these approaches follow. (More are discussed in Chapter 8 of *The Budget's New Clothes*.)

The value of the output of projects may sometimes be determined by a market, but frequently the output is not sold on a well-functioning market: for example, recreational services at federal parks and reservoirs are often underpriced or given away. Sometimes markets can be simulated, as one was for recreation. This method depends on the observation of associated costs, particularly the cost of traveling to a recreational site. Observing the response of quantity demanded to changes in the cost of using a facility is one way to estimate a demand curve when market-clearing prices are absent.

Transportation projects involve benefits to (a) traffic diverted to a particular means of transportation as well as (b) traffic generated by a new highway, rapid transit system, or airport. A new transportation facility often diverts users from an existing one, and thus reduces congestion. Foster and Beesley found that the major beneficiaries of the Victoria Line addition to the London Underground were nonusers: motorists, bus riders, and other Underground line users.[4] This realization is behind the increasing tendency to require motorists to subsidize mass transit. Their *quid pro quo* is reduced congestion on the roads. A key element in transportation benefit analysis is the value imputed to travel time, a subject of continuing controversy.

The general approach to measuring the benefits of education has been to estimate the present value of increased lifetime income due to education. Before-tax income is what counts. For present purposes, taxation can be viewed as simply a transfer from the earner to the government. One researcher found the rate of return to society from college education not materially different from the rate on business capital. However, because of subsidies to education, the *private* rate of return on college education has been higher than on physical capital. Any non-economic returns to education are above and beyond this.

Like expenditures for education, those for health have been regarded as preventive or remedial maintenance expenditures for human capital. But we do not undertake health expenditures solely to prevent depletion of our human capital. We wish to reduce suffering and save lives for their own sakes, not only for the sake of the net income contributed by healthy taxpayers.

Benefits of new airports or better facilities at existing airports have been measured as the reduction of "airport ineffectiveness": delays, diversions, cancellations, or accidents. The same concept of *cost savings* has been employed to estimate the benefits of syphilis treatment, and reducing mental illness.

Transportation projects such as roads in underdeveloped countries have been analyzed using input-output analysis to predict the *change in national income* due to the project.

Priorities for attacking particular diseases were determined by a combination of cost data (deaths averted vs. dollars expended) and "benefit" data (the value of curing or preventing various diseases in terms of present expected value of future earnings). The result was the following priority of attack: motor vehicle accidents (seat belts, head restraints, prevention of pedestrian injury), arthritis, driving while intoxicated, syphilis, cervical cancer, lung cancer, breast cancer, tuberculosis, the licensing of drivers, head and neck cancer, colon-rectum cancer.

One problem with forecasts of benefits is that other aspects of the environment may change as the project is being built. The demand for shipping at one port is heavily dependent on what is done simultaneously at other ports. Similarly the number of visitor-days at a recreational site is heavily dependent on access roads or other complementary transportation facilities. Price charged affects quantities demanded, yet many economists ignored this relationship when it was fashionable to say that design of public investments was independent of repayment policy.

Measurable benefits, even if relatively minor, tend to dominate an analysis of benefits and costs, and immeasurable or intangible benefits are usually ignored. If air pollution were ameliorated, certain producers—perhaps farmers and people with respiratory diseases—would benefit discernibly, but the largest benefit might be the increased psychic income to the whole society from the amenity of clean air. Usually there is no satisfactory way to measure such intangible gains, so measurable benefits dominate the analysis.

The Environmental Issue

Public investments have natural enemies. Frequently, residents oppose the taking of land through eminent domain either because they lose their land or because they are opposed to the proposed use. Lately, a new issue—concern for the natural environment—has gained legitimacy as a vehicle for their opposition.

Several recent court cases have stopped public and private developments. In July, 1971, a U.S. Court of Appeals found that the rules adopted by the Atomic Energy Commission were inadequate and that continued construction of an atomic power plant approved under the lax rules should be stopped. A proper "balancing" between economic factors and environmental considerations was lacking. Independent evaluation and balancing of certain environmental factors such as thermal effects were considered necessary:

> The Environmental Impact Statement required shall include a cost-benefit analysis which considers and balances the environmental effects of the facility and the alternatives available for reducing or avoiding adverse environmental effects, as well as the environmental, economic, technical and other benefits of the facility. . . . [T]he cost-benefit analysis shall . . . for the purposes of the National Environmental Policy Act consider the radiological effects together with the thermal effects and the other environmental effects of the facility.[5]

This decision resulted in the mitigation of the environmental effects of many riparian nuclear reactors by provision of cooling towers so that less heat was transmitted to the river water.

Other projects—including a reservoir project in Arkansas, the Cross-Florida Barge Canal, and a real estate development in Mono County, California—were at least temporarily delayed because of environmental considerations. The Arkansas reservoir project created flat-water recreational lakes at the expense of one of the last undammed rivers (the Cossatot) in the area.[6] The court, by inference, found that if the wild river were adjudged to be worth $5.5 million, the benefit-cost ratio of the proposed project would be less than unity—1.0.[7] The Florida Canal project represents a rare case of a public works project stopped after it was almost a third complete.

Giving attention to projects' effects on the natural environment implies exploration and explicit statement of effects on people other than the intended beneficiaries of the project. It does not mean that no additional effects will be tolerated. Another salubrious effect is that alternatives are required to be examined explicitly, a step that might not have been considered otherwise. For example, attention must be given to the possibility of leaving a river alone or of adding cooling towers to a nuclear electric plant.

Income distribution effects of projects have been discussed for twenty years, but the environmental quality objective has gained wide attention only recently. In fact, environmental aspects of projects are much more closely scrutinized now than the projects' effects on the distribution of income. Perhaps it is harder to get consensus on the latter.

The Water Resources Council has suggested that each project's benefits and costs be analyzed under four rubrics: National Economic Development, Environmental Quality, Regional Development, and Social Well-Being. Both beneficial and adverse effects would be listed under each rubric.[8] No one, however, has suggested a systematic way to make the net figures in these four accounts commensurable.

Program Budgeting in Practice

In observing the application of PPB in the military services, observers have noted that colonels learned the system and that some, knowing the basis on which decisions would be made, began to select and even falsify data so that budgetary decisions would be made in their favor. In effect, the operating bureaucrats who create information can refuse to collect data that show a program to be ineffective.

California school districts resisted the state's efforts to impose PPB on them. A public accounting firm handling the effort for the state tried to convince selected school districts that participation in the pilot program was to their advantage and that no straight-jacket categories were to be imposed from above. The districts would have the opportunity to formulate their objectives, to organize their teaching effort to serve these objectives, and to compose their own program structure. Despite their reassurances, many teachers were convinced that Sacramento intended to eliminate art, music, or programs considered potentially subversive, such as social studies.

New York was both the first state to adopt PPB and the first to discard it. Pennsylvania made the greatest effort to make it effective. Everywhere it has met resistance from people opposed to change.

Benefit-Cost Analysis in Practice

The present institutional context of benefit-cost analysis biases its results. Thus, the agency that will later oversee the engineering and construction of a candidate project often has done the analysis that is intended to decide which project—if any—to do. Given common organizational objectives of continued existence and growth, the agencies have an interest in a favorable prospectus. The problem is not solved when an outside consultant is engaged to make a feasibility study. Typically the consultant learns explicitly or implicitly which result will favor his client's goals. It is a rare consultant who is willing to give the client bad news.

Two projects to which benefit-cost analysis was applied offer insights into its long-run impact. One, the California Water Project (CWP) went ahead despite several negative recommendations. Another, the Supersonic Transport (SST) prototype development, was finally cancelled, perhaps in part because of the adverse findings. However, the SST project went on for eight years despite negative analyses by reputable firms and individuals. Both projects received favorable and unfavorable reviews in the course of many studies. Some studies are tactics for delay, or deflections of criticism, undertaken while the project quietly marches down its critical path.

The State of California, instead of the federal government, built the CWP in part to avoid the provision of the federal Reclamation Act of 1902 that forbids delivery of federally subsidized irrigation water to holdings in excess of 160 acres per owner. When "feasibility reports" were released before the bond election the following headlines appeared in two newspapers:

> "FEATHER RIVER PROJECT GETS SOUND RATING
> IN TWO REPORTS"
> —*Los Angeles Times*

> "STATE WATER PLAN CALLED IMPOSSIBLE"
> —*San Francisco Chronicle*

Clearly, it was possible for both papers to read what they wanted into the reports. The Feather River Project survived. The Oroville Reservoir and the California Aqueduct are completed. (As this is being written, however, a Peripheral Canal to take surplus Sacramento River water south is still under debate.) One element, the Dos Rios Reservoir, was eliminated despite a claimed benefit-cost ratio of 1.9. Thus it seems that *who* gets the benefits is more important to decision-makers than how the benefits compare numerically with the costs. Sometimes wealthy landowners are favored. Other times (if rarely) the poor are favored, but economic efficiency is rarely persuasive.

President John F. Kennedy committed the country to the development of a Supersonic Transport (SST) in 1963 despite a Stanford Research Institute report that advised against federal subsidy. Later, an Institute for Defense Analyses report was pessimistic on demand for SST's. Despite these negative (and courageous) conclusions, the Federal Aviation Administration continued to advocate the program, commissioning other consultants to counter the views of its negative consultants.

When President Nixon took office, he appointed an *ad hoc* committee to advise him on the subject. Several members of that committee later testified that their views were misrepresented by an Undersecretary of Transportation, who championed the project. Subcommittees on economics, balance of payments, and environmental and sociological effects all reported negatively. A subcommittee on technological spillovers reported them to be minor. In 1971 the federal government ended its subsidy of prototype development.

Rhetoric was dominated by allegations of impact on the environment. Senator William Proxmire had waged a vigorous campaign showing that most states would pay more in taxes for the SST development than they would benefit by it. Previous studies of the SST were certainly extant, however, having been brought together by the FAA in an *Economic Feasibility Report* (1967).

In the planning of both the CWP and the SST project, it appears that government officials did not ask, "Should the government spend money on this type of project?" They asked instead, "Do the benefits exceed the costs?" By analogy, if someone were to show that the benefits exceed the costs in producing and selling Bobby Fischer chess sets, this would indicate that government also should undertake that enterprise.

The Use of Alternatives

Typically, in public investment, one alternative is tentatively chosen and an effort is made to show that it is "feasible." Somewhere in the background there almost certainly has been consideration of other alternatives, but only the preferred one is analyzed in detail and considered publicly. But the essence of that much-overused term "systems analysis" is the use of *alternatives*. If we have several alternatives thoroughly analyzed, then we can compare them and recognize rates of exchange of economic benefits for environmental degradation; for example, all manmade structures have some environmental impacts, usually negative. We are not, of course, ready to stop building more structures, but we do wish to anticipate what each intrusion is likely to cost us, in order to help judge alternative ways of accomplishing a purpose or alternative uses of public funds. Models of good systems analyses of real alternatives are presented in works by Meyer, Kain and Wohl,[9] The U. S. Department of Transportation,[10] and Robert N. Grosse.[11] We do not necessarily agree with their conclusions, but they exemplify admirable method in seriously considering alternatives.

Benefit estimates are frequently inflated to serve the purpose of the agency doing the analysis. Cost estimates are usually at the lower limit of actual costs.[12] There is much discouraging indication that Congress cares little for economic efficiency. The Flood Control Act of 1936 required that "benefits to whomsoever they may accrue [should] exceed the costs," but not that a chosen project have the greatest net benefits among all admissible projects.[13] Perhaps the only thing Congress intended was that benefit-cost screening be adequate to exclude grossly uneconomic projects. Legislators seem to prefer to have civil servants prescreen certain types of projects so that the burden of a negative decision can be shifted from themselves.

Congress is reluctant to refuse to spend, but if it wishes to regain lost control over public expenditures it must equip itself to evaluate and cut where necessary. An analytical arm responsible only to Congress might be some improvement. It would give Congress the expertise that operating agencies now have. But there is no assurance congressmen would heed its advice. It seems that congressmen still are preoccupied with the regional distribution of federal spending. Having an analytic agency responsible to the Legislature has worked well in California. The Legislative Analyst is respected and is nonpartisan. His advice is frequently sought on implications of legislation.

Limitations of the Benefit-Cost Approach

Benefit-cost analysis is more effective in *comparing* projects than in deciding whether or not to pursue a single project. Analysis has not been an effective sieve, but it has served the purposes of the agency doing the analysis. Only recently, with the advent of environmental issues, have some proposed projects been pared.

Decision-making strictly according to the results of benefit-cost analysis is better adapted to those functions of government that are most similar to business, especially public utilities such as water, waste disposal, power production, and transportation projects. But in human resource fields, analysis can only be a partial aid to decision-making. Further, quantitative evaluation is more useful for intraprogram choices (for example, choosing which of several harbor-deepening projects to pursue) than for interprogram choices (for example, choosing harbor-deepening at the expense of medical research).

A Concluding Comment: Formulating Alternative Choices

One function of administrators can be called intelligence: gathering information for problem solving. A second function is design: the formulation or invention of alternative courses of action among which choices can then be made. Executives spend the least amount of time on the third step, the actual choice, and most of their time on design.[14]

The function of design and formulation of alternatives is crucially important. Further, it is far more fruitful to spend time exploring, developing and formulating alternative uses of resources than it is to investigate a single use exhaustively. Accordingly, benefit-cost analysis should be much more heavily employed in the design function, and less in the final choice among alternatives. Choosing among alternatives is relatively easy. The generation of imaginative choices should come first, and ranks first in importance.

Notes

1. U.S. Office of Management and Budget, *Circular No. A-11, Revised, Transmittal Memorandum No. 38* (Washington, D.C.: June 21, 1971).

2. U.S. Bureau of the Budget, *Bulletin No. 68-2* (Washington, D.C.: July 18, 1967).

3. Aaron Wildavsky and Arthur Hammann, "Comprehensive Versus Incremental Budgeting in the Department of Agriculture," in Fremont J. Lyden and Ernest G. Miller, ed., *Planning Programming Budgeting: A Systems Approach to Management* (Chicago: Markham, 1967), p. 161.

4. C. D. Foster and M. E. Beesley, "Estimating the Social Benefit of Constructing an Underground Railway in London," *Journal of the Royal Statistical Society* vol. 126, (1963) pp. 46–58.

5. *Federal Register* XXXVI: 175, 9 Sept. 1971, p. 10872.

6. *Environmental Defense Fund, et al, v. Corps of Engineers of U.S. Army, et al.,* 325 *Fed. Supplement* 728 (1971). The injunction was dissolved after a new impact statement was filed, 4 *Environmental Reporter Cases,* December 8, 1972.

7. 325 *Fed. Supplement* 757 (1971). A benefit-cost ratio of unity or above does not necessarily imply that a project should be undertaken.

8. *Federal Register* XXXVI: 245, 21 Dec. 1971, p. 24144.

9. *The Urban Transportation Problem* (Cambridge: Harvard University Press, 1965).

10. Urban Commutation Alternatives Special Analysis Study" reprinted in Joint Economic Committee, *The Analysis and Evaluation of Public Expenditures* vol. 2, pp. 698–733 (Washington, D. C.: 1969).

11. R. H. Haveman and Julius Margolis, *Public Expenditures and Policy Analysis* (Chicago: Markham, 1970) pp. 518–48.

12. See Leonard Merewitz, "Cost Overruns in Public Works," in *Benefit-Cost and Policy Analysis Annual* (Chicago: Aldine, 1973).

13. Congress' wording seems to suggest satisficing or choosing a "good enough" alternative rather than maximizing.

14. John Dewey, *How We Think,* Chapter 8 (New York: Heath, 1910).

Management
by Objectives

3

Management by objectives (MBO) has been widely used in the
private sector and has received significant attention in the public
sector in the United States. The concepts of management by
objectives are extensions of the normal management functions
of planning and control. Managers plan what they hope to
accomplish, then use their plans to control progress toward their
goals. The difference between MBO and good, common-sense
management lies in the rigor with which the planning and control
is carried out.

Henry Tosi and Stephen Carroll have suggested three
activities involved in management by objectives: (1) goal setting,
(2) participation, and (3) feedback.[1] The development of clear
goals—particularly goals that can be achieved—can be a strong
motivator. This is especially true if subordinates are involved in
setting the goals and developing plans to achieve them. MBO
assumes that participation leads to greater commitment to
organizational goals and encourages people within an organization
to work harder to achieve those goals. Feedback is necessary to

permit the organization to adapt to new circumstances than can affect a plan's effectiveness.

Many advocates of MBO have stressed the role of participation. The editor of a symposium issue of the *Public Administration Review* devoted to public sector MBO viewed participation as the key aspect of the technique:

> For our purposes, we define management by objectives as a process whereby organizational goals and objectives are set through the participation of organizational members in terms of results expected. . . . Although participation in the goal-setting process is not a panacea for effective management, the existing literature supports the idea that participative management can increase individual motivation toward organizational objectives, promote interdependence between managers and subordinates, and create more flexibility, increased efficiency, and greater job satisfaction.[2]

We would expect, therefore, that an environment open to decentralization of authority would produce the most benefits through MBO.

Instead, the federal government's experience with MBO suggested that management by objectives was a way of centralizing control rather than a way of decentralizing it to make government more productive. Still, few would disagree with the logic of management by objectives. It appears to be simply codified common sense. MBO seems to be what good managers have done intuitively for years.

The basic MBO cycle as used in the federal government during the early seventies appears in figure 1. This diagram suggests that the mission and goals of an agency are supplied by superiors in the hierarchy or by statute. Analysis of agency problems—subject to all the problems of analysis raised in the Merewitz and Sosnick article[3]—indicates areas of management concern. Specific objectives are developed and tied to agency goals; suitable indicators to determine whether the objectives are being achieved must be developed. Agency activities are related to goals and resources through planning. Reporting systems provide the feedback necessary to change plans and programs. Program success is evaluated by the degree to which the activities achieve the stated objectives.

The objective-setting phase is supposed to tie the subordinates to the organization's objectives through participation. But just as private sector objectives in MBO are often dictated by the hierarchy with minimal reference to participation,[4] so too were those in the

Figure 1
MBO in Federal Government

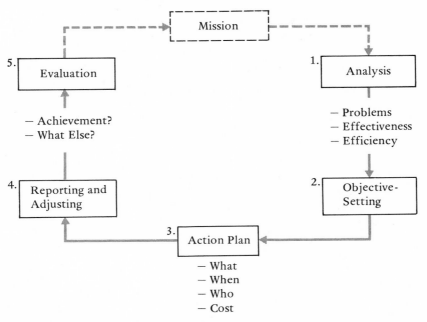

Modified from diagram appearing in William L. Ginnodo, "A View of MBO . . . From the Middle," *Civil Service Journal* vol. 16, no. 1 (July–September 1975), p. 14.

federal government. At the top levels, the Office of Management and Budget did the dictating. This filtered down until operating officials responsible for meeting the objectives were given the orders. As one bureaucrat said: "They force-feed their objectives on us, and we don't swallow."[5]

If it is generally the case that MBO in government operates in a unilateral, authoritarian fashion with the central budgeting agency enforcing objectives that it has determined, then the participative promise of management by objectives is not going to be realized. This does not mean that MBO should be assigned to the circular file of administrative reform efforts that have failed. What passes for MBO in government might still fulfill meaningful planning and control functions, but principally for centralized decision makers.

Even in governmental agencies where objectives are force-fed to the subordinates, there is often participation in developing the action plan for achieving those objectives. Of course, it is difficult to say whether the MBO process itself contributes something new in this action-planning phase or whether such planning went on before MBO. Surely, there is nothing in the action-planning phase that would disrupt smooth management unless the action plans are subject to such extensive, time-consuming review that the original planning becomes a paper-pushing exercise.

Successful management by objectives demands that indicators or measures of achievement be developed for programs. Often social service agencies hide behind the claim that no one can measure what they do. In this section, John C. Aplin and Peter P. Schoderbek explore some of the reasons why this is done and suggest ways to measure such programs. Rodney H. Brady, who was a key figure in implementing the MBO system in the Department of Health, Education, and Welfare, presents a positive view of how MBO worked in his agency. Frank P. Sherwood and William J. Page raise some serious political and organizational questions regarding MBO.

Notes

1. Henry L. Tosi and Stephen Carroll, "Management by Objectives," in Jay M. Shafritz, *A New World: Readings on Modern Public Personnel Management* (Chicago: International Personnel Management Association, 1975), pp. 179–83.

2. Jong S. Jun, "Management by Objectives in the Public Sector," *Public Administration Review* vol. 36, no. 1 (January–February, 1976), p. 3.

3. Selection 4, supra.

4. Wendell French, *The Personnel Management Process Human Resources Administration*, 3rd ed. (Boston: Houghton Mifflin, 1974), p. 385.

5. Joel Havemann, "Is MBO Becoming SOP at OSHA?" *National Journal Reports*, vol. 7 (July 26, 1975), p. 1075. Also see Jerry McCaffery, "MBO and the Federal Budgetary Process," *Public Administration Review* vol. 36, no. 1 (January–February 1976), p. 37.

How to Measure MBO

John C. Aplin, Jr. and Peter P. Schoderbek

Since the early 1950s, formal objective based planning and control systems have been extremely popular in private enterprise. It has been roughly estimated that management by objectives (MBO) programs have been employed by over 80% of the industrial firms in the United States. With the success of MBO in private industry and the frequent movement of industrial managers into public organizations, it was only a matter of time before administrators attempted to apply MBO in public agencies. Indeed, in recent years, MBO programs have been reported in educational institutions,[1] health care centers,[2] state and local governments,[3] as well as numerous other federal agencies.[4] Most of the recent articles and books in the MBO field devote entire sections to public sector applications of management by objectives. Unfortunately, in spite of the increasing use of MBO in public organizations and the apparent acceptance of MBO among senior administrators, management by objectives has yet to achieve its potential in the public sector. Anyone experienced with public MBO is aware that traditional "profit-oriented" MBO is more difficult to operationalize in the "service-oriented" organization. In recognition of this problem, the following paper was designed to describe a number of techniques the authors have found that facilitate the use and measurement of MBO in the public sector. However, it is necessary to begin by discussing the major obstacles or barriers limiting the successful use of MBO in public organizations.

From *Public Personnel Management*, March–April 1976, pp. 88–95. Reprinted by permission of the International Personnel Management Association, 1313 East 60th Street, Chicago, Illinois 60637.

Obstacles or Barriers

The environment facing the public organization today differs immensely from that surrounding the profit-seeking organization. Consequently, a number of "environmental factors" can arise and interfere with the operation of MBO in the public sector. It is important to consider these forces since they have on occasion thwarted efforts to develop MBO programs. Unfortunately, these barriers are often difficult or impossible to attack directly and must be dealt with accordingly.

The authors have recently conducted an extensive study of the use of MBO in public organizations. In this study over 200 administrators who had experience with public MBO were surveyed. The results of the survey revealed a number of these constraints. Throughout this paper the examples and illustrations will refer to social service agencies, which account for nearly 75% of all governmental expenditures. It is felt, however, that these examples have direct parallels in all others public agencies as well.

1. Philosophical Attitude Toward the Measurement of Social Services

Once an idea has been conceptualized, it is nearly impossible to reconceptualize. So it has been with social services. Since the inception of publicly financed services, it has been deemed impractical, if not impossible, to attempt to measure achievements or evaluate total unit effectiveness. Efforts to do so led to outcries by politicians and administrators alike. For the most part, casual observation of agency activity reports and cursory examinations of programs served as the routine evaluation procedure. Administrators defended this practice, claiming that their services were of a human nature, and efforts to measure these services would adversely affect their quality. This perceived uniqueness led many administrators to strenuously resist periodic endeavors by external groups to assess program or organizational accomplishments. Without question, this philosophical stance is antithetical to the basic tenets underlying the objective approach.

The MBO process endeavors to give unambiguous meaning to the accomplishments of an organization or individual. It is premised upon the measurement of results, which in turn requires the definition of outputs. The intensity of feeding of some administrators, who resist the spread of MBO, is reflected in the following comment received in response to our recent MBO survey:

... professionals in our own field for many years have been trying to develop units of service and have been largely unsuccessful . . . *you simply cannot measure our contribution to society.*

The resistance based on this philosophical perspective, although diminished somewhat in recent years, stands as a major barrier to the widespread acceptance of MBO, particularly among "long-term" public officials. Hopefully, with continued experimentation, administrators will come to view MBO as a tool to "assist" them in improving their managerial performance rather than a "control" system that interferes with their daily activities.

2. Lack of Power to Force Compliance

Typically, administrators in the public sector do not have the same degree of power as their counterparts in the private sector. In industrial firms the threat of discipline or the possibility of dismissal can substantially increase the superior's power over his subordinates. This is not the case in public organizations. Federal and state merit employment systems have been intentionally structured to protect public employees from the actions of capricious politicians. In the process, an unusually secure employment environment has been created. This situation has tended to reduce power differentials between superiors and subordinates and has enabled individuals to insulate themselves from threats by their superiors.

In most governmental agencies, it is extremely difficult to terminate an employee for failure to attain objectives. This is especially true if he or she may have accumulated a lengthy history of acceptable performance prior to the introduction of an MBO system. Furthermore, experienced administrators, being aware that even personnel at lower levels may have patrons, are inclined to maintain the status quo. In short, public employees commonly develop referent power bases to protect themselves from actions their superior may take if they fail to establish and attain job-related objectives.

3. Inability to Monetarily Reward Differential Levels of Performance

Reduced to its simplest form, MBO is a complete system that includes setting task objectives, measuring performance, and rewarding accomplishments. Experience has shown that failure to positively reinforce (reward) desired behavior will lead to eventual extinction of the behavior. When an organization's reward system fails to reinforce an individual for achieving objectives, it is impossible to sustain any long-term interest in establishing or attaining goals. The charge has often been made that salary increases to public employees have fallen behind general increases in the cost of living, a factor that has led many administrators to distribute salary increases on a straight percentage basis irrespective of performance. Such a procedure may be laudable from a humanitarian standpoint; it nonetheless can destroy the results-reward cycle essential to the success of an MBO program.

This fact was amply demonstrated by the result of the author's survey. Of 198 administrators responding, 163 (82%) had formally established job objectives. Nearly 90% of the administrators using MBO felt their future evaluations and rewards would be based on success in achieving goals. Interestingly, less than 3% of the individuals who had not established goals felt their future evaluations and rewards would be effected. These results, summarized in Table 1, underscore the importance of integrating the MBO system with the evaluation and reward system. Clearly, if an individual did not perceive a relationship between success in achieving goals and future rewards, he or she would not even establish goals.

In summary, the financial reward structure for local, state, and federal employees has traditionally been fixed by legislative action. In most instances employees can be awarded *minor* salary increases when they demonstrate exceptionally meritorious performance. However, given the financial rigidities, the only *meaningful* rewards that can be anticipated are increased responsibility, personal recognition, and/or transfer to a higher position or better job assignment. Whatever the financial constraints of the specific public agency, if MBO is to be even minimally successful it must be integrated with either the financial reward system, the promotion system, or both.

4. Rapidity of Change in the Public Sector Environment

Without question our society has become exceedingly complex. Widespread drug abuse, inadequacies in health care delivery to the elderly, and urban blight have stimulated drug-treatment programs, Medicare/Medicaid, and numerous urban renewal projects. To cope with these major societal problems, the public demands a government that is responsive, flexible, and, above all, innovative. This desire

Table 1
Administrators' Perceptions of the Relationship of Evaluations and Rewards to MBO (N = 198)

Are You Currently Using MBO?	Will your future evaluations and rewards be based on your performance under MBO?		
	Yes	*No*	*Not Sure*
Yes (82%)	86.5%	13.5%	0%
No (18%)	2.8%	77.1%	20.1%

for flexibility and responsiveness gives rise to a final obstacle that can intervene and adversely affect the functioning of an MBO program.

As specific problems become urgent, legislators respond, and with the assistance of many groups, design legislation to mitigate the long-term consequences of the problem. Since problems seem to emerge daily, an incessant flow of programs results and induces a continual shifting of priorities among existing programs. These shifting priorities complicate administrators' efforts to establish a semi-stable MBO program. Furthermore, legislation hurriedly passed is typically couched in vague and ambiguous terms, and administrators charged with implementing such legislation have difficulty interpreting intent. To be successful, MBO requires a hierarchy of relative stable specific goals. Unless legislative or governing bodies take care in defining desired outputs, it can be impossible to effectively employ MBO.

The four constraints that have been discussed are by no means exhaustive, but do reflect the *major* issues faced by any individual or organization attempting to implement MBO in the public sector. Unfortunately, these four constraints often are "binding" and cannot be overcome in practice. They must be "skirted" rather than directly confronted. It is hoped that awareness of their existence and possible adverse consequences will help to minimize their dysfunctional aspects.

Assuming that these issues have been addressed, if not resolved, the remainder of the paper turns to a number of specific recommendations intended to facilitate the measurement of MBO in the public sector. Many of the operational difficulties of public MBO can be linked to the development of criteria and the design of a measurement system.

Techniques to Facilitate MBO Measurement

The management by objectives process employed by managers and administrators is in essence a management cybernetic system. In theory and practice, the minimum requirements for a cybernetic system are the definition of a system's "goal" (desired state), the development of means or capabilities to attain the goal (transform unit), the establishment of criteria to evaluate goal attainment, and finally a system designed to monitor or measure the output level or the system's achievements. This cybernetic model can be employed to detect deficiencies in an MBO program and "fine-tune" an existing MBO program.

Many of the problems with public MBO, particularly measurement problems, relate to only three of the components in the cybernetic model. The fourth element, the design of delivery programs, does not cause substantial problems for the inherent operation of a public MBO program. The remainder of this paper will focus on three elements of the public MBO process: the initial formulation of strategic and operating objectives; the determination of appropriate evaluation criteria; and the development of an information-gathering capability.

1. Initial Formulation of Strategic and Operating Objectives

In private enterprises, the formulation of strategic goals is more of degree than kind. Generally, their strategic goals are in the areas of sales, growth, return, and market share. Variations among firms involve the magnitude of these goals and the instrumental goals that guide short-run decisions. In the profit-oriented firm, the majority of effort and time is devoted to developing strategies and plans to achieve strategic goals rather than the formulation of the strategic goals themselves.

In public organizations the strategic goals have seldom been articulated. Congress is currently debating the responsibilities, objectives, and activities of such sacrosanct agencies as the CIA, the FBI, and the Department of Agriculture. Debate has revealed a noticeable lack of agreement as to the "strategic" purposes of these agencies and the legality of their means. For many administrators the most difficult question, but one which must be answered, is: "Why does my organization exist, and what will it be held responsible for?" Fortunately, a number of attempts have been made to grapple with questions of this type.

During the 1st Session of the 90th Congress, the Senate Committee on Governmental Operations addressed these questions. In an effort to clarify the role of state, local and federal governmental bodies, the committee grouped the major government activities into various categories. They described seven "major program areas" and an additional "administrative support area." These efforts reflect the need to define "key-result" areas for public organizations, and can provide an excellent basis to begin the public MBO process. The committee's deliverations produced the following areas:

- *Major Program Areas*
  1. Personal safety
     a. Law enforcement
     b. Fire protection
  2. Health care delivery
  3. Intellectual development and personal enrichment
  4. Satisfactory home and community environment
  5. Economic satisfaction and work opportunities
  6. Satisfactory leisure-time opportunities
  7. Transportation–communication–location
- *Administrative Support Areas:*
  1. General administration and support[7]

To illustrate the type of strategic goals deemed necessary, the committee wrote example objectives in each of the eight areas. To illustrate, the following objective related to the personal safety area:

> . . . To reduce the amount and effects of external harm to individuals and in general to maintain an atmosphere of personal security from external events.[8]

The personal safety area was subdivided into law enforcement and fire protection. The global goal related to fire protection was, ". . . to reduce the number of fires and loss due to fires." (A complete report of the committee's suggested objectives may be found in *Criteria for Evaluation in Planning State and Local Programs: A Study Submitted By the Committee on Intergovernmental Relations,* United States Senate, 90th Congress [U.S. Government Printing Office: Washington, D.C., 1967].

The activities of the committee can be described as an attempt to provide a framework for jurisdictions that plan to establish strategic goals. Robert Anthony, in addressing planning and control, describes strategic planning as "the process having to do with the formulation of long-range, strategic, policy-type plans that change the character or direction of the organization."[9] The strategic goals and plans should serve as the integrating mechanism for the activities of public organizations.

To attain the objectives established by the "strategic plan," another level of operational goals and plans is required. This level, synonomous with "management control" includes all the short-run activities, processes, and functions required to successfully reach strategic goals. In the public sector, the subordinate agencies charged with implementing legislation must establish operational goals and the plans required to achieve these goals.

In practice, the operational objectives and tactical programs established at the management control level do not flow smoothly out of the strategic plans and goals. Consequently, public agencies must impute meaning to the strategic goals and design their activities accordingly. In reality one finds substantial diversity in the activities of different agencies implementing the same legislation. Confounding this problem is the tendency for legislative bodies to assume their directives are unambiguous and will be precisely implemented by the various agencies. The complete planning process is lengthy enough without wasting effort rehashing, reforming, and redefining the strategic plan in order to establish operational objectives.

In summary, a prerequisite to measurement of public MBO is the successful formulation of strategic goals by legislators or policy makers. Once these goals are established, they must be communicated to those responsible for their attainment. At this point, the strategic planners and program implementers must jointly agree upon operational objectives to insure their congruency with strategic objectives.

What is needed in the public sector is a closer working relationship between agency heads and legislative bodies to insure consistency between strategic and operational objectives.

Once the goals have been established it becomes necessary to develop "yardsticks" or criteria to evaluate the level of achievement. The following section will address the criterion problem directly.

2. Determination of Appropriate Evaluation Criteria

Once strategic and operational objectives have been established, it becomes necessary to identify criteria to evaluate unit/individual performance. Unless specific goal-related criteria are developed, evaluators use readily available data to establish criteria. In essence, many criteria are established because of the availability of information, not the requirements of the previously established goals.

Historically, the most readily accessible data has been either cost-based or workload-based. This does not accurately reflect accomplishments or goal attainment, only levels of expenditures and activities. Criteria based solely on data of this type have a number of inherent limitations.

Cost data (readily obtainable from budget and expense records) permit two types of evaluation: cost relative to a similar agency or cost over time. Neither of these measures addresses or reveals the accomplishments of the agency. Workload data (based on numbers treated or activities performed) are concerned with volume or quantity of services and disclose little about the quality of service provided. Frequently these figures will be manipulated to provide unit/cost data, but again these statistics can be grossly misleading, and tend to overstate accomplishments of an individual or organization.

The criteria used to evaluate goal attainment should be concerned with costs and quantity of services, but must also accurately reflect the quality and consequences of the agency's output. In this light, two types of criteria are required to evaluate the performance of a public organization—monetary and nonmonetary. Monetary criteria have become especially important during recent periods of scarce resources and increasing pressures to maintain fiscal control. The focus of this discussion, however, will be the development of nonmonetary criteria to assess goal attainment.

In a study prepared by the National Commission on Productivity, a disturbing fact was noted. Only four of thirty major cities surveyed have attempted to measure organizational effectiveness or impact. The commission concluded that the difficulty faced by these cities has been twofold: the conceptual problem of what to measure has not been resolved and the capability to collect output data has not been developed.[10] These conclusions have profound implications for the MBO process and emphasize the strides that must be made before public MBO can be even marginally successful.

Given the scope of goals established by public organizations, the number of possible criteria to evaluate performance is infinite. Therefore, it is impossible in the scope of a single paper to discuss all conceivable criteria that could be used to evaluate a public organization. It is possible, however, to relate in general terms a number of criteria requirements.

All public organizations are charged with two major responsibilities. First, they must design and manage an efficient organization capable of responding to changing public service demands. Second, they must develop specific programs and delivery systems to provide the clientele of the organization with services at a cost to the public commensurate with the benefits received. In the majority of organizations, only in the latter area are goals even considered. In the management area, few goals are established in terms of public responsiveness, flexibility, employee development, morale, and retention. Obviously these areas are interrelated. It would be difficult to conceive of an instance where an organization could achieve goals in service delivery without having a well-managed agency. The tendency of public organizations to establish only "program" goals leads to "fire-fighting" complaints, considerable upheaval when new programs are required, and public complaints that only a few "special interest" groups are being served by the agency.

In terms of program delivery a number of criteria should be defined. Assuming that strategic goals have been established, and that operational goals and plans are delineated, the administrator must decide what criteria will allow program evaluators to measure goal attainment. In simple form, public programs involve the delivery of a certain type of service to some target population or clientele. Criteria design for any service program should at a minimum include:

1. Definition of the type of service to be provided (i.e., delivery of meals to elderly people in their homes).

2. Specification of quality of service delivered (i.e., meeting 100 percent of minimum daily caloric and vitamin requirements of elderly individual).

3. Estimation of all *major* consequences or outputs of the organization's activities related to service delivery.

4. Definition of the target group—area of coverage/responsibility (in essence, determination of total clientele possible for service).

5. Establishment of desired clientele penetration levels (i.e., reach 35 percent of eligible recipients).

6. Economic constraints (i.e., within parameters dictated by funding and administrative support).

7. Time dimensions—a future point in time when evaluation and replanning is to occur.

These guidelines are not meant to be rigid prescriptions for behavior; rather they are concerns to be addressed when establishing criteria. It should be noted that seldom will a single criterion suffice to evaluate achievement against a single objective.

The information gathering system should be reactive to the criterion formulation process. Historically, as was noted, performance criteria have been based on cost and workload data. The resultant measurement systems have been "accounting" oriented. Public organizations have developed elaborate MIS [management information systems] (many computer based), which only account for activities, not results, as demanded by MBO. The final section of this paper examines the information gathering requirements of a public organization using MBO.

3. Development of Information-Gathering Capability

Ultimately the evaluation of a governmental unit must be linked to its ability to address and solve the problems that occasioned its creation. This necessarily implies that the information must not only be internally focused (activity-oriented), it must also actively seek external environmental information (results-oriented). Information relevant to the criteria can only be secured by going to the clientele of the organization. Quality of service is relative to the clients' experience, and cannot be assessed without feedback from numerous external sources.

An important point, frequently overlooked by administrators, is that more sophisticated data processing equipment is not likely to improve measurement under MBO. It is more apt to force evaluation to activities and costs per unit of service. The focus on internal information has led many administrators to conclude they were performing effectively, when in reality none of the organization's goals were being achieved.

An extensive elaboration of information systems has not been undertaken in this paper, because this is not where the most pressing problems lie. Information system design is a relatively simple technical consideration that can be addressed once criterion formulation becomes more effective. In the words of the Commission on Productivity, ". . . in most cases, the conceptual problems of *what* to measure have yet to be resolved and any government undertaking work in this area has to first wrestle with these problems before attacking the more mundane data (collection) problems."[11]

In summary, MBO systems require externally based results-oriented data, not internal cost or activity data. The problem of securing such information is more technical than conceptual, and can only be attacked when the question of what to measure is answered.

Summary

Management by objectives programs, developed in profit-oriented enterprises, have recently been introduced within a variety of public organizations. Unfortunately, the widespread industrial success with MBO has not been duplicated in public agencies. In part, MBO's lack of outstanding success in public enterprises can be attributed to inexperience with service-oriented-objective systems. Numerous attempts to apply profit-based systems directly to public organizations without modification have ended in failure.

Improvements in public MBO can be expected when more attention is devoted to the formulation of strategic objectives for governmental units and programs. Past failures to clearly articulate legislative intent have led to misinterpretation of strategic goals and formulation of operational goals that were inappropriate. Further needed to improve measurement is the delineation of performance criteria reflective of the objectives established. Finally, the logistical problem of information gathering, storage, and retrieval must be addressed before management by objectives can reach its potential in the public sector.

Notes

1. Merrill H. Arnold, "Management by Objectives and the School System," *The School Administrator*, 32:15–16 (1972).

2. Robert C. Gronbach, "Management by Agreement: Hartford Hospital's Approach to MBO," 3, *Management by Objectives*, no. 3:31–34.

3. C. J. Hancock, "MBO Raises Management Effectiveness in Government Service," 3, *Management by Objectives*, 4:9–16.

4. Rodney H. Brady, "MBO Goes to Work in the Public Sector," 51, *Harvard Business Review*, 2:65–74 (March–April, 1973).

5. Title 45—Public Welfare, Chapter IX, Administration on Aging, *Federal Register*, vol. 38, no. 196, 28040 (October 11, 1973).

6. *The Budget of the United States Government* (U.S. Office of Management and Budget, 1974).

7. Committee on Government Operations: U.S. Senate, *Criteria for Evaluation in Planning State and Local Programs* (90th Congress, 1st Session, July 21, 1967).

8. *Ibid.*, pp. 23–24.

9. R. N. Anthony, J. Dearden, and R. F. Vancil, *Management Control Systems* (Homewood, Ill.: Richard D. Irwin, Inc., 1965), p. 4.

10. H. P. Hatry and D. M. Fisk, *Improving Productivity and Productivity Measurement in Local Governments* (A Report Prepared for the National Commission on Productivity, June 1971).

11. *Ibid.*, p. 28.

MBO Goes to Work
in the Public Sector

Rodney H. Brady

The nation's largest organization in terms of spending power—the United States Department of Health, Education, and Welfare (HEW)—has been called unmanageable. It may have been at one time, but an important step toward making HEW more manageable has been the development and implementation of one of the most far-reaching management by objectives (MBO) systems in operation anywhere.

Although MBO is a familiar management tool in the private business sector, it had been used sparingly in the public sector prior to being introduced at HEW. The department turned to MBO as a means of coping with a veritable explosion in the size and scope of its operations. HEW's budget authority for the 1973 fiscal year is $87 billion—an increase of 70% over its budget of just four years ago, and the first civilian-agency budget in modern U.S. history to eclipse that of the Department of Defense. More than one third of all the money dispensed by the federal government this fiscal year will flow through HEW.

Prior to becoming the chief administrative and management officer of HEW in late 1970, I had been a senior executive and a management consultant in the private business sector and had discovered firsthand the value of MBO as an effective tool for managing large, complex organizations. However, the imponderable question facing me and my staff as we sought to implement a de-

Reprinted from *Harvard Business Review;* Vol. 51 (March–April, 1973), pp. 65–74. © 1973 by the President and Fellows of Harvard College; all rights reserved.

partmentwide MBO system at HEW was whether this method of management, believed by many to depend on the discipline of a profit and loss statement for successful operation, could be adapted to an organization that must ultimately measure success in terms of improving the quality of life.

Now, after over two years of experience with MBO, we have learned not only that this technique will indeed work at HEW but also that it has applicability to many other large, public-sector organizations. It is the objective of this article to (a) explain some major differences in introducing MBO to a public, as opposed to a private, sector organization; (b) briefly describe the MBO approach that has evolved at HEW and summarize the lessons we have learned in applying it; and (c) provide guidelines for other public- and private-sector organizations that may wish to adopt this management tool.

Private and Public MBO

In 1954, Peter F. Drucker gave form to the concept of MBO in his book, *The Practice of Management.*[1] Ten years later, in giving the concept substance, he could still complain that "the foundation for systematic, purposeful performance of the specific task and function of business enterprise is . . . still missing."[2] Today, however, MBO is installed in numerous private companies and its premises are familiar to many business managers.[3] The strength of these premises lies in their simplicity:

• The clearer the idea of what one wants to accomplish, the greater the chances of accomplishing it.

• Real progress can only be measured in relation to what one is trying to make progress toward.

In other words, if one knows where he is going, he finds it easier to get there, he can get there faster, and he will know it when he arrives.

Although the premises of MBO have been tested and proven in the private sector, it has taken the public sector considerably longer to effectively incorporate them. Executives in the federal government have long grasped the *need* for more effective management, but for the most part they have failed to develop and implement systems such as MBO. This is one reason why they are so often frustrated in their attempts to manage large federal departments.

As John Gardner, who spent three years at the helm of HEW, put it: "When you figure out how to hold a middle-level bureaucrat accountable, it'll be comparable to landing on the moon."[4]

Similarly, Senator Abraham Ribicoff, HEW Secretary in 1961, remarked that "no matter how brilliant he is, no Secretary can handle the job with distinction because of the enormity of the task of managing billions of dollars worth of programs spanning the wide range of social needs in the United States."[5]

Former Secretary Ribicoff would have been quite correct if he had added that no Secretary can manage HEW with distinction unless he is given the management tools required to do the job. I am convinced that MBO is foremost among these tools. But before it can be used effectively, some problems that are unique to the public sector must be overcome. These include (a) defining objectives, (b) measuring benefits, and (c) the operating cycle.

The Objectives Problem

In the private-sector organizations, the primary objective traditionally has been defined by the stockholders and board of directors as maximizing return on investment. This main objective is often supplemented by subobjectives such as rate of growth, development of new products, provisions for executive succession, and contributions to society.[6] Except for the latter (and even that to a large extent), all of these subobjectives focus directly on the primary goal of maximizing return on investment. It is possible, therefore, to translate the overall objective and each of its subobjectives into consistent, measurable, and mathematically relatable components. Thus, a single management system can be implemented throughout the enterprise to create a model of goal congruence.

In the public sector organization, however, there is no such single return-on-investment objective to which subobjectives can easily be tied. Unanimity on an overall objective for HEW, for example, does not exist among the 209 million Americans who are the department's "stockholders" as well as its "customers." Nor is such agreement to be found among those who cast the proxy votes for these stockholders—the decision-makers in the legislative and executive branches, and even the judicial branch, of the federal government.

Moreover, on the rare occasions when these parties agree on subobjectives for HEW, the subobjectives are usually nebulous, difficult to measure, and lacking in the summing qualities that characterize the return-on-investment subobjectives common to the private sector.

The Benefits Problem

Measuring cost/benefits in the public sector is also more difficult than in private industry. One can calculate the dollar cost of teaching a disadvantaged child to read, for example, but how does one measure the "profitability" of this service to society? There is no single criterion for success when the benefit gained is in terms of newly unleashed human potential.

Although the department is continuing to seek ways to measure a dollar's effectiveness in, say, rehabilitating handicapped workers or reducing juvenile delinquency, such measurement is still a very rough science. In most cases, it will be years before the real benefits toward which these objectives are aimed can be evaluated effectively.

The Operating-Cycle Problem

A necessarily short operating cycle is another limited factor when introducing MBO into a public-sector organization. Although federal agencies like HEW have their own long-range goals, these goals are more likely to be upset than those in private industry. There are three reasons for this:

1. Federal agencies are budgeted annually in a complex process that too frequently is unpredictable.

2. A high rate of turnover among top-level, decision-making personnel is characteristic of the federal government.

3. Objectives set by public-sector managers in today's political setting will likely be deemed inadequate in tomorrow's political setting.

The MBO process in HEW is based on a one-year operating cycle—the federal fiscal year. Even given this relatively short time frame, the department's objectives for the year are subject to change, based on new or altered legislative mandates and/or new executive initiatives.

Yet, despite these not unexpected difficulties in establishing objectives and the allied difficulties of measuring progress toward their achievement, MBO has proved to be extremely helpful in managing the affairs of HEW. In the next section, I shall discuss how MBO actually operates in the department; but first, a closer look at HEW may help explain why a rigorous, formalized management system is essential if such a large, politically sensitive organization is to be managed effectively. Accordingly, the HEW structure and mission are described in Figure 1.

Figure 1
The Structure and the Mission of HEW

HEW is charged with the responsibility for administering federal programs in the fields of health, education, income security, and social services. The department has over 100,000 employees, and it administers some 300 programs, ranging from cancer research to vocational education to family planning. Owing in part to the shift of national priorities away from defense spending and toward human-resources spending, HEW has recently been caught in a stream of national debate. It has been forced to operate in an atmosphere characterized by such highly political issues as school desegregation, busing, and welfare reform.

HEW is divided into seven major agencies and ten regional offices located across the country from Boston to Seattle. The staff of the Office of the Secretary provides advise to the Secretary as well as centralized support to the agencies and regional offices. The seven agencies and their basic missions are:

1. *National Institutes of Health* (NIH), which conducts and sponsors biomedical research and health-education programs.
2. *Health Services and Mental Health Administration* (HSMHA), which provides and sponsors health services, and conducts and sponsors research in the field of mental health.
3. *Food and Drug Administration* (FDA), which is a regulatory agency charged with ensuring that food, drugs, and other substances and devices utilized by consumers are safe and effective.
4. *Office of Education* (OE), which promotes the establishment of an effective and efficient educational system throughout the nation.
5. *Social Security Administration* (SSA), which operates the nation's system of social insurance through receiving contributions, processing claims, and making payments to beneficiaries; it also administers the Medicare program.
6. *Social and Rehabilitation Service* (SRS), which manages the federal social service and assistance payments programs.
7. *Office of Child Development.* (OCD), which acts as an advocate for children and coordinates federal programs specifically aimed at children, youth, and their families.

While each of these agencies administers assigned programs, many of these programs require the cooperation of two or more agencies. For example, drug abuse prevention requires significant participation by nearly every agency.

Figure 1—*Continued*

> The ten regional offices and the field staffs of each of the agencies oversee the delivery of services at the local level and maintain close contact with states, local governments, and grantees receiving funds from HEW. In this regard, it is important to note that less than 10% of HEW's money is spent on direct operations. More than 90% goes to Social Security beneficiaries or is dispersed to some 40,000 grantees, including state and local governments and educational or other non-profit institutions.

Application at HEW

Before MBO was introduced, the HEW operating cycle failed in several ways to systematically control the implementation of policy and budget decisions. For example:

- There was no adequate provision for stating program objectives that were based on specific, measurable results. Consequently, program success often was measured on the wrong criteria (e.g., the number of grants awarded rather than the number of people served or problems solved).

- There was no effective formal mechanism to ensure a continuing dialogue, throughout the operating cycle, between policy makers and program managers regarding the problems and successes encountered during the implementation phase. Consequently, there was both a lack of information for policy developers and a lack of guidance for managers.

Part A of Figure 2 shows the HEW operating cycle prior to the introduction of MBO; Part B of the figure shows the operating cycle after MBO was introduced. Accordingly, when the system was implemented at HEW, its major operational goals were:

- To identify clear, measurable objectives.
- To monitor progress toward objectives that had been agreed on by both managers and policy makers.
- To effectively evaluate results.

Figure 2
Comparison of HEW Operating Cycles

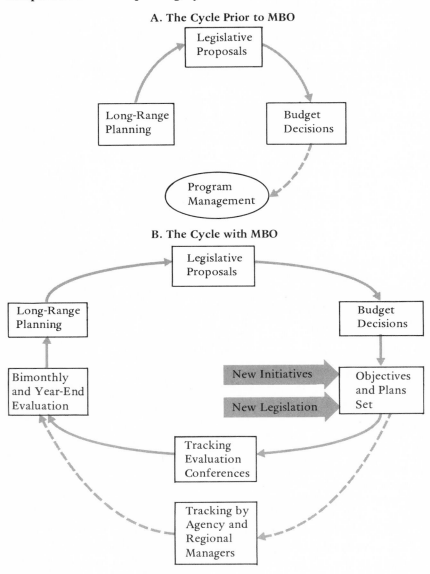

A. The Cycle Prior to MBO

Legislative Proposals

Long-Range Planning

Budget Decisions

Program Management

B. The Cycle with MBO

Legislative Proposals

Long-Range Planning

Budget Decisions

Bimonthly and Year-End Evaluation

New Initiatives

New Legislation

Objectives and Plans Set

Tracking Evaluation Conferences

Tracking by Agency and Regional Managers

Later I shall discuss how well the system met these goals. But first, let us take a closer look at how it actually works.

Setting Objectives

The annual MBO cycle begins when the department formulates its budget and makes the key resource and fund-allocation decisions for the coming fiscal year. Program managers are urged to accompany each request for funds with a list of measurable, results-oriented objectives.

By linking fund requests to the specific results the funds are intended to accomplish, HEW seeks to avoid awarding money on the basis of vague, projected activities. As mentioned earlier, this is a particularly acute problem in the public sector. To overcome it, HEW has instituted a six-stage, objective-setting procedure:

1. The Secretary employs the initial proposals as a starting point. He determines specifically what he wants the department to accomplish during the coming year and how the dpartment's short-range goals will contribute to long-range objectives. He works closely with agency heads to refine their objectives and their requests for funds in the light of these goals. (Figure 3 contains a typical dialogue between the Secretary and one of his managers as they attempt to formulate a results-oriented objective.)

2. The staff of the Secretary draws up the department's budget and then forwards it to the President and Congress for action.

3. The Secretary, who has determined priorities during the budgeting process, then formalizes them in a document that provides planning guidance to agency heads and regional managers.

4. These executives then review and alter their preliminary objectives to conform to changed budget priorities and overall department goals, typically selecting eight to ten objectives that represent the most important results expected of their respective programs.

5. Just prior to the start of the fiscal year, agency heads and regional managers submit these objectives, along with outlines of milestones that must be reached and resources that must be expended for their accomplishment, to the Office of the Secretary, where they are given careful analysis by his staff.

6. From this list of objectives, the Secretary selects those he will personally track. He also has the option of adding other objectives to the department's list (either at the start of the cycle or during the year), depending on his perception of HEW's changing mandate, the

Figure 3
An Objective-Setting Meeting at HEW

Here is a typical dialogue between former Secretary Elliot L. Richardson HEW and an agency head as they formulated an objective.

Agency head: One of our agency's most important initiatives this year will be to focus our efforts in the area of alcoholism and to treat an additional 10,000 alcoholics. Given last year's funding of 41 alcoholism treatment centers and the direction of other resources at the state and local level, we feel that this is an achievable objective.

Secretary : Are these 41 centers operating independently or are they linked to other service organizations in their communities? In other words, are we treating the whole problem of alcoholism, including its employment, mental health and welfare aspects, or are we just treating the *symptoms* of alcoholism?

Agency head: A program requirement for getting funds is that the services involved must be linked in an integrated fashion with these other resources.

Secretary: I am not interested in just looking at the number of alcoholics that are treated. Our goal ought to be the actual rehabilitation of these patients. Do you have data to enable you to restate the objective in terms of that goal?

Agency head: As a matter of fact, Mr. Secretary, we have developed a management information and evaluation system in which each grantee will be providing quarterly data on the number of alcoholics treated, as well as on the number of alcoholics who are actually rehabilitated.

Secretary: How do you define "rehabilitated"?

Agency head: If they are gainfully employed one year after treatment, we regard them as being rehabilitated.

Secretary: Please revise this objective, then, to enable us to track progress on how effective these programs really are in treating the disease of alcoholism and in rehabilitating alcoholics.

---

passage of new legislation, executive initiative, or other developments that affect the department's role. Obviously, the Secretary cannot personally track all objectives. Many are tracked on a continuing basis by HEW agency leaders and managers at several organizational levels. In addition to the 70 objectives personally tracked by the Secretary last year, HEW agency heads and regional directors tracked approximately 300 objectives, and agency bureaus tracked about 1,500.

Monitoring Progress

The Office of the Secretary and the staff workers in each agency monitor progress in meeting objectives. The ongoing review process is facilitated by milestone charts that are prepared for each objective.

Of course, interim progress cannot always be expressed in terms of the final result. Yet by carefully selecting intermediate milestones that logic says must be achieved to accomplish the end result, one can in effect measure interim progress.

For example, one objective of the Health Services and Mental Health Administration (HSMHA) during 1971 was to increase the capacity of institutions receiving HSMHA support to provide family planning services for an additional 800,000 low-income patients. Figure 4 shows a detailed plan, including eight major milestones, that was outlined for accomplishing this objective. This was the status of the objective in October of 1971; since then, the other milestones have been reached and the objective has been completed.

The progress of objectives that are narrower in scope can usually be expressed more readily throughout the year in terms of final results. An example is the section of a HSMHA objective which called for providing immunizations to eight million children. It was relatively easy to determine how many immunizations had been completed as the year progressed and to know by the end of the year that the objective had, in fact, been met.

Management Conferences Managers are encouraged to maintain close contact with the Office of the Secretary and to seek advice or assistance in meeting their goals. In addition to this informal dialogue, the Secretary holds a bimonthly management conference with each agency head and regional director. These conferences, which are also attended by principal staff aids, are the keystone to the success of the entire MBO system.

It has been charged that the typical MBO system, characterized by such periodic appraisals, "perpetuates and intensifies hostility, resentment, and distrust between a manager and subordinates."[7] This may be the case in some instances, but it does not have to be. At HEW, for example, a publication entitled *Focus* is distributed to managers who are, or will be, participating in the bimonthly review conferences. It emphasizes that these are not "knuckle-rapping sessions" and states:

"They are undertaken with the understanding that circumstances change; that, given the best will, spirit, and effort possible, *the things*

121

Figure 4
Operating Plan for HSMHA Family Planning Objective

Resources Committed: $88,815,000

Completion Date

Milestones	July-Aug.	Sept.-Oct.	Nov.-Dec.	Jan.-Feb.	Mar.-Apr.	May-June
1. Expand and transfer OEO projects to increase capacity by 25,000 patients	◀ (Completed)					
2. Establish regional coordinating councils	◀ (Completed)					
3. Fund new projects, expand and transfer projects to increase capacity by 200,000 patients		◁ (Not completed)				
4. Report to Congress on five-year plan			◁ (Not completed)			
5. Fund new projects, expand and transfer projects to increase capacity by 250,000 patients				◁ (Not completed)		
6. Develop evaluation strategy for fiscal year 1973					◁ (Not completed)	
7. Fund new projects, expand and transfer projects to increase capacity by 325,000 patients					◁ (Not completed)	
8. Prepare final report					◁ (Not completed)	

Health Priority — Family Planning Objective

Key
Completed ◀
Not completed ◁

122

we do, unfortunately, do not always *produce the results* intelligent men predict of them."[8]

Ten days prior to each management conference, an agency head or regional director submits to the Secretary a status report and evaluation on all objectives for which he is responsible. If a milestone has been accomplished on time and no problems are anticipated with future steps, the manager simply fills in the triangle representing the completion date of scheduled milestone (see Figure 4). If, however, a milestone has not been completed on schedule or a future milestone is not likely to be completed on schedule, the agency head or regional director indicates the anticipated completion deadline by adding a triangle in the column which corresponds to the new planned month of accomplishment.

Managers also submit an evaluation of the status of each objective. This is based on a three-level classification system:

1. Satisfactory—no problem exists, nor is any anticipated, that will hinder the accomplishment of the objective on schedule.

2. Minor problem—although there is a problem, it does not presently jeopardize accomplishment of the objective.

3. Major problem—there is a distinct possibility that the objective will not be achieved in the absence of major corrective action.

The conference provides a dialogue between the Secretary and the manager, giving them a joint opportunity to identify and resolve management problems. Its agenda, planned jointly by the Secretary and the manager, centers on the objectives of the manager's agency. However, the conference is also used to familiarize both parties with changes inside or outside the agency that will affect its work. Even the objectives themselves may be changed to conform to new initiatives, thus resulting in a dynamic rather than a static process.

This ability to quickly change directions, even to the point of abandoning or drastically altering prior objectives, is a must in the public sector. Contrast this with the following statement on objectives by the former chairman of the board of Avis: "Once . . . objectives are agreed on, the leader must be merciless on himself and on his people. If an idea that pops into his head or out of their mouths is outside the objectives of the company, he kills it without a trial."[9]

Following each management conference, a detailed report is provided to the Secretary and other key participants. The report outlines the discussion items, decisions, and specific assignments. The status of each assignment is then reviewed at each succeeding conference until the action is completed.

Evaluating Results

In addition to the bimonthly reports just described, each manager submits a year-end evaluation to the Office of the Secretary which describes successes and failures in meeting objectives. The annual report details such things as revisions of objectives during the year, reasons for failure in fulfilling any objective, and steps taken to ensure that the same problems will not arise again. These evaluations are used in the long-range planning process to help make the department's future objectives more realistic as well as to help obviate potential problems.

Problems Along the Way

The cliché that old ways are not easily changed is particularly apt in the federal bureaucracy. This is true for a number of reasons, most of which are inherent in the nature of a system governed by a mixture of politically appointed personnel and professional personnel. In theory, the latter are subject to the policy decisions of the former. In reality, it is no secret that this is not always the case. Presidents and heads of departments come and go; yet the bureaucracy remains behind to keep the wheels of government turning.

The primary constraint to the success of MBO at HEW has been an attitude on the part of some managers that the regular attention required of them by such a system is either (a) not consistent with their roles or (b) not as effective a way to manage as some other approach. Some managers have viewed their roles as principally involving policy making, development of legislation, and defense of their budget requests. The intricacies of formalized management planning and control have taken a secondary role to these other functions. Too often, top-level managers have become preoccupied with handling crises in their agencies and have dealt with management issues on an ad hoc, rather than on an anticipatory, results-oriented basis.

Ironically, the fact that MBO gives managers access to the highest level of the department has been a hindrance, as well as a help, in gaining acceptance of the system. A common belief among managers in organizations of all types is that you have somehow failed if you have to bring your problems to the head of the organization. Thus, at HEW, some managers have proposed only those areas for control under MBO which would not prove a source of embarrassment in face-to-face dialogue at management conferences.

A related problem has been getting managers not only to adequately define problem areas but also to "stretch" in setting their objectives in those areas. In some cases, managers have established easily achievable objectives whose accomplishment is almost a foregone conclusion. Last year, for example, one HEW agency set a goal of decreasing by 2% the number of persons, in thirteen selected geographical areas, who would need rehabilitative assistance of a certain type. By the end of the year, the goal had not only been met but had been exceeded ten times over.

Old ways can, however, be changed, as long as one can demonstrate good reasons for such change. Department leaders are satisfied that, in spite of the aforementioned obstacles, MBO has taken hold and is being genuinely accepted throughout the department.

Benefits of the System

Although HEW still has significant problems, measurable results to date document some substantial benefits from the three-year-old MBO system. For example:

• During fiscal year 1972, the Food and Drug Administration (FDA) determined that, within existing resources, it would attempt to increase by 50% the number of import products inspected. This objective was met despite the delay and disruption to shipping caused by the Eastern Seaboard dock strike.

• In fiscal year 1971, the first full year of MBO in operation in the department, an objective of a program run by the Social and Rehabilitation Service (SRS) was to train and place 35,000 welfare recipients in meaningful jobs. SRS faced the need to convince the state agencies, which are the conduits for rehabilitation funds, that such concentration on public assistance recipients was warranted. It also faced the fact that the rehabilitation of welfare recipients is not an easy task. By establishing a results-oriented objective, carefully planning for its accomplishment, and communicating it to all levels of government, SRS actually exceeded its goal. It trained more than 40,000 welfare recipients and offered them a productive future by taking them off welfare rolls and putting them on payrolls.

Moreover, the rehabilitation objective in fiscal year 1973 is to move from a level of approximately 50,000 recipients per year to a level of 69,000. This planned 38% increase is approximately double the normally expected figure based on projected historical trend lines.

Further, the department plans to achieve this objective with only a 14% increase in resources.

In addition to the short-term benefits from HEW's adaptation of MBO, there have been improvements in overall management. A key role the Secretary plays in regular management conferences is to ensure that the department is responding on an integrated basis to social problems, which rarely cut cleanly along jurisdictional lines of public agencies. In particular, he can use the conferences to communicate successes and problems identified elsewhere in HEW that have relevance to conferees.

For example, in its initial presentation of proposed fiscal year 1973 objectives, the Office of Child Development (OCD) indicated it would establish a new category of day care worker. The new position, to be called "child development associate," will be filled by competent individuals who do not have special education or college degrees but who, nonetheless, are able to work well with children. The Secretary was able to receive assurances that this objective would be developed in such a way that it would provide a basis for similar categories of workers in other HEW programs.

Conclusion

MBO as a concept is simple—deceptively so. It is much easier to explain this technique than it is to introduce it to an organization, especially one as complex as HEW. Although the department is now in its third year of utilizing MBO as a primary management device, it is still building toward achieving a fully institutionalized, short-term management and control system that is used by all of its key managers.

Many lessons have been gleaned from HEW's experience with MBO that both add to the knowledge of the concept as used in the public sector and reinforce lessons already learned in the private sector. I shall conclude this discussion by grouping the lessons we have learned into four broad categories.

1. *Differences in public-sector approach:*

• While effective objectives can be established in public sector organizations, the process of developing the objectives is often more complex and requires broader coordination and participation of interested parties than in the private sector.

- Objectives in the public sector must take a different form from those in the private sector. In the former, the objectives must usually be stated in terms of interim results; in the latter, objectives can normally be stated in terms of the ultimate objective of "return on investment."

- Although progress toward achieving many public sector objectives is difficult to measure, few meaningful objectives are beyond effective measurement. Through utilization of milestone charts, which document accomplishments to be achieved by established dates, progress toward achieving almost any objective can be measured.

2. *Role of the top executive:*

- A chief executive officer who has both the will and the capacity to manage is essential to the effective utilization of an MBO system.

- MBO must be tailored to the chief executive's style of managing. One leader might take a decisive role in the operation of the system, while another leader might well have a different style of operating. Resistance to modifying the system to fit the style can destroy the MBO process.

- The chief executive officer must communicate clearly to other organizational components what he feels the general goals and priorities of the organization ought to be. Without such guidance, the subordinates' development of initial objectives for submission to the boss tends to be wasteful and counterproductive.

- The chief executive's attitude affects the spirit in which the system functions, and it will determine whether MBO encourages the defining and solving of problems or the hiding of problems. If MBO is perceived by a chief executive as a problem-solving and goal-reaching device (rather than as an opportunity to point an accusing finger at one of his subordinates), the subordinates themselves are likely to take this view.

3. *Managerial relationships:*

- The establishment of objectives must be a cooperative venture between subordinate and superior. Moreover, unless both parties feel that the objective is important, challenging, and achievable, even cooperative activity will become only meaningless exercise.

- Managers must be persuaded that the primary function of MBO is to enable them to manage more effectively, not to use the management conference to reach the ear of the chief executive on random issues of particular momentary interest to the manager.

• To be effective, the MBO system must operate on a line manager-to-subordinate basis, not on a staff-to-staff basis. Although staff assistance is essential to keep the system functioning, staff must serve as a facilitator of the system and not its operator. To operate otherwise invites confusion in lines of authority and causes a breakdown in accountability.

• Unless the superior and subordinate have regular face-to-face reviews of interim progress, the importance of the system begins to be questioned, there is danger of misunderstanding, and much of the motivational value of the system is lost. Prior to such interim review meetings, it is essential that the superior's staff prepare him to ask the right questions and to avoid being "snowed" by the subordinate.

4. *General strategy considerations:*

• It is important to receive a detailed plan for accomplishing an objective at the same time the objective itself is submitted for approval. Otherwise, proposed objectives too often will not be well thought out in advance, and the possibility for eventual success will ultimately be decreased.

• A middle ground must be found between holding personnel too rigidly to their objectives and allowing them to alter the objectives at will. HEW's method has been to (a) have the Secretary himself approve all proposed changes and (b) ensure that such changes are evaluated in each agency's annual performance report.

• If an organization is consistently accomplishing 100% of its objectives, there is probably reason for concern rather than celebration. Objectives are not really effective unless an organization must "stretch" to reach them. During the last fiscal year, for example, approximately one fourth of HEW's objectives were only partially achieved and another one eighth fell far short of expectation. This is probably not an unhealthy balance.

• It is a mistake to try to make MBO so systematic and rigid that it precludes discussion of important matters not contained in formalized objectives. In fact, MBO should be expected to trigger ad hoc discussions of matters that are not included in stated objectives but are nonetheless vital to the success of the organization.

• MBO is perhaps better perceived as a muscle than as merely a tool. The more it is used, the stronger and more necessary it becomes. However, if MBO is merely a management system on paper and is not allowed to be exercised as an integral part of running an organization, it will atrophy and become useless.

Notes

1. New York, Harper & Row, 1954.

2. Peter F. Drucker, *Managing for Results* (New York, Harper & Row, 1964), Introduction, p. x.

3. For more detail on both the theory behind MBO and its practical application in private companies, see "Managing by—and with—Objectives," *The Conference Board Record* (1968). Also see John B. Lasagna, "Make Your MBO Pragmatic," HBR November–December 1971, p. 64.

4. Quoted in Robert Sherrill, "The Hatchetman and the Hatchetmyth," *Potomac* (Sunday Supplement to the Washington Post), February 6, 1972, pp. 13, 26.

5. Quoted in Robert Sherrill, "The Real Robert Finch Stands Up," *The New York Times Magazine*, July 5, 1970, p. 19.

6. For a discussion of social contributions in the private sector, see Raymond A. Bauer and Dan H. Fenn, Jr., "What *Is* a Corporate Social Audit?" HBR January–February 1973, p. 37.

7. Harry Levinson, "Management by Whose Objectives?" HBR July–August 1970, p. 125.

8. Department of Health, Education and Welfare, March 1972, Introduction, p. x.

9. See Robert Townsend, *Up The Organization* (New York, Alfred A. Knopf, Inc. 1970), p. 130.

MBO and Public Management

Frank P. Sherwood and William J. Page, Jr.

Look at the right book, film, or government directive, and the message will be clear; management by objectives (MBO) is the answer to your managerial problem. Advocates argue that it is the successor to Taylor's "Mental Revolution"—a new way ot thinking about, and engaging in, collective effort.

In 1973 and 1974, MBO was gospel for a Harvard Business School-dominated Washington bureaucracy. MBO would produce better strategies, higher quality decisions, less red tape, enhanced motivation, and a better ability to control things by the governmental executive.

Enthusiastic adherents (first in planning-programming-budgeting, then in MBO) felt a way had been found to cope with complexity, rigidity, and other regularly identified ailments. Now, a time has come for a move balanced view. MBO does have its attractions: it can make its contributions to more effective management of public services. However, it is not a "whole" system for managing. It is an instrument with basic elements of planning, coordination, and appraisal of performance. In public and private organizations, MBO is used primarily for short-range (tactical) planning of operations.

MBO is a relatively neutral instrument, whether in decentralized or centralized systems of managerial control. It is applicable in conditions of scarce or plentiful resources, and has utility in such vastly different arenas as public social services, water resources development, and industrial production.

From *Public Administration Review*, vol. 36, no. 1 (January–February 1976), pp. 5–12. Reprinted from *Public Administration Review* © 1976 by the American Society for Public Administration, 1225 Connecticut Avenue, N.W., Washington, D.C. All rights reserved. With permission of authors and publisher.

MBO as a tactical and instrumental means of dealing with certain managerial needs is fairly straightforward. Important to MBO are: specificity in stating objectives, establishment of feasibility, short time frame (not usually more than one year), measurability of progress and results, definitive resource allocations in terms of operational plan, tracking and evaluation, and reassessment and replanning of objectives.

MBO must be seen in terms of its use as a managerial tactic, not as a management system. In our analysis we will be concerned with gaps between promise and performance, while specifying the assumptions of an "ideal world" that are preconditions to escalation of MBO into a whole system.

Background

A number of ideas set the stage for the coming of MBO. The history of ideas relating to MBO can be traced at least as far back as the work of Frederick Taylor. Taylor's interest in quantification, with its heavy emphasis on the capacity to state an objective in unambiguous terms and to measure progress toward it, can be seen as one of these ideas.

The public sector was fairly heavily involved in MBO-type activity in the '30s when serious efforts at activity measurement were undertaken. The Ridley and Simon monograph, *Measuring Municipal Activities*,[1] laid great stress on the definition of objectives as the rationale for measurement. Similar undertakings were undertaken by certain federal agencies, notably the Forest Service and the then-new Social Security Administration (SSA).

The SSA's program for evaluating and rewarding individual performance was an early effort in the government to build MBO ideas into the fabric of an organization. The system attempted to encompass the total goal constellation of the agency and to provide a functional base for the measurement of the performance of the individual employee, rather than narrow efficiency and/or economy criteria. As a result, SSA developed an image as a humane and helping organization.

The performance budgeting movement, launched by the First Hoover Commission in 1948, was unlike the later program budgeting in that it was not primarily an approach to allocating resources. Like MBO, it emphasized defining objectives and measuring progress toward anticipated results. Performance budgeting tended to be tactical, whereas program budgeting tended to be concerned with strategies of allocation. A famous example of performance budgeting in the early '50s in municipal administration concerned the painting of light standards. The issue was not *how many* light standards should be painted but rather one of definitiveness of goals, resource allocation consistent with goals, and measurement of results achieved.

In 1954, Peter Drucker's *Practice of Management* was published. With his popularization of the term management by objectives in that book, MBO was now on track. It is important to realize that the tenets of the *Practice of Management* were empirically derived, mostly from General Motors and Sears Roebuck. However, in Drucker's opinion (correctly, we believe), MBO's early conceptual and practical development owes more to governmental than private experience.

MBO's heirs are numerous. George Odiorne has become management's modern healer. John Humble, a British consultant, has sought to enlighten Americans with his Bureau of National Affairs material, and has also introduced MBO to India. His book, *Improving Business Results*, is called "the definitive work on management by objectives."

Drucker's message came through to the public sector most clearly in California. Under Neeley Gardner, the California State Training Office began to push MBO (called "program management") in the mid-'50s. A major goal then was to free the manager to be accountable for *results* and not just the number of paper clips used. The drive sought to create processes whereby the top manager could feel himself in control (through results) without having to check time reports. MBO was conceived as an on-going management process; it was not a strategy for allocating and organizing resources.

In 1970 a seminar on MBO was held at the Federal Executive Institute. From the various federal executives there, it was found that MBO was then utilized by a number of federal agencies, among them the Internal Revenue Service, the General Accounting Office, the National Park Service, and the Federal Aviation Agency; the Social Security Administration used MBO's tactics to control error rates and other aspects of claiming and processing benefits. Tactical planning was a major part of the SSA's response to revision of benefit payments.

One major resource of the seminar was Al Kelly, then Midwest regional commissioner of the IRS. Interestingly, Kelly essentially renounced measurement and specificity as the guiding beacons of MBO. Kelly indicated IRS was already awash with numbers and computers. His concern was to find a place for humans in IRS. Kelly engaged in lengthy sessions with his subordinates, and expected them to do likewise.

The Nixon MBO

The Nixon term seems to mark the point at which MBO took on whole system pretensions in the federal government. It was part of an orientation that found societal good in the private sector and evil in the public. Harvard Business School became newly glorious. The attitude of the Nixon top management was one of low trust and contempt toward civil servants. Control and dominance of the system became particularly central concerns in his second term. There was a drive to introduce managerial techniques to assure continued control of policy, money, and manpower according to the classic business model. The second phase of the strategy was to obtain legislative and staffing changes to institutionalize and make permanent the new look.

It was in the Department of Health, Education, and Welfare that MBO became an allocation strategy, rather than only a tactic. Under Deputy Undersecretary Fred Malek, MBO received considerable notoriety as the answer to streamlined federal grants-in-aid programs. MBO's success in HEW was reported in the *Harvard Business Review* by Rodney Brady, who served briefly as successor to Malek as assistant secretary. Brady claimed that, in 1973, his department had "one of the most far-reaching management by objectives . . . systems in operation anywhere."[2] However, the program, labelled "Operation Planning System," was getting mixed notices in the department itself. Four basic problems were cited: (a) enormous paperwork burden; (b) application of resources consistent with stated objectives difficult to achieve; (c) objectives out of time phase with the budget; and (d) heavy dependence on state and local governments for delivery of services while objectives were set unilaterally by the federal government.

Brady did concede that MBO could get off the track. But that was essentially a people problem. He saw the "primary constraint" on MBO in HEW as ". . . attitude on part of some managers that the regular attention required of them by such a system is either (a) not consistent with their roles; or (b) not as effective a way to manage as some other approach."[3] Because MBO was seen in whole system terms, Brady apparently saw no opportunity for varying approaches to organizational and managerial problems.

It is fair to say that MBO in HEW did reveal advantages. It was supportive of top management's efforts to control a large, complex organization. The emphasis on objective setting appeared to enhance communication and may have even helped to get a few things on track. Certainly, the persistent query, "Why?" did strip out some useless paper in grants programs. What really emerged was a more elaborated information system (tracking) and a formal review process that supported the leadership in control. There is no evidence that MBO had a significant effect on allocation strategies in the department.

MBO promulgated for the entire government by Malek as deputy director of the Office of Management and Budget in 1973 seemed substantially similar to the HEW effort. With the support of his superior, Roy Ash (another Harvard Business School graduate), Malek gave the allocation dimension emphasis. Goals and objectives were to be proposed upward; decisions reached on proposals were to be the bases for resource allocations. In turn, the tracking was in terms of achievement of the objectives and concurrency of resource usage with levels of accomplishment. Though proclaimed a participative process, government-wide MBO should be more properly identified as a strategy for hierarchical control. Proposals were made from lower to higher echelons, but it was up to the boss to decide. It was seen as an advance that the boss now had some clear "options" and could make known to subordinates exactly what he wanted. Furthermore, in the President's case, an elaborate staff activity was established in the OMB to give him support in control and enforcement. A group of "management associates" was recruited, in the main youths out of prestigious business schools, to ensure that agencies observed the process.[4]

In developing a perspective on this period, it is important to realize this was the time of "the manager," defined as someone who gets things done. The manager is in charge. He seeks goal clarity; his system of thinking begins after someone else has told him what is to be done. In no sense can MBO be thought of as an allocation strategy as it suggests no approach to the tough problem of choice. Yet in the objective-setting rhetoric, it was implied that managers were now mystically able to put things on proper course. Essentially, it was a restatement of hierarchical accountability, with ambiguity removed.

In many respects the effort to attach mystique to management was most troublesome. Management is technique, both Brady and Malek imply. It is value-neutral, universalistic, applicable in all cases, and best functions when the situation is unambiguous and clear cut. If the situation is not that way, make it so. Demands were made on the Federal Executive Institute, for example, that technical knowledge be taught to the exclusion of discussion of executive values, moorings, and obligations.

As perhaps has already become evident, the way one thinks about MBO is greatly affected by the way one conceives of the world.

A basic assumption in MBO is that human behavior is rational. The rational model accepts macro-policy decisions (e.g., goals of "New Federalism" or economic stability without wage and price controls) as the parameters for analysis and decision making about objectives; and value of activities depends on their consistency with, and support for, the broad policies that have been established authoritatively. Behind this commitment to a rational objective-setting process lie several other assumptions: (a) objectives can be stated precisely; (b) organizations are essentially "closed" and participants in the decision (objective setting) process are easily identified; (c) sufficient information is available to administrators to enable objectivity in analysis, decision making, and evaluation of outcomes; and (d) organizational members at all levels will internalize prescribed objectives and cooperate in securing their achievement.

The key question, obviously, is the extent to which such goal clarity can be achieved. Rational behavior, in the instrumental sense, depends on understanding objectives with sufficient specificity to construct behaviors that are consistent with, and supportive of, their achievement.

Yet we frequently cannot even identify the authoritative decision maker in our complex system. While much public policy begins with messages and statements of purpose from executives and legislators, it is clear that those policy statements are not necessarily accepted as national goals. The system of checks and balances, with some exceptions, operates to enforce consensual establishment of major policies. Examples abound in environmental protection, social welfare, and national security. The effect is that an operational macro-goal may be nearly impossible to achieve (or sustain) in the absence of crisis. Further, a national goal or policy may be accepted and supported by a majority but effectively resisted by a particular geographic area or interest group. Civil Rights Act implementation was and is affected by regional variance, manifested in Old South and more recently in old and new urban Northern differences.

Indeed, the analogy of MBO to private business seems least applicable in public goal-setting. Deep differences in the role and function of public and private organizations exist; and substantive rationality in government may produce behavior that is quite removed from an MBO view of instrumental rationality, as the following conditions illustrate:

1. *Work frequently is allocated to the public sector because lack of knowledge or uncertainty makes it infeasible or too risky for performance in the private sector.*

Risk and infeasibility frequently derive from inadequate knowledge of the nature of a social problem, its incidence and prevalence, and methods for coping. Services initially developed by government (directly or through research grants) have been shifted to the private sector after being developed, tested, and routinized by governmental agencies. Prevention of communicable diseases is an example of an area in which initial government intervention and financial support led ultimately to private performance of essential human services.

2. *The stated objective may not be the real objective.*

C. W. Churchman suggests that the management scientist apply a test: Will the system sacrifice other objectives to attain the stated objective?[5] A common fallacy, Churchman notes, is to "emphasize the obvious" in stating objectives. Pressure for precision, quantification, and measurability produces statements of objectives which are susceptible to precise expression, though they may not be important. One conceals real objectives when there is questionable legitimacy of the real intent. An agency is pledged to reduce a problem by *n* per cent, though the overriding fiscal policy is to drop expenditures or contain outlays within a dollar ceiling substantially below the amount appropriated for the service. The Congressional Budget and Impoundment Control Act of 1974 was precipitated by such practices.

3. *There are no commonly accepted standards for monitoring performance or measuring achievements of many public objectives.*

Objectives of process, as distinct from output, tend to be particularly resistant to precision, quantification, and valuation of results. How does one measure the value of monthly income maintenance payments to the elderly and unemployable? Devotees of precision and quantification faced with such problems have chosen to concentrate on "quality control" objectives, which monitor and sanction errors in determining eligibility for, and levels of, payments. This process objective presumably improves fiscal accountability, but does not permit assignment of subjective values for products. In the MBO process, one may not establish or defend the objective on a basis of social merit; this is seen as subjective.

Fuzzy objectives may be politically and socially advantageous, just as lack of specificity in expressing statutory purpose frequently is beneficial. Ambiguous objectives frequently are useful products in political compromise. For example, certain health and social service programs of the 1940s and 1950s had a *real* objective of birth control for persons who desired such services. Public funds appropriated annually for birth control were spent covertly in most areas as legal, political, or social considerations weighed against services.

Finally, rationality depends on the technical ability to write objectives that can be operationalized. There has been the rather common complaint that statements of objectives are ambiguous and not amenable to results tracking. It is not a coincidence that most of the literature's examples (a) are easily quantifiable, (b) have face validity in terms of the mission and broad goals of the organization, and (c) are usually routine.

Data and Objectivity

The MBO process evokes the greatest response from persons who value "hard" information and objectivity. High valuation of hard facts runs into difficulty when relevant data are scarce or untimely. A second limitation occurs in meanings or interpretations, which vary from one organization or profession to another. Alienation occurs when an outcome that is cherished by a particular unit is absolutely or relatively devalued by a decision-maker who establishes priorities among many objectives.

Problems also arise in the analytical process, at which point judgments have to be made about progress towards goals. Thus the analyst can have much to say in respect to the valuation of performance. His assumptions and values will affect the outcome. William Capron, former federal budget executive now at Harvard, has advised top executives to be certain that assumptions of the analysts are made explicit and that they employ alternative assumptions.[6]

The essence of instrumental rationality is that the choice of ends (objectives) governs methods to be used in achieving objectives. Methods are presumably neutral and subject to analysis and conclusion. But that is seldom true in the practical situation, and not just because of assumptive analysts. As Watergate has shown, how we do things is as important as what we do. Charles Schultze has written:

> . . . there is no simple division of labor in which the "politicians" achieve consensus on . . . objectives while the "analysts" design and evaluate—from efficiency and effectiveness criteria—alternative means of achieving those objectives. . . . choice of means, particularly among domestic programs, is almost equally as freighted with political values as is the choice ends.[7]

A Closed System

The MBO process is much more manageable when an organization is perceived as having quite distinct boundaries. Then the setting and tracking of objectives occur within a known arena, subject to control by the leaders. When forces outside the immediate organization are seen as having an increased salience for internal behavior, less viable is the notion of separateness and independence in both the goal setting and the implementation process.

In terms of their sensitivity to these environmental forces, managers seem to come in two sets. On one side, there is the individual who is practically disabled by the mingling of his concerns with externalities. He tends to reject efforts at a definite statement of objectives for his organization because of the forces outside that he views as massively uncertain. Constitutionally this person cannot accept MBO even as a managerial tactic.

Conversely, there is the manager who is completely closed—both in respect to his organization and to himself. He ignores the interdependencies of the system with its complex environment, implying that a public agency can set specific objectives, perform its work, and place a value on its products or services without regard for politics (bureaucratic or partisan), economic situation, or public opinion. Such a person is a good candidate to lead the charge for MBO as a whole managerial system. In his view the approach makes good sense because all the variables are subject to leadership control.

In fact, most government organizations are neither fully vulnerable nor invulnerable. The expression, pursuit, and achievement of objectives of a governmental unit are frequently and significantly conditioned by external phenomena. For example, intergovernmental program management (which now occurs at all levels of government) is a continuing experience of the open character of systems. External phenomena include legislators, clientele groups, decisions of other governmental units, mass communication media, economic conditions, courts, special interests, and other private organizations.

With the change in the role imperatives of public managers toward interdependence and collaboration with a wide variety of official and non-official organizations, the relatively straightforward MBO view of getting on with the task seems altogether too simplistic. One must exercise influence outside as well as within the system.

Leadership

It is important to emphasize again that the values and situational factors that operate in the private sector do not necessarily provide a base for thinking about leadership in the public sector. In the necessarily open system of government, the market values of efficiency and effectiveness must always take second place to the maintenance of democratic government, in which the public interest is sought through wide participation in the goal-setting process. If the ideals of democracy are to be taken seriously, it is evident that formal, hierarchical authority will generally have less relevance in the public setting. The system will be subject to more forms of influence; the leader's object will be to support these efforts to influence rather than to make judgments unilaterally.

Thus it seems fair to say that the personality attributes we may expect of a successful leader in a private sector MBO effort may differ appreciably from his counterpart in the public sector. In a scalar analysis of human behavior, Clare Graves[8] provides a basis for understanding this difference in table 1.

The manager who depends mainly on techniques, including MBO, when there is consensus on fairly routinized activities, would most appropriately be classed at level 4. But public service bureaucracies have neither clarity nor stability of objectives. Their high professionalism requires considerable discretion both in deciding what to do and also in determining how to do it. Professionals can perform well only with leadership corresponding to their behavioral scheme. A level 4 executive attempting to manage a level 6 or 7 work force is a mismatch. Professionals demand more freedom, institutional support, mutual trust, and respect than is likely to be allowed by the "management expert."

Recent initiatives to establish MBO in the federal government reflected inadequate understanding of both leadership and organizational dynamics in public settings. MBO and related managerial controls were inaugurated without necessary understanding of motivation, authority, and power in public organizations.

In a highly professionalized work force, with expertise in specific programmatic specialities, knowledge frequently offsets hierarchical subordination. Increments of program expertise and attendant recognition are major factors in career progression. The manager whose special knowledge is methodological, rather than substantive, traditionally has had lower status than the expert in programs in the U.S. government.

MBO as practiced in the federal government has tended to deny this professional orientation. Emphasis on techniques and procedures, evaluations of unit performance by persons who knew little about programs, and the "top down" allocation of goals and objectives elicited hostility and counter-productive behavior. It was a simplistic, methodological approach which took no account of an organization culture which is, and must be, heavily professionalized.

Table 1

Nature of Existence	Motivational System	Value System	Appropriate Managerial System
7. Pacificistic, individualistic	Information	Cognitive	Acceptance and support
8. Aggressive, individualistic	Self-esteem	Personal	Goal-setting without prescribing means to goals
4. Agressive	Master	Amoral	Personal, prescriptive, and hard bargaining
1. Autistic	Psychological	Amoral	Close care and nurturing

The new bosses sought mastery in order to be prescriptive in their MBO strategy. The civil servants sought recognition for their contribution and support for the values and activities in which they had already invested. The mastery-prescriptive managerial style associated with the MBO effort was not at all compatible with the real organization world in which the strategy was attempted.

It is necessary to assume a world that is knowable, stable, predictable, and compliant in order to conceive MBO as a "whole system" approach to management. The only way a technique such as MBO can claim to deal with the ambiguities that characterize the public sector is to declare them non-existent.

Conclusion: The Future

MBO continues to have considerable visibility in the federal government partly because of its own merits and also because Malek-Ash people continue to hold important positions. Publicity, such as the Brady article, continues to generate enthusiasm at the state and local level.

The idea of MBO (as distinguished from ritualized process) must always be central to management action and thought. Managers in the public and private sectors alike share common aspirations in their desire to accomplish organizational tasks. The better these can be specified, the more likely the manager is to feel in control.

In the public sector there is a special push toward what is termed accountability. Abuse of governmental powers in the early 1970s and disappointing governmental performance in the 1960s have left legislators and the public skeptical of the intentions and abilities of public officials and organizations. MBO has the potential for reassuring legislators and the polity that government units actually are committed to specifying objectives and to reporting progress achieved toward them.

Though government has traditionally taken on many of the high risk tasks in society, scarcity of tax dollars is causing decision-makers at all levels to become less accepting of "blank check" appropriations. Legislators want more specificity of anticipated outcomes, and they are demanding increased amounts of data on performance in respect to stated objectives. Incrementally, we will undoubtedly be moving to specify intentions and measure achievements in areas such as human services.

It is likely that MBO will find its greatest expression as a tactic in a hierarchical strategy of leadership. Despite pressures for a more humanistic value orientation in society, the fact is that hierarchical patterns of leadership will dominate our organizations. MBO is an advantageous strategy in its goal clarity, in eliciting achievement motivations as objectives become clear, in its tracking wherein high achievers can see results of work, in improved capability to exercise data-based control, and in increased capability to provide rewards (often material benefits in the private sector) in terms of demonstrated performance.

Can we expect that the total system view of MBO will gain greater numbers of adherents? It is altogether likely that the federal push has not yet had its full impact on the governments of the nation. Yet the change in leadership in the OMB and the noticeable disenchantment with MBO as a panacea in the government makes it likely that remaining efforts will be tactical within a hierarchical strategy.

Another scenerio could be developed which would assume a greater discontinuity in management action and more acceptance of the philosophy of Douglas McGregor. It might include:

- A seeking of substantive rather than instrumental rationality.

- Recognition that high goal clarity can have the negative effect of enforcing conformity.

- Awareness that the collection and analysis of data are normative acts.

• Acceptance that organizations are open systems and in heavy traffic with their environments, which they influence and which, in turn, influence them.

• Cooperation as a function of interdependence and felt mutual interests.

• Prizing of leaders who help to create environments in which decisions can be made, rather than prescribed.

• A climate in which achievement and affiliative motives dominate, rather than power motivations.

Obviously, this implies a totally different management strategy. The outer trappings of MBO in this circumstance might not appear vastly different; but the dynamics of the process and the "feel" certainly would be. The real task would be to negotiate organizational approaches that reflect multiple interests, in which commitment to a decision or objective would have at least equal importance with its quality. It is in (a) value—the legitimacy of a diversity of interests in the organization—and in (b) a skill—to work collaboratively in interdependent situations—that MBO would find a new home. Whether MBO moves in such a radically discontinuous direction really depends on the degree to which we are prepared to recognize organizational goal structures in their full complexity and are prepared to develop managerial strategies reflective of such understanding and awareness.

Notes

1. Clarence Ridley and Herbert Simon, *Measuring Municipal Activities* (Chicago: International City Management Association, 1938).

2. Rodney H. Brady, "MBO Goes to Work in the Public Sector," *Harvard Business Review* (March–April 1973).

3. *Ibid.*, p. 71.

4. The recruitment of these management associates showed rather clearly the extent of the Nixon Administration bias. In an interview in March 1974, Fred Malek stated that managers in the private sector were preferred because their opportunity to learn managerial techniques was better than that of their counterparts in the public service. The interview, interestingly, was videotaped for presentation to an audience of federal administrators.

5. C. W. Churchman, *The Systems Approach* (New York: Dell, 1968), pp. 30–31.

6. William N. Capron, "The Impact of Analysis on Bargaining in Government," in Alan A. Altschuler (ed.), *The Politics of the Federal Bureaucracy* (New York: Dodd, Mead and Company, 1968), p. 201.

7. Charles L. Schultze, *The Politics and Economics of Public Spending* (Washington, D.C.: The Brookings Institution, 1968), pp. 2–3.

8. Clare W. Graves, "Deterioration of Work Standards," *Harvard Business Review* (September–October, 1966) (Reprint).

Zero-Base Budgeting

4

While the Office of Management and Budget was force-feeding management by objectives to agencies of the federal government, a "new" budgeting technique was being developed and implemented in the private sector and in a few governmental jurisdictions. That technique, zero-base budgeting (ZBB), became Jimmy Carter's symbol of good management, and many elected officials at all levels of government looked to ZBB as the way to control government expenditure through better management technique. As with other systems and techniques that we have discussed, ZBB was supposed to centralize budgetary decision making by routinely giving superiors in the hierarchy better information concerning tentative decisions made at lower levels.

Zero-base budgeting, as developed by Peter Pyhrr for the state of Georgia and the federal government, seeks to allow virtually all programs—both old and new—to be reviewed through the budgetary process.[1] ZBB involves several steps, which are presented in Figure 1. The first step is the identification of *decision units*. Decision units are the lowest level at which meaningful management decisions are made. An organization implementing ZBB has considerable flexibility in determining what "meaningful"

Figure 1
Steps to Zero-Base Budgeting

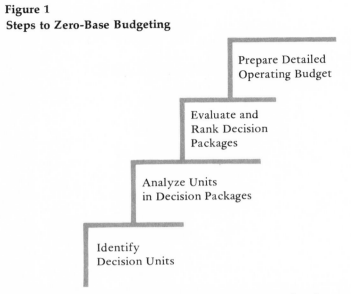

Prepare Detailed
Operating Budget

Evaluate and
Rank Decision
Packages

Analyze Units
in Decision Packages

Identify
Decision Units

means. Therefore, decision units are not completely synonymous with the program elements of program budgeting. Implicitly, in zero-base budgeting all the decision units of government when logically grouped for review at higher levels constitute a program structure.

The second step in the zero-base budgeting process demands that each decision unit develop several *decision packages* for aspects of its programs. Each decision package spells out the detailed description of program objectives, ties the objectives to the amount of resources needed to carry out the program, and presents a cost-benefit analysis to justify each aspect of the program. There are two roles for decision-package development. The first is to suggest alternative ways of performing existing functions, and the second is to analyze the impact of performing existing functions in the same ways but at different levels of activity. For example, if a "meals on wheels" program is part of the responsibility of a particular decision unit, one decision package might consider using a centralized kitchen and delivering the food to the elderly in small vans. An alternative package might analyze the costs and benefits of having the food cooked on the road in converted recreation vehicles that could also be used for the delivery. A package dealing with the level of activity might analyze the costs and benefits of providing meals to 35% of the target population. Another decision package might consider the costs and benefits of expanding the service to include an additional 5% of the target group.

The third step in ZBB involves ranking each decision package. The manager of each decision unit ranks his or her decision packages. All the packages ranked by first-level managers are sent up the hierarchy to be reviewed and ranked against decision packages from other decision units. In the course of this review, superiors can change the rankings of decision packages sent up by any decision-unit manager. If all the decision packages were reviewed and ranked against all others as they went through the review process, ZBB would be caught in a deluge of paper. Although Jimmy Carter stated that all programs would have to be justified from a zero base,[2] the practical problems of implementing the technique have forced the agencies to concentrate their review on decision packages whose incremental costs exceed some arbitrarily set percentage of last year's appropriation. In effect, this means that zero-base budgeting is not operating from a base of zero dollars, but rather from a base that is some percentage —usually 65 or 75 percent—of last year's appropriation.

Just as the base in traditional budgeting virtually eliminated review of established programs, decision packages that fall within the 65 to 75 percent of the previous year's appropriations are immune from review at higher levels. The higher levels concentrate their review and ranking efforts on the decision packages whose costs exceed the arbitrary cumulative cost level.

Zero-base budgeting, therefore, is not as thorough as its name indicates. In practice, it does not mean justifying programs from a zero base. A budgeting system that used a real zero base was tried in the United States Department of Agriculture (USDA) in the early 1960s. It proved to be too time-consuming and had relatively little pay-off in better decisions. ZBB as now practiced grants managers a solid base. Programs whose costs fall within the base figure are not routinely reviewed by higher authorities. ZBB therefore presents managers who want to subvert the system the chance to bury poor programs within the 65 to 75 percent base in much the same way that program managers in traditional budgeting hid questionable programs in their base.

Graeme Taylor, a management consultant who has worked with PPBS, MBO, and ZBB, presents a clear explanation of how zero-base budgeting is supposed to work. David Singleton, Bruce A. Smith, and James R. Cleaveland discuss the use of ZBB in Wilmington, Delaware. And Thomas P. Lauth deals with some of the political problems that affected the acceptance of ZBB in Georgia.

Notes

1. Peter A. Phyrr, *Zero-Base Budgeting: A Practical Management Tool for Evaluating Expenses* (New York: John Wiley & Sons, 1973), chapters 3, 4, and 5. Also see his "Zero-Base Approach to Governmental Budgeting," *Public Administration Review* vol. 37, no. 1 (January–February 1977), pp. 1–8.

2. Jimmy Carter, "Jimmy Carter Tells Why He Will Use Zero-Based Budgeting," *Nation's Business* vol. 65, no. 1 (January 1977), p. 24.

Introduction to
Zero-Base Budgeting

Graeme M. Taylor

The term "zero-base budgeting" is not new. In the most literal sense, zero-base budgeting implies constructing a budget without reference to what has gone before, based on a total reappraisal of purposes, methods, and resources.

This interpretation has been roundly condemned as naïve and impractical, if not downright mischievous. The U.S. Department of Agriculture's attempt at this sort of zero-base for FY 1964 was widely regarded as a failure. As Allen Schick has remarked, even a teenager doesn't have an identity crisis every year. Or, as Dean Acheson pointed out in another context, we can't have a foreign policy if we pull it up every year to examine its roots.

But there is another version of zero-base budgeting. Developed originally at Texas Instruments by Peter A. Pyhrr as a method of controlling overhead costs, and later implemented by Jimmy Carter in Georgia, this latter day zero-base budgeting provides a practical way of involving line managers in a systematic evaluation of budget priorities. On April 19, 1977, the Office of Management and Budget issued Bulletin 77-9 to implement this approach to zero-base budgeting in the federal government, and it is this version of zero-base budgeting that is the subject of this article.

Although the basic concepts of zero-base budgeting are indeed simple, putting them into practice is difficult, complex, and demanding. Many organizations, however, apparently believe the results are worth the effort. Within the past three years, at least 100 major corporations have applied zero-base budgeting to portions of their operating budgets. A handful of states and several local governments have adopted zero-base budgeting. A few federal agencies introduced zero-base budgeting on a limited basis even before the election.

Some of the growing popularity of zero-base budgeting must no doubt be attributed to the President's support of the process. But it would be a mistake to think that the "bandwagon syndrome" is the main reason for ZBB's adoption. The real explanation lies in certain intrinsic features of the process itself, coupled fortuitously with the needs of the times.

Industry views zero-base budgeting as a more rational approach to the perennial problem of controlling overhead. The recent recession forced most companies to reappraise their discretionary costs, and many found ZBB an instrument ideally suited to the task.

In the public sector, the example of New York City looms like a severed head on a spike as an awful warning. Today virtually everyone is a fiscal conservative. There is a growing realization that program initiatives to meet public needs must go hand-in-hand with sound financial management. As the President pointed out in *Nation's Business* (January 1977): ". . . there is no inherent conflict between careful planning, tight budgeting, and constant management reassessment on the one hand, and compassionate concern for the deprived and afflicted on the other. Waste and inefficiency never fed a hungry child, provided a job for a willing worker, or educated a deserving student."

Zero-base budgeting has come a long way since its origins at Texas Instruments and in Georgia. These early models have been substantially improved upon and refined in later, less-publicized applications, while still retaining the original fundamental principles. Experience indicates that there are almost limitless ways to adapt the basic ZBB concepts to the varying decisional needs of different organizations. This should come as no surprise. Zero-base budgeting is, after all, a management-oriented approach to budgeting. It follows, then, that its basic principles must be adapted to fit each organization's unique management structure and culture.

This article will attempt, somewhat boldly, to summarize the state of a complex and rapidly evolving art. The writer's viewpoint is not that of a scholar, but rather that of a practitioner, one who has been actively involved in helping organizations design and implement zero-base budgeting.

The reader will therefore not find much in the way of public administration theory, nor any glittering generalities to serve as a conceptual framework. If any apology is needed, it would be this: it is too early to predict the ultimate fate of zero-base budgeting in the public sector. It could evolve in many different ways to serve different needs in different government organizations. Many versions of zero-base budgeting could comfortably coexist in Washington, in the states, and in city halls. Different approaches may be quite appropriate even within the same government, at different levels and for different kinds of programs. No unified theory is likely to emerge; certainly none can be discerned at this time.

Principles and Elements of Zero-Base Budgeting

The distinctive and essential hallmark of zero-base budgeting is its focus on the total budget request. The current spending level is not regarded as an inviolate base, immune from detailed scrutiny. Existing activities are examined along with proposed new activities.

In traditional budgeting systems, all participants behave as if the relevant question was: "At the margin, is an increase in Program A more important than an increase in Program B?" Decision-makers are essentially forced to accept or reject a program increase, or to reduce its amount. This so-called "incremental" budgeting effectively denies decision-makers the option of trading off a requested increase in one activity against a reduction in another.

Zero-base budgeting places a premium on offering decision-makers a range of choices among alternate funding levels. The relevant budget question is: "At the margin, is an increase in Program A more important than an increase in Program B or a previously funded item in Programs A, B, C. . . .?" It is explicitly *not* assumed that present activities must necessarily be continued. Given budget constraints, an existing activity may be reduced or eliminated entirely to make way for new activities, or one program may be cut back to permit another to expand.

The three basic elements of zero-base budgeting are:

A. Identification of "decision units."

B. Analysis of decision units and the formulation of "decision packages."

C. Ranking.

A. The decision units are the lowest level entities for which budgets are prepared. Decision units may be programs, functions, cost centers, organizational units, or, in certain cases, line items or appropriation items. One important requirement is that each decision unit have an identifiable manager with the necessary authority to establish priorities and prepare budgets for all activities within the decision unit.

B. ZBB calls for two kinds of analysis. First is the analysis that most truly deserves the name "zero-base"—a reexamination of the purposes, activities, and operations of the decision unit. In this analytic phase, questions such as the following are addressed:

- What would be the consequence if the decision unit were entirely eliminated?
- How can the decision unit's purposes be achieved in a more cost-effective manner?
- How can the decision unit's operations be improved?

Following the zero-base review of purposes, activities, and operations, the decision unit manager then segments the decision unit's activities into a series of decision packages. The first package contains those activities, or portions of activities, deemed highest priority. The second contains the next most important items, and so on. The costs and consequences of each package are documented for higher level review.

C. The third basic element of ZBB is "ranking," the process whereby higher level managers establish priorities for all decision packages from all subordinate decision units.

Decision Units, Decision Packages, and the Ranking Process

Identifying and Defining Decision Units

A key consideration in selecting decision units is the organization's "responsibility structure." Decision units should generally be selected to parallel the flow of responsibility for budgetary decision-making within the organization.

To illustrate this point, consider an organization that operates neighborhood health centers, each of which offers a variety of health services such as tuberculosis control, venereal disease control, lead poisoning control, maternal and child health clinics, and so forth. The decision units may variously be (a) each center, encompassing all health services provided within the center, (b) each separate health service provided in each center, or (c) each health service aggregated across all centers.

If each center has a manager who is responsible for resource allocation within the center, then the individual centers may be logically selected as decision units. If each health service within a center has an identifiable manager responsible for resource allocation within that service, each service within a center could be viewed as a separate decision unit. On the other hand, if resource allocation decisions within health services are made system-wide by identifiable managers at the organization's headquarters, then the individual health services aggregated across all centers would be logical decision units. The key criterion is how responsibility for resource allocation decisions is distributed.

There is, of course, a fourth option: the entire health organization may be considered a single decision unit. This option would make sense if all resource allocation decisions are made by the organization's chief executive, or if other considerations become important, such as the relative size of the organization with respect to the government of which it forms a part. For example, if an entire city is engaged in zero-base budgeting, then, from the standpoint of the mayor, the entire neighborhood health center program might be logically one single decision unit. Relative size, therefore, is a second important consideration in identifying decision units.

The availability of data often constrains the choice of decision units. The organization's accounting system may not provide reliable cost data for the "ideal" decision unit structure. Compromises may have to be made, or the accounting system may be modified so that something approaching the ideal structure may become feasible at a later time.

Analytic Emphasis

Some organizations emphasize a fundamental reexamination of each decision unit before its manager is permitted to formulate decision packages. In other instances, only perfunctory attention is paid to the questioning of objectives, activities, and operating methods, so decision packages simply reflect a priority listing of the status quo. The relative emphasis on each type of analysis is decided by the architects and users of the zero-base budgeting system. Both types of analysis are useful, but time, practicality, and available analytic skills sometimes dictate that the former be sacrificed and attention be concentrated on the latter.

Formulation of Decision Packages

The decision unit manager formulates, in priority order, a series of decision packages that together equal the total of his budget request for the decision unit. Each decision package consists of a discrete set of services, activities, or expenditure items.

The first, or highest priority, package addresses the most important activities performed by the decision unit, i.e., those that produce the highest priority services or meet the most critical needs of the decision unit's target population. The cost of this first package is usually well below the current level of funding for the decision unit, and is often thought of as the "minimum level" or "survival level" for the decision unit.

In some cases decision unit managers are allowed complete freedom in determining the size of the first package, subject only to the constraint that it cost less than the current funding level. In other cases, guidelines are provided in the form of a percentage of the current level; for example: "The first package should be less than 75% of current," or "The first package should be between 40% and 60% of current."

In most cases, no firm rule is established for the total number of packages for each decision unit. In practice, the number can usually be expected to vary between a minimum of three and a maximum of around ten.

Typically, packages become smaller and more discrete as their cumulative total cost approaches and exceeds the decision unit's current funding level. This offers decision-makers a more practical range of flexibility in the subsequent ranking process.

The decision unit manager's analysis of decision packages is communicated on a series of forms, using a separate form for each decision package. Each form documents:

● Precisely what services are to be provided, or activities performed, if this package is funded.

● The resource requirements of the package and their cost.

● A quantitative expression of workload, output, or results anticipated if the package is funded.

In some cases, the decision unit manager is asked to identify additional information on each decision package form, such as "benefits of funding this package," "consequences of not funding this package," "present services that would not be provided if only this package and those that precede it are funded," "support required from other decision units if this package is funded," and the like.

Ranking

Ranking is the process in which a manager reviews all decision packages (from all decision units reporting to him) and establishes their relative priority. A "ranking table" is prepared, listing all decision packages in descending order of priority. A running cumulative total is kept to indicate the total budget request for the sum of each package plus all preceding (higher priority) packages.

Ranking may be performed in a variety of ways—for example, unilaterally by a single manager, or in committee fashion where the manager meets with his decision unit managers.

Depending on the size and complexity of the organization, a series of rankings by successively higher levels of management may be required to produce a single, consolidated ranking table for the entire organization.

To avoid overwhelming higher levels of management with excessive detail, the ranked decision packages are often consolidated into a smaller number of "super packages" for review and ranking by the next managerial level.

Designing and Implementing Zero-Base Budgeting

Before embarking on zero-base budgeting, an organization must carefully weigh several factors:

- What are the strengths and weaknesses of the existing budget process?
- What are the organization's objectives and expectations for zero-base budgeting?
- Who is the principal intended "consumer" of the information generated by the zero-base budgeting process?
- What implementation strategies shall be followed?
- What degree of linkage to existing management systems is appropriate?
- What particular ZBB "technology" shall be employed?

Any decision to launch zero-base budgeting normally should be preceded by a systematic appraisal of the strengths and weaknesses of the existing budget process. This review may be thought of as a "budget audit" during which managers assess the degree to which the current budget process serves or fails to serve the organization's planning, management, and control needs. Design of the approach to zero-base budgeting can then attempt to build on existing strengths and correct deficiencies in the current process.

The organization should next address explicitly the question of what it hopes to achieve by implementing zero-base budgeting. Different organizations may have quite different objectives and expectations for zero-base budgeting. Some of the more common are:

- Cut budgets rationally.
- Reallocate resources from lower to higher priority areas.
- Yield better information or more credible justifications to support budget requests.
- Forge a better link between budgeting and operational planning and control.
- Provide top management with better insights into the detailed workings of the organization.
- Create more substantive involvement by line managers in budget formulation.
- Achieve various "organizational development" objectives (such as improved communication between managerial levels, greater sense of participation, more identification with the organization's mission).

Finally, the organization must design the technical and procedural aspects of the zero-base budgeting process. Particular attention must be paid to the following:

- The logic by which decision units are identified and defined.
- The type of analysis to be emphasized.
- The particular forms, procedures, timetable, guidelines, and instructions to be used in implementing the process.
- The type and amount of training and technical assistance to be provided.

The users of zero-base budgeting must also decide how to modify the process in the second and later cycles following the first year. Priorities may be reviewed to ensure that they are still relevant, decision units may be added or deleted as appropriate, new decision packages may be formulated to meet newly identified needs, and cost and output data may be refined and updated. But it is usually not necessary to repeat the considerable development normally required in the first year. Illustratively, the focus can shift to areas of the budget not included the first year, or the process can be driven deeper in the organization, or the reliability of data can be improved, or the process can be more selective in concentrating analytic efforts on particular issues.

The Future of Zero-Base Budgeting in the Federal Government

Strengths and Weaknesses of the Existing Federal Budget Process

The federal budget process works. It comprehensively reconciles the competing claims of a myriad of programs into a unified whole. Each party understands the rules of the game, and open conflict is kept to a minimum.

Some weaknesses are, however, apparent. Budget justifications focus almost exclusively on increments—the additional positions and dollars requested above the "adjusted base." Neither the President nor Congress is routinely provided the opportunity of examining whether objectives should be changed, or whether the same objectives could be attained more economically, or what would be the consequences of funding a given program at varying levels. Interagency trade-off opportunities within the same general program area are difficult to examine without special analyses. The link between costs and services provided is hard to discern. Often, cuts are imposed without any explicit recognition of which services will be reduced by what amounts. Agencies are frequently expected to "absorb" cuts and still, somehow, maintain the present level of operations.

Objectives for Zero-Base Budgeting in the Federal Government

A tentative set of primary objectives for zero-base budgeting in the executive branch of the federal government might be as follows:

• Provide the President [with] a range of choices within a given program so he can ensure that the total resources correspond to his policy preferences for that program.

• Yield more credible budget justifications, at all levels within the executive branch, in support of total budget requests, and not merely with respect to proposed changes from the prior year. The information should be structured so as to illuminate the consequences of various levels of funding, both above and below current levels.

• Encourage agency operating managers to surface recommendations for improved methods of operation as part of the formal budget process.

Consumers

There are many potential consumers of the results of zero-base budgeting in the federal government . . . the Congress (its substantive, budget, and appropriations committees, as well as the Congressional Budget Office and the GAO); the President and his Office of Management and Budget; agency heads and their policy, planning, and budget staffs; and the several levels of operating "line" managers within each agency.

Implementation Strategies

The central problem is to identify the most productive targets of opportunity for zero-base budgeting and then determine how best to implement the process in the selected areas.

Although the President's budget embraces virtually all federal expenditures, zero-base budgeting may not be equally appropriate for all types of expenditure.

The interest on the national debt is hardly susceptible to annual zero-base review.

A variety of income and other transfers, such as social security payments, veterans' benefits, welfare payments, and general revenue-sharing, are controllable only in the long run and can be changed only if there is a significant shift in the political consensus.

Other major expenditures have powerful constituencies; it would take more than a new budget process to affect significantly expenditures from the Highway Trust Fund or the various agricultural price support programs.

Stability and credibility in national security and foreign affairs require a degree of continuity in the scale and distribution of resources commitment.

Significant or abrupt changes in long-range procurement or construction programs, both civilian and military, could cause severe economic dislocations even if decision-makers are persuaded to ignore sunk costs.

But in the long run nothing is fixed. In the short run much is, at least within the realm of practical politics. This is not to say that programs such as those cited in the previous paragraphs should not be thoroughly reappraised from time to time. Of course they must be, but the annual budget process may not be the proper forum for the debate.

There are, however, several classes of Federal expenditures ideally suited to the type of zero-base budgeting described in this article:

• The overhead agencies of government, i.e., those agencies providing services not to the public but to government itself (e.g., GSA [General Services Administration], the Civil Service Commission, parts of Treasury and Justice, etc.).

• The overhead (administrative and support) activities of agencies, in Washington and in countless field offices. This is a very diverse category including a multitude of functions such as legal, ADP, personnel, training, accounting, research, planning, procurement, printing, communications, transportation, etc.

• Virtually all formula and project grant programs.

• Many operating programs of government, where the government itself acts directly as the provider of service, without any intermediaries. This group would include organizations such as the National Park Service, Forest Service, VA Hospitals, Customs Service, FAA, FDA, and so forth.

A fundamental implementation issue to be resolved is the relationship of zero-base budgeting to the overall federal budget process. Zero-base budgeting could be implemented as a supplement to the existing budget process, it could substitute for the existing budget process, or elements of the zero-base budgeting process could be incorporated into the existing budget process.

The first option would leave undisturbed the normal routines of budgeting, and therein lies both its advantages and disadvantages. Treating zero-base budgeting as supplementary to the existing budget process would cause the least disruption for both OMB and the agencies. True, it would generate an additional workload, but this could be accommodated. OMB and the agencies would in all likelihood set up special staffs to handle zero-base budgeting, effectively insulating it from the "real" budget process. This, of course, is precisely what happened to PPB (the earlier planning-programming-budgeting system).

The second option is only superficially a real option. The concept of "replacing" the existing budget process with zero-base budgeting is wrongheaded. In the first place, the budget process serves many purposes other than those for which zero-base budgeting is suited. Besides, a budget process is not an integrated circuit module that can be unplugged or reconnected at will.

The third option is a real one, in fact the only one that makes sense. The basic principles of zero-base budgeting could be made an integral part of the agency budget formulation process and could form the basis for both the Spring Preview and Director's Review. (This, in fact, is the approach taken by the Office of Management and

Budget; see OMB Bulletin No. 77-9, dated April 19, 1977.) The formats of detailed supporting budget schedules need not be altered necessarily, but the schedules probably would be completed only after basic program allocations are made by OMB.

It is probable that at least three overlapping zero-base budgeting cycles would operate, each with a different focus. The first cycle would operate at the most detailed level within the agency. At this stage, operating managers would formulate zero-based budget requests, which through a successive ranking process would flow upwards to the various line assistant secretaries. During the second cycle, the agency head would formulate the agency-wide budget and review it with OMB. The third cycle would involve OMB's own zero-base analysis and preparation of priority-ranked budget proposals for consideration by the President.

In practice, of course, the process would not be as simple and sequential as suggested above. Several iterations might be required, each cycle operating within a framework of planning and policy guidelines . . . much as in the present process.

Zero-Base Budgeting Technology

As this article has attempted to emphasize, zero-base budgeting may be variously implemented for different reasons, in different ways, and to serve the needs of different users. The federal government is so diverse that no one ZBB "technology" can suffice. What constitutes a decision unit in one part of one agency will not apply in other parts of the same agency or at different levels in the same agency, still less in other agencies. The decision variables governing the formulation of decision packages will vary within and among programs and agencies.

It would be possible, however, to develop models, standards, or guidelines to deal with similar classes of programs or activities commonly found throughout the Federal Government. Several agencies operate hospitals, for example; similar approaches to zero-base budgeting would probably be applicable regardless of the agency. Again, at a more detailed level, similar approaches could be used in different agencies to deal with functions such as maintenance, ADP operations, and the like. Within OMB it doubtless would be desirable to develop a consistent framework to analyze programs from different agencies within the same general program area.

Can ZBB Do the Job?

Zero-base budgeting has proved, in diverse settings, that it can make a useful contribution to the art and practice of management. Whether it can be equally helpful if applied extensively in the federal government is an open question. Its success will largely depend on how agencies respond to the challenge of adapting the principles of zero-base budgeting to their own decision-making needs.

Now that zero-base budgeting is being launched on a broad scale, it is to be hoped that it will be viewed as an *approach* to resource allocation rather than as a uniform set of procedures to be applied by rote regardless of the nature of the program, organizational level, or management's needs.

Finally, what will be the lasting impact of zero-base budgeting? PPB is no longer a formal, government-wide system, but its effects are very much with us. The legacy of PPB has been a demonstrable improvement in the amount and quality of policy, program, and budgetary analysis, in the federal government and in state and local governments throughout the nation.

Zero-Based Budgeting
in Wilmington, Delaware

*David W. Singleton, Bruce A. Smith,
and James R. Cleaveland*

In recent years, governments at every level have shown growing interest in adopting progressive management techniques. These techniques are in stark contrast to such factors as tradition and political considerations, which have historically played a central role in governmental management. The rapid growth in governmental expenditures in recent years, and the fiscal crises confronting many governmental units, have contributed significantly to the growing interest in adopting these modern approaches to management.

As in the private sector, the fundamental area of management in the public sector is the planning-budgeting-accountability process. Consequently, it is in this area that a large share of public sector management concern and improvement has taken place. Executive budgeting, performance budgeting and the planning-programming-budgeting system (PPBS) all represent innovations—and advances—in this field.

One of the major drawbacks in most budgeting systems is their primary focus on the increases from year to year in various accounting categories, with little systematic regard for programmatic priorities and results. A relatively new approach to planning and budgeting—zero-base budgeting—aims to overcome this drawback by subjecting all proposed activities and expenditures to the type of intensive scrutiny normally reserved for proposed new programs. Zero-base budgeting, or ZBB, originated in the private sector and has

From *Governmental Finance*, vol. 5, no. 3 (August 1976), pp. 20–29. Reprinted with permission of municipal Finance Officers Association.

been little used in the public sector. This article presents a case history of its implementation in the municipal government of Wilmington, Delaware.

With a resident population of 80,000, and a daily commuter influx from the suburbs of another 60,000, Wilmington is far and away Delaware's largest city, and its commercial hub. The city also houses half of the state's welfare recipients, a quarter of the senior citizens, a quarter of the persons with incomes below the poverty line, and nearly a third of the crime—although it represents only 15% of the state's population. Since 1960, the city's resident population has declined 17%.

For fiscal 1976, Wilmington's general operating budget was $34.8 million, of which $9.1 million was an operating subsidy to the local school district. In addition, the city operates separate funds for its water, sewer and Marine Terminal operations, totaling $11.3 million in Fiscal 1976, and administers another $10.2 million annually in federal, state and private grant funds. The city's capital budget for Fiscal 1976 amounted to $12.5 million.

Wilmington's governmental structure, under home-rule charter, is characterized as "strong mayor-council" form. The present mayor, Thomas C. Maloney, had held office since 1973. During that time, Maloney has established a national reputation for fiscal restraint, limiting the growth in the city's operating budget to only 18.9% for all four of his budgets combined—compared to 16% annually under his predecessor. A mainstay of Maloney's approach has been improved management of resources, and dramatic productivity improvements in a variety of city services.

In their continuing review of the planning-budgeting-accountability process in Wilmington, Mayor Maloney and his staff had identified a variety of disadvantages with the existing process—a fairly typical, although heavily detailed, line-item approach. Among the more significant difficulties were:

• *Insufficient Information:* The existing budget process provided little useful information about the nature and level of services provided, the reason for providing the service, the beneficiaries of the service, or the resources needed to provide a specific level of service.

• *Existing Level Assumed:* In general, the budgeting process took as given the level of funding from the current year, and focused almost entirely on the increase sought for the coming year. Expenditures included in previous budgets usually required no significant justification.

• *No Trade-offs:* Although the city did not have sufficient resources to fund all services at the requested—or even current—level,
there was no meaningful process available to make choices and
trade-offs among the city's different services on anything even approaching a cost/benefit basis.

• *Impact of Change Unclear:* There was no mechanism to predict
the impact of significant changes in the funding of particular services,
and no systematic way to identify the absolute minimum level of
service (if any) which the city must provide. Similarly, there was no
way to project the likely benefits of significant funding increases in a
particular service.

Although these problems are relatively common to all levels of
government, they were exacerbated in Wilmington's case by the severe and continuing fiscal problems which beset Wilmington and so
many of America's older cities:

• Little or no growth in existing revenue sources, coupled with a
high level of inflation and excessive unemployment.

• Locked-in union wage settlements in the 5–7.5% range.

• Relatively "fixed" expenses, such as pensions, debt service,
insurance, and the public school subsidy, consuming roughly half the
available revenues.

• Continuing demands for new programs (or continuation of
programs formerly federally funded), particularly social services.

• Strong aversion to any tax increases, which tend to accelerate
the erosion of the city's tax base.

As a result of these concerns, members of Mayor Maloney's staff
were attracted by the concept when they learned of the successful use
of ZBB in the private sector.[1] After further research, discussions with
a consulting firm having considerable ZBB experience, and con-
sultation with city officials in Garland, Texas, one of the few
public jurisdictions which had utilized ZBB, a decision was made
in the late autumn of 1975 to promptly implement ZBB in
Wilmington.

In most organizations, the one type of budget request certain to
receive intensive screening and analysis is the one that proposes to
establish a new service. It is likely to be reviewed as to desirability and
need for the service, beneficiaries of the service, reasonableness of
proposed costs, potential future implications, and availability of
funds—often in terms of relative priority of all proposed new services. Zero-base budgeting aims to apply this same type of process, in
a more sophisticated manner, to all proposed expenditures.

Essentially, ZBB seeks to accomplish this through a process that divides all proposed activities (and expenditures) into cohesive units of manageable size, subjects them to detailed scrutiny, and ultimately establishes a rank-order of those units which, given unlimited resources, would be funded. A selected level of expenditure is then matched against the final rank ordering, and if funds are not sufficient to cover the entire listing, lowest priority items are left unfunded until the cumulative total of the funded priority list exactly matches the level of funding that is available. The final priority list, balanced with available funds, then becomes the budget.

ZBB is a sophisticated management tool which provides a systematic method of reviewing and evaluating all operations of the organization, current or proposed; allows for budget reductions and expansions in a planned, rational manner; and encourages the reallocation of resources from low to high priority programs. Because of the nature of the process involved, ZBB also tends to have some important fringe benefits, such as involving more managers in the budgeting process, providing more information and options to decision-makers, and establishing a systematic basis for management by objectives and priorities.

The foundation of ZBB is a four-step analytic process. Conceptually, the steps are:

1. *Establish Budget Units:* A budget unit is a grouping of existing or proposed activities which might be identified as a "program." It may consist of only one distinct activity, as in the case of trash collection in Wilmington's budget, or it may consist of a group of closely related activities, as in the case of Wilmington's recreation program. In nearly every case in Wilmington, the budget units were smaller than a department, consisting of the previously established divisions within most departments. As a result, the budget units did not create a new and unfamiliar organizational structure, and each budget unit had a readily identifiable manager.

2. *Divide Budget Units into Service Levels:* Since the variety, quantity and quality of service to be provided is usually a more realistic question than whether or not a given budget unit will be funded at all, each budget unit is divided into several alternative levels of service. In most cases in Wilmington, this began with a level at about half of current, and advanced in steps through a slightly reduced level, the current level, and a possible expanded level. Each level represents a forecast of the cost and service consequences of operating at that level. In Wilmington's budget, the 61 budget units were eventually divided into a total of 194 service levels, with from 1 to 7 levels per budget unit.

3. *Analyze Service Levels:* Given the relatively small size and programmatic cohesiveness of the budget units and the service levels, it is then possible to analyze each segment of the proposed budget in considerable detail. The need to provide a given level of a particular service may be explored. Potential alternative approaches to meet a particular need may be identified. The manpower and other costs proposed to provide a given level of service may be examined for reasonableness. A given level of marginal cost may be compared to a given marginal increase in the quality or quantity of service.

4. *Priority Ranking of all Service Levels:* Following the analytic process, all of the potentially desirable service levels from all of the budget units, as revised and finalized, are rank-ordered into a single list. The basic concept is that a given service level is ranked higher than all of the service levels that would be foregone, if necessary, to make available the funds for that given service level. Meanwhile, a level of expenditure (typically the projection of revenue from existing sources) is selected. Since, generally, revenues are not sufficient to cover the entire list, the priority rankings determine which service levels will be funded and which will not.

In practice, the ZBB process is considerably more complex than this conceptual framework. Wilmington's experience with ZBB, in chronological order, is presented in the following sections.

Following Mayor Maloney's decision in the late autumn of 1975 to implement ZBB in Wilmington, a variety of planning and decision-making became necessary. In recognition of the priority ascribed to the project by the mayor, two members of the mayor's staff were, from the outset, given essentially full-time responsibility for ZBB. Also, a consulting firm was retained to assist.

The first step was the development of a detailed timetable, from the starting point in mid-November, 1975 to the charter-mandated City Council submission date, April 1, 1976. From the outset, it was recognized that the schedule was tight, with little allowance for slippage.

The major milestones of the schedule were:

Task	Completion
Determination of Agencies to be Included	December 5
Review and Approval of Budget Manual	December 12
Training Program	December 19
Preliminary Departmental ZBB Submissions	January 16
Final Departmental ZBB Submissions	January 30
Departmental Hearings	February 27

Preliminary Ranking and Revenue Estimate   March 5
Mayor's Approval of Final Ranking   March 19
Presentation of Budget to Council   April 1
Approval of Budget by Council   June 1

A fundamental decision was the comprehensiveness of the ZBB process. The possibility of including only some departments or only certain expenditures (such as personnel costs) was discussed. However, the ranking process which culminates ZBB was judged to be far more meaningful if all requests competing for the General Fund were ranked competitively.

While Wilmington's water, sewer and Marine Terminal funds are maintained independently of the General Fund, it was decided to include all of these funds in the ZBB process—although they would be ranked separately. This was done both to strengthen the overall resource allocation process, and also because any year-end surpluses in these funds are transferred to the General Fund, thus giving expenditures in these funds a direct impact on the General Fund.

Likewise, federal and state grant funds, which had never previously been included in the budgeting process (except for federal revenue sharing) were to be included. In each case, federal and state grant funds were to be identified as such, but shown as part of the relevant budget unit and service level. The inclusion of grant funds would provide significant additional information, not previously available to decision-makers in a systematic manner. In many cases, this data would show major activities which had been little known to decision-makers because they used no city funds. In some cases, the data identify critical areas with heavy dependence on grant funds, which might have to be assumed by city funds upon expiration of the grants.

The major exclusion from ZBB was to be the operating subsidy to the local school district. In view of the limited time available, the relative autonomy of the Board of Education, and the fact that the bulk of the schools' funding comes directly from state appropriations, it was considered infeasible to include the schools in the first implementation of ZBB.

The other significant exclusion from ZBB was to be so-called "fixed" expenses. Due to the lack of short-term control and discretion over these expenditures, items such as pensions, debt service and insurance were omitted from the process.

Once the extent of inclusion in ZBB had been determined, it was necessary to identify budget units. In the great majority of cases, budget units were selected to correspond with the established divisions within city departments. Thus, for example, Wilmington's Public Works Department was divided into eleven budget units, corresponding to its eleven divisions; Planning and Development was assigned four budget units, matching its established divisional structure; and the Auditing and Treasurer's Departments were each assigned one budget unit, since there were no established divisions within those departments. In a few cases of very large divisions with highly varied functions, budget units were established to subdivide the established divisions. Thus, in the Department of Public Safety, the police and fire divisions were sub-divided into, respectively, six and three budget units.

A critical step in the planning process was the development of forms. The unique needs of every jurisdiction make it improbable that any set of standardized forms can be used for ZBB. In Wilmington's case, consideration was given to such local factors as past budget practice, accounting system needs, availability of data and other factors in developing ZBB forms. Where possible, the forms were designed to resemble the previously used budget forms. A total of seven forms were designed and utilized, although later experience suggests that the process can and should be somewhat simplified, with the number of forms reduced.

The final planning step was the preparation of a budget manual, containing ZBB instructions as well as traditional data, such as salary scales, hospitalization insurance premiums, and submission deadlines. Although it was recognized that the manual would have to be supplemented with training and technical assistance support, the manual did serve a useful purpose as the only written compendium of ZBB forms and instructions.

Recognizing the need for technical assistance, a team of nine budget analysts was assembled from the Mayor's Office, the Finance Department, the Department of Planning and Development and City Council's staff. All had past experience in fiscal analysis. After a period of intensive training, one of the budget analysts was to be assigned to each city department, to assist them in responding to the demands of ZBB.

With these steps completed, ZBB was ready for presentation to the city's departments for implementation.

The impending implementation of ZBB was formally announced to Wilmington's department heads by the mayor in late November, 1975. Although—as with any radical departure from the past practice—there was some criticism and resistance, cooperation and support from the departments generally proved to be excellent.

Actually, the first involvement by most departments had been in early November, when the city's consultants met with department heads to gather their impressions of the former budget process, suggestions to improve the process, and sufficient information regarding departmental operations to identify budget units. This information was all used in developing Wilmington's ZBB format.

Following the formal announcement, department heads and budget unit managers (usually division managers) were split into two workshops, of about 25 participants each, for training. Each group received two half-day training sessions, at which budget manuals and forms were also distributed. The first session was an orientation to ZBB concepts and general procedures, while the second session was used to review specific instructions in the manual and to discuss samples of completed forms.

The first major process for departments—the preliminary analysis—focused largely on the definition of service levels. As the most radical and fundamental concept of ZBB, it is essential that service levels be soundly developed. Departments were given some guidance in defining service levels, but functioned largely on their own. For each service level of each budget unit, departments were asked to submit basic information as shown on the sample form B-2 (see figure 1).

Some departments felt that a reduced service level might be misconstrued as a recommendation to operate at that level, and resisted proposing reduced levels. As a result, all budget unit managers were instructed that service levels represented options, not recommendations, and the first level must not exceed 40–60% of the current expenditure level. Generally, a second level below current service was to be proposed, then the current level, and finally an improved level of service (when desirable), yielding a recommended minimum of four service levels. In fact, budget units ultimately submitted averaged three service levels each.

The structuring of service levels is cumulative. If a given service level is funded for a department, those that precede it will also be funded—although those that follow will not necessarily be funded. This assumption means that the costs for each level are costs to be added to prior levels in a department in order to produce the higher level of service.

Service levels vary either the quantity or the quality of a department's operations, or both. For example, in firefighting, the first service level might either: *Quantity Variation*—Reduce by 50% the number of fire companies, but maintain manning on each company as at present; *Quality Variation*—Maintain the same number of fire companies as at present, but reduce by 50% the manning on each;

Figure 1
Preliminary Service Level Description

PRELIMINARY
SERVICE LEVEL DESCRIPTION

B-2 **Page 4 of 9**

Department	Division	Budget Unit
Planning & Develop.	Development	Development

Rank	Service Level Title
3	Extensive Planning & Development Activities

Describe Services Provided and Activities Performed in this Service Level

Update Urban Renewal plans and the comprehensive plan for areas of the city, and prepare zoning ordinance amendments. Prepare plans for the expenditure of Community Development funds and coordinate the execution of those plans. Prepare designs for simple capital improvement projects. Develop housing programs and initiate downtown business improvement projects.

Briefly Describe Resources to be Used in this Service Level

1 Senior Planner
1 Community Development Coordinator
1 Renewal Technician
1 Draftsperson
Total Personal Services $57,797
"CURRENT LEVEL"

	Est. Fiscal 1977	
	City	Non-City
No. Pos.	2	2
Cost	$29	$29

Rank	Service Level Title

Describe Services Provided and Activities Performed in this Service Level

Briefly Describe Resources to be Used in this Service Level

	Est. Fiscal 1977	
	City	Non-City
No. Pos.		
Cost		

Both—Reduce both the number of companies and the manning on each by 25%.

Service levels were devised in all of these manners in Wilmington. Sanitation, in Public Works, varied primarily the frequency, and thus the quality, of service:

- Level 1: Once weekly pick-up at curb
- Level 2: Twice weekly pick-up at curb
- Level 3: Pick-up from rear or side yard, plus special services and school pick-up (current level)

The department apparently did not see sufficient marginal improvement to show possible service expansion to a fourth level (which could have been three times a week pick-up).

Other departments defined service levels largely in terms of the quantity of services provided on a prioritized basis, holding quality relatively constant. For example, the police patrol division budget unit in Public Safety divided current and proposed services into six levels:

- Level 1: Basic patrol and preliminary investigation of major crimes
- Level 2: Preliminary investigation of all criminal complaints; response to priority non-criminal calls
- Level 3: Follow-up on all criminal and non-criminal calls: operation of jail and selective parking enforcement
- Level 4: Increased parking enforcement; full-service response to noncriminal calls
- Level 5: Additional patrols, school crossing guards (current level)
- Level 6: Expansion of patrol, parking enforcement and school crossing functions

Here, the department saw sufficient marginal improvement to show expansion to a sixth service level.

Whatever the approach, the objective was to show the department's assessment of what services should be provided if only a certain level of funding was available.

Once levels were defined, an estimated cost for each level was calculated. This did not prove to be difficult, since the bulk of the costs were personnel and fringe benefits, which could be readily correlated with the manner in which personnel were divided among the levels. The service levels and costs, along with certain additional data and a preliminary ranking by the department head, were submitted by the departments in mid-January, 1976. This provided the mayor's staff with an estimate of the total budget, and an opportunity to discuss possible revisions in the service level structure and priority rankings with the departments. As a result of this process, several significant revisions were made.

In the latter part of January, departments completed the detailed final service level descriptions, as shown on the sample form B-3 (see figure 2). In addition to the information reported in the preliminary phase, more precise data and certain supplemental information were required for the final submission.

A unique feature of ZBB is the "program measures" reported for each service level. Up to seven measures could be selected for each budget unit, which would be repeated for each service level and reflect the increasing quality or quantity of services provided at each higher service level. Unfortunately, many departments had not accumulated such data, and were unable to provide the desired level of documentation of program measures. However this process has established a foundation for future years, and has led to efforts by several departments as well as the mayor's staff to begin the accumulation of more useful data.

The final service level description was accompanied by a detailed line-item listing of all costs associated with that service level, including personnel, fringe benefits, materials, supplies, and equipment. These forms resulted in a considerable bulk of paperwork and a significant workload to the departments, although the work was more time consuming than onerous.

In addition to the service level and line-item listings, each department also submitted a departmental priority ranking of all budget units and all service levels within the department. A running cumulative total was included to show the amount required to fund the department to a particular priority level. Also, departments were asked to include a memorandum indicating the rationale for the order of prioritization selected.

The focus then shifted to the mayor's staff for the preparation of the city's consolidated budget.

The Mayor's Office review of departmental budget submissions began with a preliminary assessment of the city's financial position. Departmental general fund requests,[2] including requests for new or expanded services, amounted to $19.9 million, an increase of 15.6% over the existing budget. With a 1–2% revenue growth likely, requests would exceed revenues by roughly $2.6 million.

Wilmington's ZBB process presented a number of alternatives, which could be used singly or in combination to deal with the $2.6

Figure 2
Service Level Analysis

SERVICE LEVEL ANALYSIS

B-3					RANK:	5	

Department Planning	Division Prog. Anal. & Admin.	Budget Unit Program Analysis	Service Level Title Administrative, Budgeting, Plan & Grant Preparation	Bud Acct # 01-17-00			
					Department	2 of 15	
					Division	1 of 4	
					Budget Unit	1 of 4	

Describe Services Provided and Activities Performed in this Service Level
—general administration of the Dept. of Plan. & Devel.
—preparation of the Criminal Justice Plan
—preparation of the Capital Budget
—preparation of federal & state grant applications
—collection of data & other pertinent information necessary to complete the above mentioned tasks
—Fiscal management of Department Federal Grants
—Collection & dissemination of the facts about the City
—Secretarial support for above functions

Justification of Need for this Service Level

Preparation of the Criminal Justice Comprehensive Plan is required by contract #10-07-000-01-76 with DARC. Preparation of the Capital Budget and program is an essential activity of city government. Section 5-700 (e) of the City Charter states that the Department of Planning will prepare and submit the capital budget and program to the Planning Commission.

The city benefits substantially from the use of federal and state funds obtained by grant applications. Fiscal & operational management of federal grants is necessary for effective and efficient utilization of funds. In order for the above mentioned functions to be completed effectively, data collection and analysis must be carried out. Overall department administration of the varied activities is necessary for effective management and control.

SUMMARY BUDGET DATA ($000's)

	This Serv. Level		Cumulative*	
	City	Non-City	Total	% FY76
No. Bud. Pos.	4	2	4	80
Pers. Serv.	86	38	86	96
M. S. E.	47	39	56	110
Total	142	77	142	101

PROGRAM MEASURES

Description	This Serv. L	Cumulative	
		Total	% FY76
1. Federal Grants Prepared	7	7	100
2. Value, Federal Grants	3,900	3,900	74
3. Special studies	1	1	NA
4. Capital Budget prep	1	1	100
5. Criminal Justice Plan	1	1	100
6. Program Budgets Prep.	0	0	0
7. Programs Evaluated	0	0	0

Describe and Justify Resources Required in this Service Level
1 Planning Director—needed for overall administrative control and expertise for all divisions and special projects.
1 Grants & Contracts Manager—needed for fiscal management of federal grants, other financial matters in department, and maintenance of census data and other Management Information Systems.
1 Criminal Justice Coordinator—prepares criminal justice plans and serves as expert on crime trends in Wilm.
1 Program Analyst   )—It is necessary to have these two people to prepare capital budget
1 Director of Program Analysis) & assist in data collection for other activities.
1 Clerk Stenographer III—Secretarial functions for above-mentioned professionals.
Contractual/other services: $87,645   Equipment: $1,000
Materials/supplies: $5,950

*Cumulative for City funds only.

173

million gap: 1) raise taxes to increase revenues; 2) reduce the cost of providing a specified level of service; or 3) not fund lowest priority service levels.

The first alternative is generally least desirable. For policy reasons, it was ruled out in Wilmington at this time.

The second alternative is generally most desirable, in that it tends to represent an increase in efficiency or productivity. In practice, this approach is most similar to traditional budgeting, with the prime emphasis on large or unusual expenditures, and expenditures showing significant increases from the current budget. Ultimately, Wilmington was successful in reducing the departmental budget requests by approximately $900,000, or 4.5%, through these line-item cuts.

Once revenues are established, and the cost of each service level has been reduced as much as possible, the third alternative—prioritizing—comes into play. This alternative represents the unique characteristic of ZBB. For Wilmington, this provided the mechanism for identifying $1.2 million in departmental requests that were of lowest priority, and would not be funded.

A major portion of the administration review process was consumed by departmental budget hearings. Each department was afforded a session of 3–6 hours duration, attended by both members of the mayor's staff and representatives of City Council Finance Committee. At the hearings, discussions focused on opportunities to reduce the cost of providing a specified level of service, as well as on the rationale for the structuring of the service levels and the prioritization of the department's service levels. Numerous minor changes in the costs of service levels were made at the hearings, generally with the consent of the department head. Changes in prioritization were not made at the hearings, although areas of disagreement with a department head's rankings were identified. Budget hearing discussions also covered program measures, beneficiaries of the service, involvement of grant funds and marginal cost of increasing service levels.

The consensus of both departmental officials and members of the mayor's staff was that with the introduction of ZBB, the hearings provided a more comprehensive and penetrating view of a department's activities than hearings in previous years. Specifically, the basis for proposed expenditures was usually related much more directly and rationally to services provided than in the past. Also, more discussion of the value of specific services, and the need for specific services, was possible.

Separately from the hearings, members of the mayor's staff also reviewed the departmental submissions for completeness, clarity, arithmetic accuracy, and other largely technical considerations. This process, along with the hearings, resulted in minor adjustments to the total cost for most of the service levels.

Formal ranking of priorities is the crucial and distinctive step in ZBB. A variety of criteria may be used, both formally and informally. Some criteria are relatively general, probably applicable to any jurisdiction, while some are more related to local goals and objectives. Key criteria considered in Wilmington include:

• Importance of the service level in terms of the perceived health, welfare, safety and satisfaction of city residents

• Statutory, charter, and contractual commitments met by the service level

• Potential consequences of not providing the service level

• Federal and state funds received dependent on a particular expenditure of city funds

• Informal assessment of the quality of the service provided

• Cost effectiveness of the service level

• Preference, where feasible, to direct services to the public over administrative costs

The final analysis and ranking process began with the decision to lump together a group of services identified as essential, without further prioritization. Little benefit was seen in discussing whether the most fundamental service levels of police, fire or sanitation service is more important. Clearly, all of these services will be provided, at least at the first level of service. Thus, 34 of the 196 service levels were lumped together as a "basic" group, and ranked above all other services. Since most budget units had developed a first service level of 40 to 60% of the existing funding level, the total cost of the "basic" group amounted to $10.0 million.

After isolating the "basic" group, $9.0 million in requested service levels remained, as against only $7.8 million in forecasted revenue. Efforts focused on analysis and ranking of the 162 service levels remaining.

Numerical ranking of 162 separate items is quite difficult—particularly when the 162 items are as varied as the service levels in Wilmington's budget. Consequently, the process began by dividing the remaining service levels into four groups: high priority; medium priority; low priority; and service levels not to be funded for policy reasons[3].

The initial ranking of the remaining service levels showed that revenues were sufficient to cover the entire "high" and "medium" priority groups and part of the "low" priority group. Service levels undesirable for policy reasons were ranked below the "low" priority group, but were effectively eliminated from further consideration.

With the number of service levels to be ranked now reduced to groups of manageable size, all of the service levels in each group were then numerically prioritized. For the "high" and "medium" groups, this was somewhat academic, since revenues were sufficient to fund all of the service levels in the group. However, it was judged important to establish these rankings as the first organized, comprehensive statement of the city's priorities.

For the "low" priority group the specific numerical ranking was of critical importance. Of the 56 service levels within the group, funds were sufficient for only about half. After rankings were assigned, a cumulative funding total was calculated to determine the point at which revenues were exhausted. An analysis of the rankings showed that many of the service levels below the cut-off point were new or expanded levels of service, although 21 levels of service currently being provided also fell below the cut-off. Two levels of new or expanded service ended up above the cut-off.

The complete rankings, as proposed by the mayor's staff, were then presented to the mayor for his consideration. The mayor directed a number of minor changes, but generally expressed satisfaction with the priority order. However, the mayor was concerned that a number of existing service levels involving incumbent employees fell below the cut-off, necessitating immediate layoffs and service cutbacks.

As an alternative, the mayor's staff developed a factor known as "special attrition." A factor had already been allowed for normal attrition, representing funds that would not be spent for salaries and fringe benefits during the period positions remain vacant between incumbents. Now, in order to avoid layoffs and abrupt service cutbacks, an additional factor was calculated representing anticipated savings from positions which would be left unfilled for the balance of the fiscal year when they become vacant. Although this may still entail modest service cutbacks unless compensating productivity increases are achieved, they would occur on a scattered basis throughout the year. While the exact positions to be left vacant could not be identified, past turnover experience indicated that the savings budgeted for "special attrition" were reasonable and attainable.

Following the addition of "special attrition" and minor priority adjustments, the ranking was finalized. No layoffs would be required, although some existing services without incumbent personnel still fell below the cut-off. All told, the "basic" group and ranks 1-110 were shown as funded; ranks 111-162 were shown as not funded.

With the completion of prioritization, the budget was then ready for final housekeeping details, printing and submission to City Council.

In a radical departure from most jurisdictions which have implemented ZBB, Mayor Maloney decided that the Council should receive the actual ZBB documentation. Other jurisdictions using ZBB have recast their budget in traditional format for legislative consideration and public distribution. Although this decision was sure to significantly increase the complexity of City Council's work, Mayor Maloney regarded Council's involvement in the actual ZBB process as ciritical.

City Council's exposure to ZBB had actually begun at the very start of the city's involvement. The councilmen were thoroughly briefed before the decision was made to adopt the process, and had registered their support by adoption of a resolution. In addition, Council's Finance Committee Chairman and a staff member had attended all of the departmental hearings.

Council's consideration of the completed ZBB budget began with an orientation session, devoted to both the process and the output of ZBB. The ZBB budget represented such a total departure from past budgeting practice—in process as well as appearance—that a thorough orientation was essential.

As in past years, Council then proceeded to hold public budget hearings for each department. The hearings, which lasted from one to three hours each, repeated some of the discussion from the administration's budget hearings, but primarily served as a forum for the discussion of concerns of particular relevance to the councilmen. Several departments used the hearing to appeal either a ranking or a line item cut made earlier by the administration. In a number of cases, members of the public or city employees raised questions about specific items in the budget. Members of the mayor's staff attended all of the hearings, and were often asked to explain the rationale behind the prioritization of a particular service level.

Prior to the hearings, Council agreed that no actual changes in the rankings would be discussed until all of the hearings were complete and all comments were heard. This avoided moving service levels up and down the ranking until all the hearings were completed and the Council could put all the levels in perspective.

Initially many of the councilmen approached the budget much as they had approached past budgets. Most of the discussion concerned the incremental changes to line-items. However, as the hearings proceeded, greater and greater attention focused on ZBB considerations. The rationale for a particular ranking, for example, was discussed more and more frequently. Much interest centered on the federal and state grant funds—information which the Council had never before had available in a systematic manner. There was also steadily increasing discussion of program measures and the marginal costs associated with a higher level of service.

One problem was the greatly expanded amount of paperwork. As part-time city officials, many of the councilmen had difficulty finding the time to digest the large volume of information on a department prior to the hearing. The line-item budget detail, a 1000-page document, was simply too heavy and bulky to be readily taken home for review.

At the conclusion of the hearings, Council's staff checked with all of the councilmen to determine what changes in the administration's budget should be considered. After all had been polled, only five changes were proposed. Three proposed changes concerned service levels, with a total cost of $15,000, which had been ranked below the cut-off point but which Council wished to see funded. One change was a line-item cut of $6,000 within a funded service level, which the department head had argued for convincingly. The final proposed change of $8,000 was a service previously provided which the department involved had not included in their budget submission.

The latter proposal was most easily resolved by the administration's commitment to continue the service with personnel under a federally-funded Summer Youth Program, thus not requiring any additional city funds.

Council met at some length to consider possible rerankings to accommodate the other desired additions to the budget. The process proved difficult. Every service level suggested for deletion, as a tradeoff, had its own supporters among the councilmen. Most of the service levels just above the cut-off point included incumbent personnel, whom the councilmen were not anxious to see laid off. A tax increase was seen as unpalatable.

Ultimately the small amount involved in the desired changes proved decisive. Council recommended to the mayor that the four service levels in question be reranked to include them in the budget, and that all service levels then be reduced by 0.1% to provide the needed funds. Since extensive line-item cutting had already been undertaken, the mayor accepted the recommendation only with the understanding that the 0.1% savings would be achieved through attrition, by slightly increasing the time a position remained vacant between incumbents. Council agreed, and the appropriate rerankings were made. With these changes, the Council soon thereafter gave its approval to the entire budget.

Generally, City Council appears to have found ZBB preferable to the city's former process. A major reason appears to be that Council now gets more information, and more useful information, than they have ever had before. The ranked service level format, although not legally binding on the mayor, provides Council with a strong moral commitment as to what services will be provided—whereas the old process had provided only a commitment as to what the line-item expenditures would be. Many councilmen have expressed a desire to continue the ZBB process in future years and possibly expand it to other areas, such as the operating subsidy to the school district and the city's capital budget.

It is important to establish the context in which zero-base budgeting was adopted in Wilmington. Essentially, it represented a logical step forward in a well-established process of fiscal restraint and improved management of resources. It followed earlier experimentation with other budgeting innovations, particularly program budgeting. It drew heavily on analytic and management staff resources that had been developed over an extended period. And it relied on the cooperation and support of the mayor, City Council, and city department heads. The process and the results could differ significantly in a different context.

Insufficient time has passed to assess fully ZBB's impact on Wilmington. However, a number of conclusions may be drawn as to the benefits already derived, and the disadvantages.

On the positive side, a key accomplishment has been the detailed identification of all the services provided by the city—regardless of funding source. Such information was never previously available in systematic form. Once identified, all programs and expenditures were reviewed to a level of detail usually reserved for proposed new programs.

Also beneficial is the establishment of a systematic prioritization of the city's services. This establishes a firm foundation for future years when the city's financial situation may require extremely difficult decisions, and helps assure that those decisions will be based on a well-developed set of priorities.

The ZBB process itself was beneficial, in that it involved nearly all management personnel in the budgeting process, considerably more than in the past. Also, as a planning *and* budgeting process, ZBB involved these personnel in a far more comprehensive resource allocation process.

The ranking of federal and state grant funds establishes a mechanism for identifying the importance of these funds to the city and anticipating the future demands to replace these funds with city funds when they expire. In effect, Wilmington has adopted a comprehensive planning and budgeting process for all its resources.

The statement of priorities and program measures by department heads serves as an excellent basis for a management by objectives program. In the past, the city's approach to management by objectives had been more general, making performance assessment more difficult. With the level of specific detail provided by ZBB, performance against objectives can be measured much more quantitatively.

ZBB has also involved City Council more meaningfully in the budget process. Specifically, it has given them a better picture of the issues involved and a direct involvement in the tradeoff process inherent to budgeting. Potentially, ZBB could serve to very significantly increase the role of the legislative branch of government by providing more effective control of the planning and resource allocation process.

ZBB also has significant disadvantages. Foremost is the large increase in the time, effort and paperwork required. Increased time devoted to the budget by city personnel, the need for consultants in the initial implementation, and increased printing costs probably resulted in a net increase of 100% in the cost of preparing the budget. The increased effort, and the high level of detail required, caused numerous complaints, especially from department heads. Particularly in the cases where a service is already rather well known to the city administration and City Council, such complaints are understandable.

The large size of the first service level in most budget units—40 to 60% of current spending—may also have provided an opportunity to effectively shelter costs which might, if listed as separate service levels, be more seriously questioned. In a number of departments it appeared that overhead-type costs were unduly heavy in the initial service level, although if more time had been available, this could have been addressed by revisions in the proposed service levels.

Another limitation is the underlying assumption that the specified level of funding must be provided in order to obtain the specified level of service. Past experience suggests that improvements in efficiency and productivity may enable a specified level of service to be provided even with reduced funding levels. While the knowledge that reducing the cost of *each* proposed service level enables more service levels to be funded tends to encourage economy and stimulate productivity improvement, the stimulus may not be sufficiently strong to produce the desired results. Thus, it is desirable to undertake separate measures to promote efficiency and productivity in combination with the implementation of ZBB.

Wilmington's experience with ZBB has generally been quite positive and seems likely to lead to further use of ZBB in Wilmington. Combined with a variety of measures geared to improved organization effectiveness and economy, ZBB appears to be making a significant contribution. While ZBB would not necessarily prove beneficial in every jurisdiction, its implementation is certainly worthy of consideration.

Notes

1. Peter A. Pyhrr, "Zero-Base Budgeting," *Harvard Business Review,* Nov.–Dec. 1970, pp. 111–121. *Zero-Base Budgeting: A Practical Management Tool for Evaluating Expenses* (New York: John Wiley & Sons, 1973).

2. Excluding fixed costs and the operating subsidy to the schools, which were not included in ZBB. These items were budgeted at $17.1 million.

3. For example, a proposed change in water billing procedure that would initially result in serious cash flow problems.

Zero-Base Budgeting
in Georgia State Government:
Myth and Reality

Introduction

This article on zero-base budgeting presents an analysis of information obtained in a series of interviews with budgetary personnel in
Georgia state government. Georgia was the first state to install zero-
base budgeting,[1] and it is currently one of the states with the most
highly developed ZBB process.[2] The Georgia system also gained national attention during the 1976 presidential campaign as the leading
example of ZBB applications in governmental budgeting.[3] For these
reasons the Georgia experience is an important source of information
about the impact of ZBB on traditional budgeting practices.

Much of the early literature dealing with ZBB focused on defining
it and describing its formal procedures.[4] Subsequent writings have
assessed the adaptability of ZBB techniques to public organization,[5]
speculated about their impact on those organizations,[6] and described
the problems attendant to installing the system.[7] Advocates of ZBB
have praised it as an innovative management tool,[8] while critics have
expressed doubt that it represents much that is new.[9] Absent from
the literature, however, is an empirical analysis of the impact of ZBB
on budgetmakers and the budgetary process. This paper provides
such an analysis.

Reprinted from *Public Administration Review*, vol. 38, no. 5 (September–October,
1978). © 1978 by The American Society for Public Administration, 1225 Connecticut
Avenue, N.W., Washington, D.C. All rights reserved. By permission of author and
publisher.

The Myths and the Rhetoric

The initial claims made on behalf of ZBB were impressive but exaggerated, with promises far exceeding the likelihood of performance. The ZBB label was in many ways its own worst enemy. The label implies *tabula rasa* budgeting—an approach which would wipe the financial slate clean at the beginning of each fiscal year by assuming that an agency has no base from the previous year upon which to predicate its budget requests for the forthcoming year. According to such an interpretation each agency would build its budget requests from the bottom up without referring to the past as either guide for, or a constraint upon the future. Taken literally, a zero-base budget would seem to imply no base at all. Each program would be on trial for its life every year.[10]

While students of public budgeting easily recognized the absurdity of such a characterization, others seem to have been less certain about the extent to which proponents of ZBB actually expected budget decisions to be made by starting at point zero.[11] Confusion over the precise meaning of "zero-base" was unfortunately compounded by the statements of the then-Governor of Georgia, Jimmy Carter—the leading public advocate of ZBB. In his 1971 Budget Message to the Georgia General Assembly Governor Carter stated:

> No longer can we take for granted the existing budget base and simply be responsible for reviewing proposed increases to continue programs and add new ones. . . . I will insist that the entire range of State services be re-examined and will cut back or eliminate established programs if they are judged to be ineffective or of low priority.[12]

On another occasion Governor Carter said: "We stripped down our budget each year to zero and we start (sic) from scratch . . . we try to optimize the service delivered to our people compared to how much it cost."[13] In 1976, presidential candidate Carter wrote: "Zero-base budgeting starts from a very different premise. (The comparison was with what he referred to as the traditional approach.) Rather than just incrementing the new on the old, the system demands a total justification of everything from scratch—from zero!"[14] While, these statements can be dismissed as political hyperbole, they did lend credence to the most exaggerated caricature of ZBB. Thus, the combined effect of the ZBB label and the statements of Jimmy Carter both as Governor of Georgia and as presidential candidate contributed to the misunderstanding about what ZBB entails for public budgetmakers.

ZBB in Georgia: An Operational Definition

In actual practice ZBB is substantially different from its caricature. As operationalized in Georgia, ZBB is a set of budget preparation techniques designed to improve managerial control over agency funding requests so as to improve efficiency within the executive branch in the allocation of available resources. This is not a new objective; nor is ZBB the only set of techniques through which improvements in efficiency can be attempted. The uniqueness of ZBB is in the way in which it formats information.

In Georgia all departments of state government are broken down into activities which in turn are divided into programs. A program is the lowest organizational subdivision at which it is considered practical to maintain cost data. The budget request for each program is formulated in a series of decision packages which identify different levels of effort as well as alternate means for performing the same function. Decision packages are ranked in order of priority at each operating level within the organization. The manager at the next organizational level reviews the rankings and produces an aggregate ranking for all packages presented to him from below. This process continues until final rankings are completed at the departmental level.[15]

The underlying assumption of ZBB is that the ranking process for the forthcoming fiscal year will operate so as to focus attention on those packages at the margin—just above and just below the funding level of the current fiscal year. The corollary assumption is that with budget request information presented in this format there is a greater likelihood of some programs being decreased at the margin rather than increased.[16] The myths and the rhetoric notwithstanding, this is the crux of the ZBB approach in Georgia. One purpose of this paper is to analyze why there is such an incongruity between the caricature of ZBB and the claims made about it, and the operational reality which developed.

ZBB: An Alternative to Incrementalism?

While the ZBB label and the Carter statements tended to cloud rather than clarify the exact meaning of zero-base budgeting, neither is as troublesome as the assertions made by George S. Minmier that zero-base budgeting brought an end to "incrementalism" in budget-making in Georgia. Minmier's writings are the most widely referenced sources of information about ZBB in practice. In his otherwise useful studies of budget reform in Georgia he writes: "Prior to the change to the zero-base budgeting system Georgia had used an incremental budgeting system." Elsewhere the idea is repeated: "Under the former incremental system," and ". . . the incremental budget system previously employed."[17] The clear implication is that at some point in time incremental decision-making stopped and a new mode of decision-making was installed.

That incremental decision-making played a very important role in the budgeting process in the State of Georgia prior to the advent of zero-base budgeting has been well documented by the research of Augustus B. Turnbull.[18] Minmier would have us believe, however, that incrementalism ceased after the installation of zero-base procedures. That is a dubious suggestion at best. Since "incrementalism" is not a set of budget procedures which are ever formally installed, but rather a concept which characterizes a set of practices used by budgetmakers to facilitate decision-making,[19] it is possible that despite the introduction of a new budget delivery process budgeters may continue to build budgets incrementally. A change in procedures does not necessarily alter behavior. Whether or not ZBB altered the behavior of budgeters is an empirical question. Thus, the second purpose of this paper is to assess the extent to which ZBB, a rational budget innovation, succeeded in penetrating the routines[20] of the traditional, incremental budgetary process in the State of Georgia.

Research Method

The research methodology employed was patterned after the approach used by Davis and Ripley in their 1965 study of U.S. Bureau of the Budget personnel.[21] Thirty-six interviews were conducted in 1977 with individuals actively involved in the budgeting process of the State of Georgia.[22] Respondents included the heads of both the Budget and Planning Divisions, Office of Planning and Budget; budget analysts and planners, Office of Planning and Budget; the Legislative Budget Analyst and the Deputy Legislative Budget Analyst; and the chief budget officers of twenty-eight executive branch agencies.[23]

Respondents were asked to reply to a series of open-ended questions about both their participation in the budget process and their interpretations of the working of the zero-base budget system. Since the ZBB approach operates almost exclusively during the preparation and submission phase of the budget cycle, the interviews focused primarily on matters related to that phase of the process. The same topics were pursued in every interview, but the precise wording of the questions and the order in which they were considered varied from one interview to the next. The length of the interviews ranged from forty-five minutes to one and one-half hours. The average interview was one hour.

Defining the "Base"

If zero-base budgeting is a non-incremental approach to budgeting, evidence of the change from incremental decision-making practices to non-incremental practices should have been evident by 1977 in the way in which budgeters described their approach to the task of budget preparation. In zero-base budgeting the preparation of decision packages is the critical decision point where changed budgeting behavior would be expected. It is at this juncture that agency program needs are articulated and cost estimates assigned to programs.

In order to assess the extent to which budget requests were being built from the ground up with basic programs rejustified annually, agency budget officers were asked to describe the manner in which they proceed in the preparation of their annual budget requests. None of the twenty-eight agency budget officers interviewed described his/her approach in terms of a systematic reconsideration of existing agency programs and operations. The notion that budget-makers start from zero or that programs and agencies are annually on trial for their lives was rejected by all of those interviewed. Without specifically using the language of incrementalism, most described an approach to budget preparation that is characteristic of the incremental approach to decision-making. Budgeters in Georgia tend to assume that agency programs will be continued at very close to, or slightly above, the current level. The following comments made by budget officers will serve to illustrate the point:[24]

> Zero-base is OK in theory, but I need to go back and find out where I am by looking at where I've been. I look at last year's budget and start from there.
>
> I look at the experience of last year's budget.
>
> We do 'continuation' budgeting.
>
> I look at last year's budget. I rely on the Auditor's report of actual expenditures, and figure in inflation. Then I figure in the number of people to be added, less the number of people to be separated; that gives you the number of people you need to pay. Salaries plus current expenses with inflation taken into account and you have it. After that we start to consider any new activities which we are not now doing.
>
> We look at last year's budget, figure inflation and required salary increases and try to anticipate likely increases in client requests.

> You have to do 'continuation' budgeting because that is the way the legislature thinks.

> We calculate the amount we want . . . that is our best guess as to what the governor would be willing to recommend to the legislature . . . add in a little for the analyst to cut—he has a job to do, I understand that. Then we develop justification for the increase over last year . . . you don't have to justify what the legislature has already given you in the past—why should you?

> We start from scratch. By that I mean we use last year's expenditures as a bench mark. Then we begin to worry with what we will need to stay up with increased costs. After that we consider expansion of our operations. How else would you do it? Now under the new zero-base system you have to do more justification for the 'new or improved' levels of service.

> Except for the new forms, there has been no change in the way I make the budget.

Budgeters operate in a complex world of conflicting values and goals in which it is often difficult to sort out the interrelationship among policies, or predict the consequences of courses of action. In order to survive in such an environment, budgetmakers in Georgia report that they have adopted strategies which aid them in making decisions. Rather than reconsidering their programs anew each year or attempting to consider the consequences of all alternative courses of action, they rely heavily on past experience. Even in ZBB the "base" is the historic base, not zero-base.

A unique feature of the zero-base budgeting format which also bears closely on the incrementalism issue is the "minimum" funding level. In Georgia, agencies are presently required to submit decision packages for each program at three levels of operations; minimum (less than 100% of the current funding level); current (continuance of last year's programs including increased costs); and new or improved (expansion of program objectives).[25] While no exact funding level is specified for the "minimum" in the budget preparation instructions given to agencies by the Office of Planning and Budget, the general consensus among both agency budget officers and OPB analysts is that the minimum level is approximately 85% of the current level. Information about the impact of the minimum level requirement is important to an understanding of the extent to which ZBB was able to penetrate the existing routines of budgeting because the very idea of recommending a funding level below the current level runs counter to the incremental strategy of protecting the base.

In order to assess the impact of the minimum level requirement on budget preparation and submission, agency budget officers were asked to comment on (1) the way in which they determine the minimum level, and (2) the impact of that requirement on the budgetary process. The following responses are indicative of the way in which budgeters view the minimum funding level requirement:

> The minimum is not very useful except that it may contribute to a more frugal attitude about the budget. I suppose that's why they have it. We have never had to live with anything close to the minimum level.

> We determine the current level first, then drop back to 80% or whatever the minimum level is supposed to be this year.

> The minimum level is not of much use . . . we work backward to get it.

> The minimum is a waste of time . . . no one looks at that. We determine where we want to be and work back to 85%.

> The minimum level is a pain in the ass. It is inconceivable that you would only fund 85% of current level.

> No one pays any attention to it. In 1975 when we had to rework our budgets because of the revenue shortage, we made cuts without any reference to the minimum. You certainly could not expect anyone to come up with say 10% in each program. Some programs are untouchable. We would get 10% department-wide by taking most of it out of a couple of less important programs.

> The minimum level is worthless. We (Legislative Budget Office) don't look at it . . . the departments merely take their 'current' and lop off 10 or 15% to satisfy the requirement of submitting a minimum funding level.

> See that machine over there? (A desk calculator) I prepare my current level which to my way of thinking is not the same dollars as this year, but what it will take to provide the same level of services . . . then I hit those keys and multiply by .85 of the current to get the minimum.

> The minimum is less threatening than you might think . . . the departments know that we (Office of Planning and Budget) don't intend to recommend that their programs be funded at that level. But, it makes them think about the possibility of a cut rather than always expecting more.

Another feature of ZBB which relates to the incrementalism issue is the ranking process. When ranking, managers usually give higher priority to the packages that satisfy essential operating requirements and lower rankings to more discretionary packages. In Georgia the "minimum" level is generally placed higher than the "current," and the "current" levels for most activities tend to be ranked ahead of "new or improved" for any other activity. As a practical matter the ranking process concentrates on only a small segment of package rankings—those which might be regarded as marginal.

The budget format in Georgia makes available to decision-makers a cumulative total for each additional decision package entered into the rank order. Decision-makers know that if they recommended, for example, the funding of a 13th ranked package, then the cumulative total will be increased from perhaps 108% (at the 12th ranked package) to perhaps 110% of last year's level. The consequences of recommending the 13th ranked package (which may actually be some "new or improved" level for a particular program) is thus known to be an increase of 2% over the next highest ranked package. It is also known that a recommended funding at the level will constitute an increase of 10% over the previous year's level for the department. The rankings depict incremental levels of effort.[26] The effect of this process is to reduce the number of packages receiving close consideration. An OPB official pointed out that in practice budget analysis is concentrated on those packages falling between 85 and 110% levels. Agency budget officers suggest that the range of OPB scrutiny is even smaller—somewhere between 95 and 110% levels.

In summary, agency budget officers reported that in building next year's budget the funding level of the previous year is a very useful starting point. Agency budgets are not reviewed as a whole every year for the purpose of reevaluating existing programs. In formulating budget requests agencies seek to protect the integrity of the existing base, and attempt to increase and expand the base by getting their share of whatever new funds are available. The requirement that a "minimum" funding level be identified seems to have little bearing on that budget preparation strategy, and the ranking process has facilitated rather than terminated marginal analysis. The budget preparation process in the State of Georgia conforms much more closely to Peter Pyhrr's idea that "a logical starting point for determining next year's needs is the current year's operations."[27] than to former Governor Carter's notion that ZBB demands "total rejustification of everything from scratch—from zero."

Incremental Outputs?

The evidence obtained from interview sources strongly suggests that actors in the budgetary process in the State of Georgia continue to build budgets incrementally despite the procedural innovation called zero-base budgeting. However, as Bailey and O'Connor have pointed out, it is important to distinguish between incrementalism as a decision-making process and incremental budget outcomes. These are "separate but theoretically linked aspects" of the same concept.[28]

Incrementalism as a *process* characterizes the behavior of decision-makers, while incrementalism as *outcomes* refers to adjustments in existing policies. The former denotes a bargaining process among actors as well as individual intellectual responses to complexity.[29] The latter denotes marginal changes in agency funding levels from one year to the next. The literature often assumes that an incremental decision-making process will result in incremental budgeting outcomes and that incremental outcomes are evidence of an incremental process. While that connection is intuitively compelling, it is not logically required.

Even though ZBB is essentially a mangerial approach to budgeting which stresses efficiency and effectiveness of operations, rather than a planning approach which purports to redirect governmental goals and objectives,[30] the ever-present implication has been that ZBB could be expected to change budgetary outcomes in Georgia.

In order to assess the extent to which services were cut back and/or established programs eliminated because they were "judged to be ineffective or of low priority,"[31] budgetary outcomes for all agencies of Georgia state government between FY 1973 (the first year of ZBB) and FY 1978 were analyzed. Table 1 summarizes the annual percent change in appropriations for each department for the fiscal years 1973 through 1978.

When the most stringent definition of incrementalism is used— change in appropriation level of less than 10%—it is discovered that 49.3% of budgetary outcomes in the State of Georgia during the era of zero-base budgeting were incremental.[32] (If a less stringent standard of 15% is used, 65.0% of all budgetary outcomes were incremental. If Wildavsky's extravagant standard of 30%[33] is used, 87.1% can be characterized as incremental.) However, of those outcomes which can be considered non-incremental according to the most stringent definition (71 of 140 cases or 50.7% of all budgetary outcomes), only 16.9% (12 of 71 cases) were reductions in appropriation levels. In short, only 8.6% (12 of 140 cases) of the budgetary outcomes in the State of Georgia during the zero-base budgeting era were non-incremental reductions in appropriation levels. The remainder of the reductions in appropriation levels were "decremental" (or less than 10%).

Further evidence of the stability of budgeting outcomes in Georgia during this period can be seen from data presented in Table 2.[34] Departments have retained a rather consistent percentage of the total annual budget between 1973 and 1978. A comparison of the rank ordering of departments according to their percent of the total budget

Table 1
Summary of Percent Change in Departmental Appropriations FY 1973–1978

Percent Change	Number of Departments Per Fiscal Year						Cumulative Total
	FY73 to FY74	FY74 to FY75	FY75 to FY76	FY76 to FY77	FY77 to FY78	Fy 73 to FY78	
0–5%	3 (11.1)	11 (40.7)	8 (28.6)	20 (71.4)	6 (20.0)	48 (34.3)	34.3
6–10%	1 (3.7)	4 (14.8)	6 (21.4)	3 (10.7)	7 (23.3)	21 (15.0)	49.3
11–15%	3 (11.1)	3 (11.1)	5 (17.9)	0 (0.0)	11 (36.7)	22 (15.7)	65.0
16–20%	4 (14.8)	3 (11.1)	2 (7.1)	2 (7.1)	3 (10.0)	14 (10.0)	75.0
21–30%	8 (29.6)	4 (14.8)	2 (7.1)	1 (3.6)	2 (6.7)	17 (12.1)	87.1
31–40%	1 (3.7)	1 (14.8)	2 (7.1)	1 (3.6)	0 (0.0)	6 (4.3)	91.4
41–50%	1 (3.7)	0 (0.0)	0 (0.0)	1 (3.6)	1 (3.3)	3 (2.1)	93.5
51–100%	2 (7.4)	1 (3.7)	1 (3.6)	0 (0.0)	0 (0.0)	4 (2.9)	96.4
100%	4 (14.8)	0 (0.0)	1 (3.6)	0 (0.0)	0 (0.0)	5 (3.5)	100.0
Total	27 (100.0)	27 (100.0)	28*(100.0)	28 (100.0)	30*(100.0)	140 (100.0)	

Source: Compiled from data presented in State of Georgia, Office of Planning and Budget, *Budget Report–Volume I, Financial Display*, FY 1974, FY 1975, FY 1976, FY 1977, FY 1978, and FY 1979.

*Variation in the number of departments for which funds were appropriated each year is explained the following ways: beginning in 1975 the GBI was budgeted as an entity separate from the Department of Public Safety; beginning in 1977 the Department of Medical Assistance was budgeted as an entity separate from the Department of Human Resources; and beginning in 1977 the Georgia Franchise Practices Commission began receiving state appropriations.

Table 2
Departmental Appropriation as Percent of Total Appropriation, 1973–78

Department	FY 73	FY 74	FY 75	FY 76	FY 77	FY 78
Administrative Services	.737	.490	.562	1.106	1.445	1.368
Agriculture	.975	.984	.943	.845	.854	.824
Banking and Finance	.071	.069	.076	.086	.097	.097
Community Development[1]	.574	.672	.515	.953	.516	.473
Comptroller	.153	.169	.165	.178	.169	.144
Defense	.169	.130	.096	.088	.086	.112
Education	35.430	34.986	35.118	35.776	35.179	35.915
Employees Retirement[3]	—	—	.047	—	—	—
Forest Research Council	.038	036	.036	.033	.031	.029
Forestry Commission	.553	526	.529	.505	.512	.532
GBI	—	—	.398	.408	.393	.040
Franchise Practices Comm.	—	—	—	—	.002	.002
Financing and Investment Comm.[3]	—	—	—	—	—	—
OPB and Governor's Office	.316	.268	.302	.303	.301	.300
Human Resources	19.691	18.544	19.836	20.587	19.850	19.289[2]
Labor	.217	.138	.139	.182	.182	.181
Law	.106	.102	.116	.118	.118	.115
Merit System[3]	—	—	—	—	—	—

Natural Resources	1.404	2.384	1.776	1.586	1.478	1.352
Offender Rehabilitation	1.993	2.483	2.077	2.537	2.564	2.790
Public Safety	1.525	1.379	1.289	1.336	1.293	1.298
Public School Emp. Retirement	.184	.448	.431	.457	.448	.393
Public Service Commission	.073	.119	.121	.122	.120	.120
Board of Regents	15.137	15.004	15.145	14.712	14.726	14.916
Revenue	1.253	1.136	1.346	.997	.993	.999
Scholarship Commission	.394	.454	.489	.517	.529	.512
Secretary of State	.346	.333	.341	.325	.335	.350
Soil and Water Conservation	.038	.029	.024	.024	.019	.018
Teacher Retirement	.030	.135	.087	.107	.104	.068
Transportation	16.634	14.156	15.253	14.201	13.279	13.657
Veteran Services	.368	.367	.391	.342	.345	.315
Workmen's Compensation Board	.066	.061	.090	.098	.104	.017
Other	1.552	4.398	2.262	1.471	8.520	3.954

[1] Beginning with FY 1979 Department of Community Development divided into Department of Community Affairs and Department of Industry and Trade

[2] Beginning with FY 1977 Department of Medical Assistance budgeted as separate department. For comparison purposes Department of Medical Assistance combined with Department of Human Resources in FY 1977 and FY 1978, in this table.

[3] Merit System funded by assessments to other State agencies; federal funds; and employer/employee health insurance contributions. It receives no direct State appropriations. The Georgia State Finance and Investment Commission is funded by service fees and no State fund appropriations are required. The Public Employees Retirement System is funded from pension accumulation funds and no direct State appropriation is received.

for the years 1973 and 1978 reveals very little difference (Spearman's Rank Correlation of .978).

The data summarized in Tables 1 and 2 provide little support for the idea that zero-base budgeting enabled Georgia budget-makers to effect substantial spending reductions through the elimination of programs. A caveat must be entered, however, regarding the use of departmental level budget output data as evidence of incremental budgeting. It is quite possible that within departments (at the division level) or within divisions (at the unit level) non-incremental changes occur from one year to the next. Indeed, Georgia OPB officials maintain that ZBB has enabled them to redirect funds at the micro-organizational level even though the savings achieved are not reflected in departmental budget totals due to the fact that the state was experiencing an overall growth in both revenue collections and expenditures between 1973 and 1978.[35] Zero-base budgeting is credited by those officials with slowing the rate of growth in the Georgia budget during that period.

There is, however, some additional evidence that suggests that departmental level data are not hiding significant spending reductions within departments. Minmier reported that through the fiscal year 1975 no apparent shift of financial resources could be identified which was attributable to zero-base budgeting. He pointed out that during the first three years of the zero-base budgeting system not a single instance could be identified where a function was funded at a level less than the previous fiscal year.[36] Eckert, using within-department budget categories, also suggested that ZBB did not significantly alter budget outcomes in Georgia through 1975.[37] Since there is no reason to expect that departmental level data are less reliable indicators for the 1975–78 period than they were for the 1973–75 period, it is unlikely that the departmental level data reported here misrepresent the impact of ZBB on budgetary outcomes in Georgia.

The Persistence of Incrementalism

In seeking an explanation for the continuation of incremental budgeting practices in Georgia despite the advent of zero-base budgeting, it is necessary to look at the political environment within which public budget-makers operate. Budget preparation decisions are the products of political pressures and constraints exerted by actors and events outside the agency. At least six political constraints have been identified which operate to promote incremental approaches to budgeting in Georgia: (1) constitutional or statutory requirements; (2) public expectations that governmental activities will be continued at close to existing levels; (3) demands from interest groups concerned with the funding of new programs or the protection of existing ones; (4) the differing roles of central budget office personnel and agency budget officers; (5) legislative budget practices and procedures; and (6) the requirements of intergovernmental grant-in-aid programs.

For example, the Georgia Constitution requires the General Assembly to appropriate to the Department of Transportation an amount for highway purposes not less than the previous year's receipts from the motor fuel tax. At least that portion of the agency's budget (approximately 84% of its state appropriation for the 1978 fiscal year) is protected from zero-base considerations. Statutory requirements were also cited as justification for the continued funding of programs by agencies charged with economic regulation or the administration of retirement and other entitlement programs. As one agency budget officer put it, "We were established by statute to regulate_____; to cut back our program would reduce our effectiveness—that would be a violation of the law." Another noted, "So much of our program is specifically required by law that I cannot conceive of any major phase of it being eliminated without closing out our agency completely." Those budget officers contended that so long as the legislature does not intervene to modify their agency's statutory authority, they are protected from budget cuts by other actors within the executive branch.

The second constraint is closely related to the first. Budget officers contend that public expectations preclude the reconsideration of the historic base each year. Certain functions of government, they believe, are simply not going to be significantly reduced (much less eliminated) for reasons of economic efficiency no matter how compelling the data and analysis. The level of public sector responsibility for ameliorating social problems and providing social amenities has evolved over many decades. The political costs of breaking faith with citizens on matters which are thought to have been resolved in the past are very high. ZBB has not altered that political reality. Those who participate in preparing the budget tend to assume that agencies will continue to do about what they have been doing because the public in some general sense expects the continuation of programs. While no precise figures are available, budget-makers in Georgia assume that a significant portion of the budget is "uncontrollable" each year.

Perhaps the most troublesome counter-claim to this line of argument is the contention that 278 government agencies were eliminated during the first year of zero-base budgeting in Georgia. The most persuasive interpretation of those events, however, is that the Executive Reorganization Plan of 1972 (which, among other things, reduced the number of state agencies from 300 to 22) happened to coincide with the initiation of the zero-base budgeting system. It should also be noted that only 65 of the 278 agencies "eliminated" were actually being funded at the time of their discontinuation. One veteran budget officer contended that only one agency (the Georgia Educational Improvement Council) was actually eliminated; all of the others were subsumed as part of the reorganization plan. It was also the opinion of most of those interviewed that ZBB should not be given credit for ferreting out the need for reorganization. An agency budget officer who had served as part of the reorganization team in 1971 noted: "We had already identified duplication and proliferation of agencies by the time the first ZBB packages were prepared in the summer of 1971— but the packages did reaffirm what had been identified by separate investigation."[38]

Interest group activity is a third constraint. Although interest group activities are perceived by budget officers to be an important part of the budgetary process, they report very few direct contacts with interest group representatives. Interest groups in Georgia tend to concentrate their efforts within the executive branch on department heads or the governor's office, rather than with agency budget officers. Nevertheless, budget-makers believe that interest groups play an important role in maintaining continued support for existing programs. The comment made by one agency budget officer captures the opinions expressed by several others: "Those people who depend on what we are doing here get with their representatives in a big hurry if it looks like our budget is in trouble."

The differing role orientations of agency budget officers and OPB analysts place an additional constraint on the zero-base budgetary process. While the precise relationship between OPB analysts and agency budget officers varies according to the personalities of the individuals involved, the nature of the relationship dictates that it will be characterized by both cooperation and conflict. These officials need each other—the analyst needs the budget officer in order to learn about the agency program, and the budget officer needs the analyst in order to interpret the governor's priorities as they relate to his department. Yet despite this mutual need, the overriding fact remains that the analyst's principal responsibility as a representative of the governor's budget office is to find ways to control agency spending by recommending cuts in requests put forth by the agency. The agency budget officer, on the other hand, is an advocate for agency programs and an interpreter of agency problems. The process of negotiation through which OPB analysts and agency budget officers reconcile the competing demands of their individual role requirements, tends to be marginal adjustment. Stated quite simply by one agency budget officer, "The analyst gets paid to cut—so I try to protect against that by making sure that there is something to cut . . . we trade around the edges."

The manner in which the General Assembly considers the budget places yet another constraint on the ability of zero-base techniques to alter budgeting practices in Georgia. The budget law of Georgia requires the governor to submit a draft appropriation bill along with the Annual Budget Report. After the bill is introduced in the House of Representatives, a "continuation" appropriation bill is substituted for the governor's recommended version. The difference between the spending level in the House substitute and the level proposed by the governor is an amount which the legislature can then redistribute, decrease or increase according to its own priorities. For the most part the legislature is guided by the governor's recommendations, and agency budget officials emphasize the importance of having their requests included in the governor's recommended funding level.[39] What finally emerges as the annual appropriation bill is an admixture of the priorities of the legislature and those of the governor. The significance of this process for an understanding of the impact of ZBB is that in the reordering of priorities the legislature focuses attention mainly on the categories of "new or improved." The legislative tendency is to fund established programs while negotiating with the governor to determine which of the new items will be funded.

In analyzing the budget, the Legislative Budget Office simply does not use ZBB. The "minimum" level information and the activity statements (which explain and support funding requests) are regarded by legislative budget analysts as "worthless." "We throw most of that stuff in the can," said one analyst. Agencies report that the LBO frequently requests information from them directly regarding their appropriation requests. The Georgia General Assembly does "continuation" budgeting and that strongly biases the total process in the direction of incrementalism in budget preparation.

Intergovernmental aid also constrains budget-makers. For the 1978 fiscal year the Georgia Department of Labor obtained less than 5% of its funds from state appropriations; the Departments of Community Development and Human Resources received approximately half of their funds from state appropriations; while the Department of Transportation received slightly less than two-thirds of its funds from state appropriations. The balance of funds in each case came largely from the federal government. Program and matching fund requirements which are part of federal grants-in-aid limit the ability of budget-makers to alter existing programs significantly from one year to the next.

In short, incremental budgeting continues amid the procedures of zero-base budgeting because it serves participants well as a useful decision premise when operating within a political environment. The pervasive characteristic of that environment is pluralism.[40] According to this interpretation of American politics, conflicts among competing interests over the distribution of socioeconomic benefits and burdens are frequently resolved by negotiated and partial accommodations with which the participants can live, at least temporarily. Many of those accommodations are recorded annually with the adoption of the budget. By assuming that existing programs will normally be continued, political accommodations arrived at on earlier occasions by previous actors are reaffirmed and the range of political conflict is restricted. By asking "How can we adjust what we are doing?" rather than abrogating prior agreements and asking anew each year "What should we be doing?" conflict over basic values and public purposes is minimized. Zero-base budgeting has had a difficult time penetrating existing budgeting practices precisely because those traditional practices have served the political interests of most of the participants in the budgetary process. In one sense ZBB did successfully penetrate the routines of building and justifying a budget in Georgia. The format and procedures of ZBB were installed throughout the government during the first year with only minor difficulties. In a more important sense, however, ZBB has failed to fundamentally change the decision rules used by those who prepare budgets in the State of Georgia.[41]

The Achievements of ZBB in Georgia

It would be easy to take the caricature of ZBB at face value[42] and conclude that it is simply a "fraud," a "farce," or "a fantasy in someone's head" (to quote three of the more cynical budgeters in Georgia). However, as another agency budget officer said: "Too many claims have been made for zero-base budgeting that are not true; unfortunately that overshadows the good points about it." What are the good points?

The most frequently cited advantage of ZBB is that it has improved both the quantity and quality of information available to managers about agency operations.[43] The following comments will serve to illustrate that point:

> Zero-base is a useful management control device. The forms require people to organize and develop their information. Managers are better able, I think, to make decisions on the basis of an improved reporting system.

> It provides good, useable information for managers. It certainly is an improvement over the way we used to do things.

> I like zero-base. We used to make up the budget in this office with very little communication with the operating people. Now the budget format makes us reach to the lowest levels for information—that has advantages for everyone even beyond putting together a budget.

> Managers have better information—that is its strength.

> The biggest advantage is the visibility which we now get of what our people are doing.

> Zero-base may not be liked by everyone (I personally had doubts about it in the first year when we had to put together all that information which we did not have on hand) but it benefits the people of Georgia because it contributes to better management.

ZBB also requires greater justification for funding requests than ever before in Georgia. Although bargaining between OPB analysts and agency budget officers continues, agency officials believe that they now have a greater burden to demonstrate why existing programs should be continued at the current level or new programs funded. Prior to ZBB the burden tended to be on the budget analyst to demonstrate why new programs should not be recommended for funding. ZBB has shifted the burden of justification to the operating agencies at the following statements will indicate:

> Zero-base requires us to justify what we are doing—even justify continuation to some extent.

> On balance it (ZBB) is an improvement . . . more justification is required. I'm not always convinced that it's an 'improvement' when we are doing it, but I guess I think that it is.

> The budgets have less fat in them . . . tighter . . . more justification for the requests.

A greater interest in evaluation is another development which can be partially attributed to ZBB. It was perhaps inevitable that an approach to budgeting so committed to achieving efficiency in government would eventually address the matter of performance evaluation. As part of the 1978 fiscal year budget preparation process state agencies were required to develop evaluation measures to be included in their decision packages. Two types of measures were developed: (1) program effectiveness—defined as the degree to which a program achieves its objectives; and (2) workload efficiency—defined as the degree to which the program economically manages the workload associated with its objectives. A considerable amount of difficulty has been encountered in formulating meaningful and operational performance measures during the first year. That is partially due to the lack of experience in some agencies in dealing with the performance evaluation concept. It is also due to the inherent difficulty in evaluating many of the kinds of things government agencies do.[44] Nevertheless, a beginning has been made. Agencies have been charged with the responsibility for developing and implementing performance measures through which managerial control can be effectively achieved. Most of the performance evaluation measures developed by the agencies are workload efficiency measures rather than program effectiveness measures. Since ZBB is largely a management approach to budgeting those measures are not inappropriate.

Finally, zero-base budgeting is, in addition to being a set of budget preparation procedures, also a state of mind. Many budgeters have acquired the habit of thinking about efficiency in on-going programs as well as alternate ways of achieving program objectives. This is perhaps best expressed by the budget official who said, "Zero-base is useful in that it causes us to think about what we are doing . . . Many other approaches to budgeting might do that, but zero-base is the one we happen to be using."

Conclusion

Those who expected ZBB to result in widespread program elimination and/or substantial cost reductions in the State of Georgia have been disappointed. The effects of ZBB have been much more moderate and subtle. Incremental budgeting persists and zero-base budgeting innovations have taken place within that constraint.

However, the most important question which this research leaves unanswered is the extent to which the marginal analysis techniques of ZBB have been successful in, and directly responsible for redistributing resources within programs at the micro-organizational level.

Some budget officials in Georgia, particularly those in the central budget office, are of the opinion that capacity for redirection is the essence of ZBB, and that significant redirections have taken place. Agency budget officers tend to be less convinced that ZBB has produced very much redirection of funds, and aggregate data analysis has been unable to reveal subtle shifts.

Before an adequate assessment of the impact of ZBB at any level of government can be made, it will be necessary to devise a research strategy to address this important question. That task should occupy a high place on our future research agenda.

Notes

1. On January 15, 1971 Governor Jimmy Carter in the annual Budget Message to the General Assembly announced his intention to install zero-base budgeting for all areas of State government. The zero-base budgeting system was first used in preparing the budget for the 1973 fiscal year.

2. Allen Schick and Robert Keith, *Zero-Base Budgeting in the States* (Lexington, Kentucky: The Council of State Governments, 1976), p. 5.

3. Governor Carter's interest in zero-base budgeting is reported to have been the result of his having read Peter Pyhrr's article in the November–December 1970 issue of the *Harvard Business Review*. In that article Pyhrr describes the use of zero-base budgeting by Texas Instruments, Inc. Pyhrr was subsequently hired as a consultant to the Georgia Budget Bureau for the purpose of installing the new budget system in State government.

4. Peter A. Pyhrr, *Zero-Base Budgeting: A Practical Management Tool for Evaluating Expenses* (New York: John Wiley and Sons, Inc., 1973); Peter A. Pyhrr, "Zero-Base Budgeting," *Harvard Business Review*, Vol. 49, (November/December 1970), pp. 111–121; Charlie B. Tyer, "Zero-Base Budgeting: A Critical Analysis," *Southern Review of Public Administration*, Vol. 1, (June 1977), pp. 88–107; and Graeme M. Taylor, "Introduction to Zero-Base Budgeting," *The Bureaucrat*, Vol. 6, (Spring 1977), pp. 33–55.

5. Peter A. Pyhrr, "The Zero-Base Approach to Government Budgeting," *Public Administration Review*, Vol. 37, (January/February 1977), pp. 1–8; Aaron Wildavsky, *Budgeting: A Comparative Theory of Budgetary Processes* (Boston: Little, Brown and Company, 1975), at pp. 278–296; and Aaron Wildavsky and Arthur Hammand, "Comprehensive Versus Incremental Budgeting in the Department of Agriculture," *Administrative Science Quarterly*, Vol. 10, (December 1965), pp. 321–346.

6. Walter D. Broadnax, "Zero-Base Budgeting: New Directions for the Bureaucracy?" *The Bureaucrat*, Vol. 6, (Spring 1977), pp. 56–66.

7. Donald F. Haider, "Zero-Base: Federal Style," *Public Administration Review*, Vol. 37, (July/August 1977), pp. 401–407; George S. Minmier *An Evaluation of the Zero-Base Budgeting System in Governmental Institutions* (Atlanta, Georgia: Publishing Services Division, School of Business Administration, Georgia State University, 1975); and George S. Minmier and Roger H. Hermanson, "A Look at Zero-Base Budgeting—The Georgia Experience," *Atlanta Economic Review*, (July/August 1976), pp. 5–12.

8. In addition to the writings of Peter A. Pyhrr, see: Herbert P. Dooskin, "Zero-Base Budgeting: A Plus for Government," *National Civic Review*, Vol. 66, (March 1977), pp. 119–121; 144.

9. Robert N. Anthony, "Zero-Base Budgeting is a Fraud," *The Wall Street Journal*, April 27, 1977.

10. For a more extensive discussion of zero-base budgeting see Wildavsky and Hammond, *op. cit.*, pp. 322–325.

11. See the Communications to the Editor from F. Ted Herbert and Peter A. Pyhrr which appear in *Public Administration Review*, Vol. 37, (July/August 1977), pp. 438–439.

12. Budget Message to General Assembly, January 15, 1971.

13. Address by Governor Jimmy Carter—Charter Property Casualty Underwriters, September 12, 1974, in Frank Daniel, Compiler, *Addresses of Jimmy Carter*, (Atlanta, Georgia: Georgia Department of Archives and History, 1975), p. 277.

14. A campaign paper written in mid-1976 and published in Logan M. Cheek, *Zero-Base Budgeting Comes of Age: What It Is and What It Takes to Make It Work* (New York: AMACOM, A Division of American Management Association, 1977), p. 297. A slightly altered version of the same statement appeared in *Nation's Business*, (January 1977), p. 24.

15. For a more specific discussion of Georgia's budget preparation procedures see: State of Georgia, *General Budget Preparation Procedures: Fiscal Year 1978 Budget Development*, June, 1976.

16. Allen Schick has written that despite the exaggerated claims, marginal analysis is the actual intent of ZBB. Allen Schick, "Zero-Base Budgeting and Sunset: Redundancy or Symbiosis?" *The Bureaucrat*, Vol. 6, (Spring 1977), p. 16.

17. Minmier and Hermanson, *op. cit.*, pp. 5 and 8, and Minmier, *op. cit.*, p. 135.

18. Augustus B. Turnbull, III, "Politics in the Budgetary Process: The Case of Georgia," (Unpublished doctoral dissertation, University of Virginia, 1967).

19. Two important works dealing with the topic of incremental decision-making are Charles E. Lindblom, "The Science of Muddling

Through,' " *Public Administration Review,* Vol. 19, (Spring 1959), pp. 79–88, and David Braybrooke and Charles E. Lindblom, *A Strategy of Decision* (New York: The Free Press, 1970). Incrementation as it applies to public budgeting is discussed in Aaron Wildavsky, *The Politics of the Budgetary Process,* Second Edition (Boston: Little, Brown and Co., 1974).

20. Allen Schick has pointed out the importance of "penetrating the vital routines of putting together and justifying a budget" if budgetary reform is to be successful. Allen Schick, "A Death in the Bureaucracy: The Demise of Federal PPB," *Public Administration Review,* Vol. 33, (March/April 1973), p. 147.

21. James Davis and Randall B. Ripley, "The Bureau of the Budget and Executive Branch Agencies: Notes on Their Interaction," *The Journal of Politics,* Vol. 29, (November 1967), pp. 749–769.

22. It is hoped that the interview technique used in this research will partially accommodate Peter A. Pyhrr's admonition that those who write about Georgia budgeting should "personally visit and evaluate the process as it actually exists in total instead of spending their time in university libraries." Peter A. Pyhrr, "Communication to the Editor," *Public Administration Review,* Vol. 37, (July/August 1977), p. 439.

23. The term "agency" is used here in the generic sense to include all those executive branch entities which for budgetary purposes are accorded separate consideration. Fifteen are actually designated as departments, the remainder are designated as boards, commissions, or systems. During the period 1973–78 the State of Georgia budgeted for thirty-two executive branch agencies. The twenty-eight agencies included in this study are highly representative of all executive branch agencies since they received 99.4 per cent of the total appropriations to the executive branch for the 1978 fiscal year and they employed 99 per cent of all executive branch personnel as of 1977.

24. No notes were taken during interviews. All quotations were derived from notes made immediately after each interview. Although quotations may slightly paraphrase the words actually spoken during the interview, great care has been exercised to ensure the accuracy of the ideas expressed. Where doubt existed as to the accuracy of the quotation, it was excluded.

It should be noted that respondents were not consistent with each other in the way they referred to the base budget year. Some referred to it as "last year," while others called it "this year" or the "current year." For the purpose of clarity a uniform reference i.e., last year, has been adopted.

25. Prior to the 1978 fiscal year decision packages for four levels of operation were submitted: minimum, base (same dollars as last year), workload (same level of program activity with cost increases reflected), and new or improved.

26. Pyhrr, "Zero-Base Budgeting," *op. cit.,* p. 113, and Pyhrr, "The Zero-Base Approach to Government Budgeting," *op. cit.,* p. 6.

27. Pyhrr, "Zero-Base Budgeting," *op. cit.*, p. 114.

28. John J. Bailey and Robert J. O'Connor, "Operationalizing Incrementalism: Measuring the Muddles," *Public Administration Review*, Vol. 35, (January/February 1975), p. 61.

29. *Ibid.*, p. 65.

30. For a discussion of the distinction between a management orientation and a planning orientation in budgeting see Allen Schick, "The Road to PPB: The Stages of Budget Reform," *Public Administration Review*, Vol. 26, (December 1966), pp. 249–253.

31. Governor Jimmy Carter, Budget Message to General Assembly, January 15, 1971.

32. The 10 per cent cutting point for incrementalism has recently been used by Steven A. Schull, "An Application of Budgetary Theory: Incrementalism Reassessed," *Georgia Political Science Association Journal*, Vol. IV, (Spring 1976), pp. 21–42.

33. Wildavsky, *The Politics of the Budgetary Process, op. cit.*, p. 14.

34. The format for this table was suggested by Turnbull's presentation of similar data. Turnbull, *op. cit.*, p. 131.

35. Net revenue collections by the Georgia Department of Revenue for the years 1973 to 1978 showed a per cent average increase per year of 12.5 per cent. During the same period the budget experienced a per cent average increase per year of 12.4 per cent. See: State of Georgia, Department of Revenue, *Statistical Report 1977*, (November 1977), and State of Georgia, Office of Planning and Budget, *Budget Report Fiscal Year 1974* and *Budget Report Fiscal Year 1979*.

36. Minmier, *op. cit.*, pp. 130–131; 154–155; and 173.

37. William Albert Eckert, "Evaluating the Impact of Zero-Base Budgeting," Unpublished paper presented at the Annual Meeting of the Midwest Political Science Association, Chicago, Illinois, April 20–22, 1978.

38. Peter A. Pyhrr has also written that the need for reorganization was recognized before the start of zero-base budgeting in Georgia. Peter A. Pyhrr, *Zero-Base Budgeting: A Practical Management Tool for Evaluating Expenses, op. cit.*, p. 113.

39. This is consistent with Sharkansky's findings regarding the reliance of legislatures on gubernatorial budget recommendations. Ira Sharkansky, "Agency Requests, Gubernatorial Support and Budget Success in State Legislatures," *The American Political Science Review*, Vol. LXII, (December 1968), pp. 1220–1231.

40. For a discussion of the relationship between pluralism and the budgetary process, see Allen Schick, "Systems Politics and Sys-

tems Budgeting," *Public Administration Review,* Vol. 29, (March/April 1969), pp. 137–151.

41. Allen Schick has recently made a similar assessment of ZBB in the federal government. Allen Schick, "The Road From ZBB," *Public Administration Review,* Vol. 38, (March/April 1978), p. 178.

42. Allen Schick has discussed the strategy of caricature as it was applied to PPB. Allen Schick, *Budget Innovation in the States* (Washington, D.C.: The Brookings Institution, 1971), pp. 200–201.

43. This amounts to a confirmation of similar findings reported by Minmier and Hermanson, *op. cit.,* p. 11.

44. For a discussion of this problem see: Harry P. Hatry et al., *Practical Program Evaluation for State and Local Government Officials* (Washington, D.C.: The Urban Institute, 1973).

Assessing Modern Budgetary Techniques

5

In the late seventies irate taxpayers mobilized to enact taxation limits in California. Muscle-flexing by similar groups in other jurisdictions signaled those in policy positions within government that many Americans would not tolerate further increases in taxes to support governmental services. If services are to be maintained at their current levels or expanded to meet new needs, governments must either develop new sources of revenue other than direct taxes[1] or increase productivity. Modern budgeting techniques promise to be powerful management tools that government policy makers can use to increase productivity. But it is questionable whether these tools can meet the reasonable expectations of their advocates and users.

Implementing major management changes in large organizations ranges from the difficult to the impossible. People in organizations are not always open to change. Often when a new system is introduced, some people feel that their past efforts are being criticized. Others may feel that they do not have the skills needed to make the new system work. They may feel that they will lose power to those who possess the new skills. People tend to be comfortable with their old habits, even when those habits fail to produce the desired results.

Behavioral scientists working under the banner of organization development (OD) seek to prepare people in organizations to accept changes that might make the organization better able to cope with its environment.[2] At the state and local levels, taxpayers fighting against tax increases while demanding better services are part of the environment in which these governments must function. Most governmental jurisdictions have neither the money nor the commitment to mount full-scale OD programs to make the participants in the budgetary process more open to change. Nevertheless, some change has come to public budgeting.

Earlier selections have suggested that implementing budget innovations in government is not so easy. The two articles in this last section raise questions concerning the assessment of these techniques. Richard Rose suggests that the spirit of the innovation may survive the form. Allen Schick argues that acceptance of the form might dilute the spirit of the innovation.

Notes

1. The taxpayer revolt happens at a time when state and local governments are getting roughly 40% of their revenues from the federal government. This is up from under 20% as late as 1966.

2. See Warren G. Bennis, *Organization Development: Its Nature, Origins, and Prospects* (Reading, Mass.: Addison-Wesley, 1969).

Implementation
and Evaporation:
The Record of MBO

Richard Rose

If the implementation of good ideas were easy to achieve, then many of the problems of governing would be headed for solution. If implementation were always doomed to fail, this would imply the existence of determinate laws of politics, and public administration would be becoming a science of the inevitable. Often the proponents of an idea that in the abstract appears desirable will face the criticism: "It's all very well, but it can never be implemented." If they prove their critics wrong by carrying out their proposals, there follows a dispute about whether the idea, as implemented, was good after all.

Analyzing the brief history of management by objectives (MBO) in the federal government in the 1970s can help us understand the indeterminate character of success and failure in the implementation of new ideas. The difficulty of deciding whether MBO has become accepted, disappeared, or simply "evaporated" illustrates how difficult it is to evaluate the implementation of a program in terms of its immediate consequences. The absorptive character of government, gradually adapting and incrementally augmenting its activities, suggests that change may more easily be measured on a time scale congenial to a forester or a geologist than to a Congress or a White House in a hurry.

From *Public Administration Review*, vol. 37, no. 1 (January–February 1977). Reprinted for *Public Administration Review*, © 1977 by The American Society for Public Administration, 1225 Connecticut Avenue, N.W., Washington, D.C. All rights reserved. By permission of author and publisher.

Problems as Problems and Solutions as Problems

It is far easier to promote a new idea when there is agreement that a problem exists than to get public officials to accept the real costs of change in exchange for the hypothetical benefits of a new idea. If the costs of maintaining the status quo are infinite, then any new course of action, however good or gimmicky its promises, is better than doing nothing. While such a strategy is immediately rational in short run cost-benefit terms, in the long run it is *not* a problem-solving technique. It simply exchanges the difficulties of coping with the immediate problem for the difficulties of implementing the intended solution.

There is no doubt that the management of the programs of the federal government has been perceived as a real and immediately pressing problem in Washington in the past decade. In 1967 a blue ribbon Presidential Task Force headed by Ben W. Heineman privately reported to President Johnson:

> Many domestic social programs are under severe attack. . . . Some criticism arises because of alleged organizational and managerial weaknesses. After several months of study, we believe the organizational criticism is justified.[1]

To symbolize the emphasis it wished to give to management, the Heineman group recommended reorganizing the Bureau of the Budget and changing its name to the Bureau of Program Development and Management. Budget officials agreed with the thrust of these recommendations. An internal staff review paper commented that future Presidents "will be forced by the nature of the problems to try to run the government as well as make policy decisions."[2] The Nixon Administration accepted the diagnosis of federal mismanagement; its top officials distrusted career civil servants, and they were out of sympathy with the objectives of the Great Society programs that attracted the most publicity for alleged mismanagement.[3] The Administration's resolve was symbolized in 1970 by reorganizing the Bureau of the Budget and relabelling it the Office of Management and Budget.

Conceptually, the Nixon Administration sought to shift attention from problems of choice to problems of management. In the Kennedy-Johnson years, economists had brought to Washington new techniques for deciding what government *ought* to do, assuming that whatever they chose would then be done. In reaction, the Nixon Administration brought management experts to Washington, to concentrate attention upon *what gets done,* that is the running of established programs and the implementation of new programs. The difference between the two approaches was emphasized by the contrasting backgrounds and political values of academic economists and business-oriented management men.

Politically, the Nixon Administration felt it had to do something to "get hold" of federal programs. Logically, the Nixon Administration had three alternatives. An *overt* political strategy defines problems in terms of conflicts about ends. The objectives of existing programs are declared undesirable or not worth their cost, and their abolition or replacement by new programs is recommended, e.g., the Nixon attack upon poverty programs. A *covert* political strategy defines problems in terms of conflicts about means. The methods of existing programs are declared undesirable, and alternative methods are recommended, e.g., financing welfare through new federalism. The attempt to avoid political controversy by declaring a consensus about ends masks but does not eliminate conflict. Policies are implemented, not by agreed good intentions about ends, but by choices among specific program means. To change means is to invite controversy, not least among those for whom the maintenance of a program has come to be an end in itself. An *apolitical* strategy assumes consensus about means and ends; problems require the discovery of technically more efficient means to implement this consensus. While any proposed change in government can be controversial from some perspective, many issues of concern to public administrators are not in fact issues that elected politicians wish to make into controversies because they are of no interest to them. The continuing reorganization efforts in Nixon's Administrative Presidency[4] is evidence of a strong impulse to action, and recurring frustrations.

The appointment of Roy Ash and Frederic V. Malek as Director and Deputy Director of OMB following the 1972 presidential election was a major step forward in the Nixon Administration's efforts to get their hands on the management of federal programs. OMB was perceived as in need of a shake-up, for a survey of federal managers, following OMB's 1970 reorganization, found "three-fourths of them could see little difference between the old Budget Bureau and the new management-oriented OMB."[5] The arguments for introducing management by objectives at this time were several. The overt political arguments started from the fact that the President, as the popularly elected head of the Executive Branch, had a right to set objectives for program managers working in "his" Administration. Republican presidential appointees from the business world wished to transfer to Washington methods that they believed had brought great benefits to management in the private sector to prove that Republicans could manage government better than Democrats could. The fact that MBO was concerned with the means of governing gave it covert political importance too. MBO's concentration upon the objectives that superiors wished realized, while leaving subordinates free to progress toward them by whatever means appropriate, was consistent with the Nixon White House's post-November 1972 strategy of gaining more power by turning to the agencies where programs are administered.

Because MBO is a management technique rather than a substantive program, it could be applied across-the-board in the federal government. Its proponents thus hoped to influence a large number of programs, a more ambitious goal than lobbying Congress to adopt a single new program in HEW, HUD, or Agriculture. At a minimum, management by objectives promised to provide some apolitical benefits, making sure that actions agreed were not lost sight of in the blinding glare of politically important firefighting tasks, and that program delays did not consume unnecessarily the goodwill and funds of federal government.

When MBO was introduced in Washington in 1973, there was broad agreement that management was an important problem of the federal government, MBO was not intended to resolve all the difficulties identified, but rather to be one of several means of keeping the White House and agencies "tracking together." The decision to introduce MBO did not dispose of the problems of governing. It simply traded in the difficulties of managing the Executive Branch with the existing system—"the problem as problem"—for the difficulties of implementing MBO—"the solution as problem."

Implementation, or Learning by Doing

Implementation does not guarantee a program's success; it is merely a pre-condition of success. In analytic terms, implementation is an intervening variable in the policy process, which starts with the statement of policy intentions or aspirations, moves through program choice to implementation and, finally, to an evaluation of the consequences of what has been done. Logically, the consequences of a program need bear no relation to the initial intentions of its sponsors, or to the expectations of those who chose to authorize it. The consequences immediately reflect what government has done to implement previous aspirations and expectations. Logically, the implementation of a program can be classified as a success, if the consequences are positively evaluated; a failure, if negatively evaluated; or a nullity, if implementation seems to have had no discernible consequences. For example, the 1921 act establishing the old Bureau of the Budget was implemented with positive consequences; the 1970 reorganization of the Budget Bureau, in the minds of veteran bureaucrats, was implemented with negative consequences; and perennial presidential "wars on waste" have been implemented with no discernible consequences.

Because program implementation does not *ipso facto* achieve desired objectives, Pressman and Wildavsky recommend "making the difficulties of objectives implementation a part of the initial formulation of policy."[6] But if all the difficulties could be foreseen in advance, then often a program would not be started. Implementation is not only a matter of forging "links in a causal chain so as to obtain the desired results";[7] it is more a matter of learning by doing—including learning what to do when the links are not closed and the chain breaks.

Ironically, many proponents of MBO nominally follow the Pressman-Wildavsky recommendation, building a careful and comprehensive description of existing shortcomings and pathologies of management into their description of the problem to which MBO is addressed. Having identified these problems, they then deduce the means by which they may be solved, and MBO is the name given to their comprehensive solution. In this way, every deficiency in the status quo becomes a further argument for adopting the new idea.[8] Problem solving by stipulation can be successful as a paper exercise, but this does not guarantee that recommendations deduced will have the desired consequences, if they are implemented. An inductive school of public administrators and political scientists, by contrast, would start by identifying problems as the obstacles to change; each difficulty then becomes an argument against adopting any new program. The inductive approach risks the blanket endorsement of the status quo as the best of all possible worlds.

Any political initiative for which funds and staff are allocated is almost certain to be implemented to some extent in some form.[9] Insofar as implementation in some form follows from a decision to act, then the problems involved are trivial. What is non-trivial is *whether implementation is successful.* But to judge success requires criteria of evaluation. The difficulties of identifying intended objectives are notorious in evaluation research, and they are no less in a program meant to improve concentration upon objectives. Examining the impact of MBO does not require any assumptions about intent but rather an investigation of observable consequences.

In the minimal sense of the term, there is no doubt that management by objectives was implemented in the federal government in 1973. By internal reorganization within OMB, Frederic Malek created thirty posts for management associates to introduce and monitor MBO. Each of twenty-one major federal agencies, together accounting for more than 95% of federal expenditure, within a year established its own MBO staff. Within five months of the initial presidential announcement, the White House received 237 objectives filed for fiscal year 1974, and in 1974 the second year's cycle produced another catalogue of more than 225 objectives.[10]

In introducing MBO, the staff at OMB consciously reacted against the experience of the attempt to introduce PPB (planning-programming-budgeting) eight years previously. MBO was not described as a scientific device for identifying or making choices, and its manpower and paperwork requirements were relatively less. Roy Ash was quoted in the *Civil Service Journal* as saying:

> I think it is reasonably clear that the approach we have taken is neither particularly new nor particularly profound. . . . Frankly, I would prefer to label it "Management by Common Sense."[11]

The initial OMB directive to the agencies welcomed the submission of objectives of any type, as long as they conformed to three broad criteria: the issue is important to the President; there is a means of determining whether it has been achieved; and no additional financial or legislative resources would be required. The refusal of OMB to lay down elaborate specifications regarding the identification of objectives led to some complaints from the agencies about its alleged fuzzy fiat. The decision to avoid detailed prescription was conscious, reflecting a belief by Ash and Malek that MBO would work only insofar as operating agencies developed and incorporated procedures suited to their own specific situation. The emphasis upon the "hearts and minds" aspect of MBO is consistent with modern management psychology. But it also made skeptics wonder whether the substitution of such an intangible objective reflected the inability to measure whether MBO also moves bodies.

The objectives sent to OMB by the agencies varied greatly in clarity and logic. Few of the statements reflected the formal logic employed in social science models. The language was that of bureaucracy, and the logic that of bureaucrats anxious, at a minimum, to produce paper to satisfy a demand from their OMB overseers. Management associates were disinclined to ask for a rigorous statement of cause and effect program designs.[12] Had they engaged in a seminar trying to define "good" objectives, the management associates would have faced a series of dilemmas. Objectives could either concentrate upon immediate achievements or long-term results; significance, however vague, or quantification; bigger or smaller achievements; or more or less controversial policies. In the event, most agencies tended to go for precise, short-term, smaller, and non-commital objectives.

The most frequently cited objectives appropriately enough concerned the improvement of agency management. Many agencies also cited objectives concerning issues of broad national concern—the economy, the environment and natural resources, and energy—complementing these statements by objectives of narrow departmental concern. Two-thirds of all objectives were immediately directed at activities within government—within the agency, or Executive Branch, or congressional legislation—and only one-third actions in the world beyond Washington. About half the objectives immediately concerned with government actions could be related indirectly to consumers outside government.[13]

The fact that agencies could produce lists of objectives refutes the assertion frequently advanced by frustrated economists and program evaluators that government does not have anything that they recognize as measurable, costable objectives, or a preference schedule of valued objectives. In aggregate, it is undoubtedly the case that any portrayal of government objectives appears confusing, contradictory, and unstable. Agencies did not bother with the grand philosophical problems arising from this fact. Instead, the OMB request for objectives was sent down the line to bureau chiefs and program managers, who in turn sent back statements concentrating attention upon their immediate organizational concerns. In effect, the top-down White House call for objectives became a bottom-up catalogue of bureau chief concerns.

Getting action on objectives is a very different matter from getting objectives listed on paper. In theory, MBO was meant to succeed by setting off a three-step sequence of events. First of all, OMB proposed holding quarterly monitoring sessions between agency heads or their deputies and the Director or Deputy Director of OMB to put pressure upon presidential appointees to improve the direction of their agency. Second, internal management conferences were to be held to prepare for agency-OMB conferences, with assistant secretaries and bureau chiefs reporting to the Secretary or his deputy. Third, the program managers responsible for getting things done were expected to pass the milestones required to attain objectives, in anticipation of the review of programs at departmental managerial conferences.

Management by objectives began to run into trouble within months after its launching, for its sponsors at OMB began to lose interest in it. The loss of interest was signalled from the top by the frequent cancellation of periodic meetings between OMB directors and agency heads to discuss progress toward their objectives. Lack of interest was also signalled by management associates going off on special assignments or "firefighting" exercises. For example, the efforts of the MBO group in the Energy and Natural Resources Division were consumed by ad hoc responses to the autumn, 1973, energy crisis. Agency heads could take their cue from OMB, and cancel internal management conferences. Doing so would not cause protests from below, for the program managers have no political incentive to encourage management procedures strengthening the hands of those who exercise oversight above them.

The best explanation for the loss of OMB interest in management by objectives is their discovery that it was only an *apolitical* reform. Analysis of the presidential objectives filed by the agencies with OMB shows that 81% for 1973 and 80% for 1974 were apolitical.[14] The objectives were noncontroversial, because they referred to consensual aims such as the prepraration of a report by a given date without any commitment as to content; the implementation of a new act of Congress that was their responsibility to fulfill; or actions that had low likelihood of causing protest by politically active groups. The absence of controversy made such objectives safe for bureaucrats to present to political superiors. But it also meant that busy Executive Office staff had no positive incentive to take an interest in them, and paid a high opportunity cost in time to monitor noncontroversial achievements of government, when there were many controversial issues to seek to influence. While wiseacres might comment "We told you so," the historical fact is that the officials responsible for promoting and implementing management by objectives only discovered its limitations by trying to make it work.

The Evaporation of MBO?

Implementation, viewed from the perspective of public administrators, has two obvious alternatives: a program is either institutionalized or it disappears.[15] In the former case, there are staff and organizations devoted to furthering it; in the latter, there is a termination order abolishing units and reassigning affected staff. There is, however, a third possibility: a program can evaporate, that is, the process of implementing it is followed by the dissipation of its "hard" statement of intentions, and the absorption of its personnel and institutions into the climate around it. In such circumstances, one can stress the disappearance of the original program, the fact that it has been transmuted into something else, or that the atmosphere that has absorbed it is more powerful than that which is absorbed.

The fate of PPBS offers an example of a program that has evaporated rather than disappeared. The PPBS program of OMB was officially closed down in 1971, six years after it was initiated, but the program analysis that it was meant to stimulate has not ceased. Whether judged by the number of planning and evaluation units, program analysts, or actual analysis done within federal agencies, there has been a substantial jump from the zero-base year of 1965. It can be argued that the concepts of PPBS have prospered more following evaporation into the Washington climate than when it was a high Executive Office priority. An ex-Budget official now at the General Accounting Office, Harry Havens, concludes:

> The formal structure of PPBS is now dead; the analytical concept is still very much alive. In fact, the analytical concept was always more important than the formal structure. The primary value of the structure was to force the use of the analytical concept.[16]

In formal terms, OMB has maintained a skeleton crew of management associates; the numbers in established posts are about half the strength of peak days. The management associates, however, no longer make MBO matters their first priority, and in the energy and natural resources division, their separate organizational status has been abolished. They are formally as well as informally absorbed by supplementing and complementing the work of examiners. In turning toward more conventional program concerns, the management associates are following the cues given them by the actions of their leaders in the Old Executive Office Building. The last government-wide circular from the President requesting agency heads to file statements of presidential objectives was sent out in 1974.

A management method praised by some[17] because it made possible a centralized, holistic review of major government objectives, today survives in the piecemeal form of decentralized management teams in the agencies. Within an agency, a familiar pattern repeats itself. MBO is potentially of greatest political interest to presidential appointees on top, for it can give them a chance to learn quickly what major priorities are within the agency, and selectively encourage progress to completion before the end of limited tenure there. Alternatively, it can be reduced to an apolitical routine, concerned with progress-chasing non-controversial activities that might otherwise be overlooked, like the amount of maintenance work undertaken on Defense Department vehicles.

MBO's current status varies widely among the agencies of the Executive Branch. The evaluation of success is more positive when judgments are given from "top side" staff appointees than when they are collated from the line managers down below.[18] Yet such is the time lag in the diffusion of knowledge in downtown Washington that in summer 1976 the Civil Service Commission can find many applicants for its training courses in MBO for line personnel, at a time when Executive Office leadership no longer wishes to talk about it.

Analysis of the varied experiences of executive agencies identifies five factors influencing the extent to which the MBO system has been accepted. First and most important is the extent to which a department had already established a system of this type *before* OMB's 1973 initiative. Second, political support from the top of the department, as in the case of Elliott Richardson at HEW, can make a management innovation be treated with respect. The institutional attributes of departments are a third factor affecting developments. The very vastness of the Defense Department requires the Office of the Secretary to pay more attention to keeping track of things than in a smaller agency. Fourth, the more readily verified are the actions of an agency, the easier it is to identify objectives as a comparison of GSA and State Department statements shows. Fifth, MBO was picked up by agencies to the extent that they saw the system as primarily benefiting their department, rather than as a channel of information and control by OMB.[19]

The prospects for strengthening MBO within the federal government are dim. Both proponents and critics agree with this, and for the same reason. The proponents of MBO, drawing primarily upon examples from the private sector, describe all the things that should be done to make MBO and management generally prosper in the public service. The skeptics about MBO accept this diagnosis—and then give the reasons why such changes will not be made:[20] objectives are either fuzzy and controversial, or fixed by statute, or both; the institutions of government divide direction of programs between the Executive Branch and Congress, rather than concentrating power in the White House; there are no pay or promotion incentives that can be given civil servants sufficient to act as incentives for producing results; and there are no political incentives for presidential appointees to concern themselves with long-term management reforms.

The claims that can be made for MBO are slight, by comparison with the grandiose promises often made for other innovations in

Washington. Yet the costs of the innovation were relatively low in money terms (about $6 million annually) and in friction between operating agencies and OMB. In the long-term history of management improvement efforts within the federal government, MBO was a "not unrealistic" attempt to respond to very real problems of managing government.

The concern about the management of an allegedly unmanageable government is, if anything, stronger today than in 1973. The "soft sell" innovations implemented under the leadership of Ash and Malek gain stature by comparison with some of the nostrums being offered in Washington in 1976. On Capitol Hill, after more than a decade of federally mandated evaluation research has been ignored in program reviews, congressmen under the leadership of Senator Edmund Muskie are promoting "sunset laws" to mandate periodic evaluation and zero-base budgeting across the bulk of the programs of the federal government.[21] The cries of congressmen were echoed, moreover, by campaign statements of opposition presidential candidate, Jimmy Carter, whose rhetoric about improving management is redolent of the days of Richard Nixon's Ash Council, and Lyndon Johnson's PPBS program.

In the White House itself, after internal difficulties caused by shifting personnel and indecision, President Ford unveiled a "mega-management" initiative on July 23, 1976, asking the heads of his major agencies to undertake more than twenty specific management reforms in organization and decision making, evaluation, deregulation, federal contracting and overhead costs, and personnel management. In a follow-up memorandum the next day, the President asked agency heads to accept that, while "it is more exciting to build a new boat than to scrape away the barnacles," the need today is "to scrape away the barnacles that build up over time around almost any program or agency."[22] OMB followed up this presidential exhortation with a memorandum setting deadlines from four to twelve weeks away for reporting progress to the associate director of management. Management by objectives was buried in an avalanche of injunctions to agency heads, unsupported by any statements about how they were to be implemented. The first of these requested that each agency head make sure that reporting to the head "in an unbiased manner" was a unit that not only determined MBO statements but also assured that "all relevant factors" were borne in mind when making important decisions; directed program impact and efficiency evaluations; obtained "complete implementation of the agency head's decisions"; and "coordinated all of the foregoing with the agency's budget process." One jaded official, after reading this lengthy list of "thou shalts," remarked, "This memorandum doesn't come from the *Harvard Business Review;* it comes from *Superman* comics."

To ask today, "What's happened to MBO?" is to raise fundamental questions about the implementation of management innovation within the federal government. Are we to say that MBO was institutionalized when there was a paper exercise in full swing in 1973–74? Are we to say that it has disappeared in default of political interest, even though there remain staff in many agencies still carrying on MBO-type activities? Perhaps it is better to turn from a legalistic determination of its status to a more atmospheric one, concluding that MBO has evaporated, becoming a part of the climate of management, albeit a part whose specific influence is limited and incapable of precise measurement. For better or worse, it thus stands in the tradition of a long line of management improvement schemes launched under the auspices of the Bureau of the Budget and OMB in the past quarter century or more.[23] As of 1 January 1977, the political process once again registers the management of government as a problem, rather than implementing a solution as the problem.

Notes

1. The President's Task Force on Government Organization, *The Organization and Management of Great Society Programs* (Washington, D.C.: Executive Office of the President, unpublished typescript, June 15, 1967), p. 1.

2. Steering Group on Evaluation, *The Roles and Mission of the Bureau of the Budget* (Washington, D.C.: Bureau of the Budget Working Paper, unpublished typescript, 1967), p. 1.

3. Cf. "Even paranoids may have real enemies," a comment quoted and evidenced by survey findings of Joel D. Aberbach and Bert A. Rockman, "Clashing Beliefs within the Executive Branch: The Nixon Administration Bureaucracy," *The American Political Science Review* vol. 70, no. 2 (June 1976), p. 467.

4. Cf. Richard Nathan, *The Plot that Failed: Nixon and the Administrative Presidency* (New York: John Wiley & Sons, 1975).

5. Quoted in Thomas R. Mullaney, "OMB Pushes Plans to Improve Federal Management: Still no Miracles," *National Journal Reports* vol. 2, no. 49 (December 4, 1971), p. 2378.

6. Jeffrey L. Pressman and Aaron B. Wildavsky, *Implementation* (Berkeley & Los Angeles: University of California Press, 1973), p. 143. The au-

thors appear at pp. xiv–xv to build evaluation into their definition of implementation. The definition given above, by contrast, treats implementation as an independent variable whose impact may or may not be positively evaluated.

7. *Ibid.,* p. xv. Cf. the case that Wildavsky has previously argued against the possibility of anticipating problems: "If Planning is Everything. Maybe It's Nothing," *Policy Sciences* vol. 4, no. 2 (1973), pp. 127–153.

8. For examples, see three articles in the MBO Symposium of *Public Administration Review,* vol. 36, no.1 (January/February 1976), pp. 1–45; Jong S. Jun, "Introduction"; Peter F. Drucker, "What Results Should You Expect? A Users' Guide to MBO"; and George S. Odiorne, "MBO in State Government."

9. Pressman and Wildavsky describe a federal program that succeeded in spending only $3 million of $23 million in authorized funds. This is not typically the case in the federal government, and thus vitiates simple generalization from their study.

10. The fullest study of the implementation of MBO can be found in Richard Rose, *Managing Presidential Objectives* (New York: The Free Press, 1976), chaps. 4–9. See also papers in the symposia published by *The Bureaucrat* vol. 2, no. 4 (Winter 1974), pp. 351–426, and *Public Administration Review* vol. 36, no. 1 (January/February 1976), pp. 1–45.

11. Roy Ash, "Good Management a Prized Commodity," *Civil Service Journal* (October–December 1973), p. 2.

12. Contrast the approach set out by Joseph S. Wholey, Joe N. Nay, John W. Scanlon, and Richard E. Schmidt, "If You Don't Care Where You Get To, Then It Doesn't Matter Which Way You Go," in Gene M. Lyons (ed.), *Social Research and Public Policies: The Dartmouth/OECD Conference* (Hanover, N.H.: Dartmouth College Public Affairs Center, 1975), pp. 175–197.

13. Rose, pp. 92, 125.

14. *Ibid.,* pp. 141ff. The study of "MBO in State Government" by George S. Odiorne indicates that there, too, MBO objectives tend to be apolitical.

15. By contrast, the Pressman and Wildavsky approach stipulates that the outcome is either a success in terms of originally hypothesized intentions, or a failure in such terms, thus confounding implementation with program evaluation.

16. Harry S. Havens, "MBO and Program Evaluation, or Whatever Happened to PPBS?" *Public Administration Review* vol. 36, no. 1 (January/February 1976), p. 43. See also Arnold J. Meltsner, *Policy Analysts in the Bureaucracy* (Berkeley and Los Angeles: University of California Press, 1976).

17. See the articles cited in footnote 8.

18. Compare the views of Rodney H. Brady, "MBO Goes to Work in the Public Sector," *Harvard Business Review* vol. 51, no. 2 (March–April 1973), pp. 65–74, and Robert H. Marik and Thomas S. McFee, "The Management Conference: Key to HEW's MBO System," *The Bureaucrat* vol. 2, no. 4 (Winter 1974), pp. 378–384, with the two-part case study of the same department's program, *Case Studies of MBO in HEW* (Cambridge, Mass.: Harvard Business School, 1972).

19. Rose, chap. 9.

20. The 1976 PAR symposium illustrates this conflict clearly, in the prescriptive optimism pervading articles by Jong S. Jun, Peter F. Drucker, and George S. Odiorne, as against the empirical realism of Frank P. Sherwood and Willaim M. Page, Jr., Chester A. Newland, and Harry S. Havens.

21. Cf. Joel Havemann, "Congress Tries to Break Ground Zero in Evaluating Federal Programs," *National Journal Reports* vol. 8, no. 21 (May 22, 1976), pp. 706–713, and Carol H. Weiss, *Evaluation Research* (Englewood Cliffs, N.J.: Prentice-Hall, 1972).

22. *Management Initiatives*, Memorandum to the Director, Office of Management and Budget, from the President, July 24, 1976, p. 1.

23. Cf. Harold Smith, *The Management of Your Government* (New York: McGraw-Hill, 1945); Marver H. Bernstein, "The Presidency and Management Improvement," *Law and Contemporary Problems* vol. 35, no. 3 (Summer 1970), pp. 505–518; and Ralph C. Bledsoe, "MBO and Federal Management: A Retrospective," *The Bureaucrat* vol. 2, no. 4 (Winter 1974), pp. 395–410.

The Road from ZBB

Allen Schick

The first president to promise a zero-base budget has delivered the most incremental financial statement since Wildavsky canonized that form of budget-making more than a dozen years ago. The fiscal 1979 budget (unveiled on January 23, 1978) hardly terminates or curtails anything of significance, continues most spending at inflation-adjusted levels, and offers few program initiatives. It projects an expenditure growth of $40 billion, all but $8 billion of which—2% of the budget total—is due to mandatory inflation and workload increases. Even this 2% overstates the amount of discretion exercised by the nation's number one budgetmaker. OMB's current service estimates assume no inflation adjustment for entitlement programs (such as veterans' benefits) which are not linked by formula to the cost of living, or for grant-in-aid programs which do not have spending increases already scheduled in law. When inflation is added for these two categories, there appears to have been almost no exercise of presidential power. Virtually every function, subfunction, and major program is funded at or slightly above its current service level. The small number of program reductions sprinkled throughout the budget certainly are not due to zero-base technology. There are fewer such reductions than in any previous 1970s budget, though this was the first one graced by the new waste-purging methods. The fiscal 1979 budget comes out just about where disembodied incrementalism would tend to.

There is a compelling political explanation for this budgetary standoff. Committed to fiscal prudence and still cherishing budgetary

Reprinted the *Public Administration Review*, vol. 38, no. 2 (March–April 1978). © 1978 by The American Society for Public Administration, 1225 Connecticut Avenue, N.W., Washington, D.C. All rights reserved. By permission of author and publisher.

balance at the end of his first term, President Carter could not afford costly program starts. But, confronted with demands for more spending in behalf of Democratic programs, the President could not try to do what his Republican predecessors (Ford and Nixon) had failed to accomplish. So the budget neither gives nor takes; it simply holds the line.

The budget is properly restrained in its claims for ZBB. The President's message states that he

> "used zero-base budget alternatives and agency rankings to compare and evaluate the many requests competing for resources. As a result of the first year's effort, we have gained a better understanding of federal programs and have made better, more even-handed judgments. Because of this system the budget includes dollar savings and improvements in the way programs are operated."

The statement concludes with the expectation that "with experience, zero-based budgeting should be even more effective in future years." These last words suggest the need for caution in appraising ZBB's first year. After all, a president who earnestly believes in the efficacy of this technique is likely to have at least three more opportunities to remake the federal budget in its image. If ZBB fails, it will not be for want of presidential support.

The Successes of ZBB

By one vital measure, ZBB was a remarkable success. The new system was speedily installed throughout the federal bureaucracy. Within months after issuance of OMB's instructions (Bulletin No. 77-9, April 19, 1977), agencies were ranking their decision packages and submitting the required documents. On cue, thousands of federal managers cast their budgets in the prescribed format, producing schedules of expenditures below, at, and above the current level. This fidelity to the techniques of ZBB belies the caricature of federal employees as foot-dragging—"we'll be here when he isn't"—subversives who instinctively resist all calls for change. The submissions which flooded OMB in the summer and fall of 1977 had the unmistakable mark of zero-base budgeting on them.

Even more astounding, ZBB was much more than an ancillary submission, merely supplementing the standard budget documents which continued to receive the lion's share of attention. The core budget estimates submitted by most federal agencies conformed to the ZBB guidelines. Unlike the planning-programming-budgeting (PPB) and management by objectives (MBO) debacles, ZBB was not divorced from the basic process of preparing agency budgets. No separate staffs were organized; ZBB was entrusted to the same offices responsible for year-round budget work. Nor was ZBB cordoned off in a separate process; the zero-based requests were formulated according to the same timetable and guidelines applicable to the basic budget estimates.

This rapid penetration of budgetary practice betrays ZBB's superficiality. ZBB could be speedily installed because it did not really change the rules by which budgetary decisions are made. It changed the terminology of budgeting, but little more. It certainly did not alter the two things that matter most in budgetary technique: the data used for making program and financial decisions and the form in which the data are classified. To have attempted either would have meant a difficult and protracted period of adjustment. It couldn't be done overnight. Even in the best of circumstances—where there is little disagreement as to the types of information that should be gathered—it takes time to implant a new data base within an on-going organization. The same federal agencies which converted instantly to ZBB went through years of negotiation, trial and error, and confusion during the 1960s and 1970s when they tried to introduce management information systems.

It can be even more difficult and painful to modify the manner in which the data are classified. Unless the new classification is mere window dressing—"for information only"—and not the decisional structure, the various parties involved in budgeting will want to assure that the proposed arrangement will not disadvantage their interests. They will fight over the appropriate budget classification much as PPBers fought a decade ago over the ideal program structure. The issue is important because an agency can have only one decision structure for budgeting. It can display budgetary data in a multiplicity of formats, but it can use only one of the classifications for deciding the budget.

ZBB was introduced quickly and painlessly because it did not alter either "the rules of evidence" for budgeting or the structure for budget choices. There is not a single bit of budgetary data unique to ZBB. Nowhere do the OMB guidelines command agencies to gather information (other than ranking scores) not already used in budgeting. Nor do the guidelines require agencies to abandon their existing decisional structures. With ZBB, the best clue to an agency's budget practices is the system it had immediately prior to ZBB's advent. Agency after agency accommodated ZBB to its existing budgetary framework. If an agency had a program budget, it selected programs as decision units; if its budget still was oriented to organizational lines, these became its ZBB categories.

This permissive approach was endorsed by OMB's April 1977 guidelines. The implicit but clear message was "anything goes" provided that agencies use the official nomenclature. As long as they have something labeled "decision units," it doesn't matter what the units consist of. Thus OMB defined a decision unit as "the program or organizational unit for which budgets are prepared." Furthermore, OMB advised that each decision unit should, "to the extent possible, reflect existing program and organizational structures that have accounting support." In other words, if the unit is already used for budgeting, it is qualified to be a decision unit. Agencies were told to select units that "are not so low in the structure as to result in excessive paperwork and review. On the other hand, the units selected should not be so high as to mask important considerations and prevent meaningful review of the work being performed." As things turned out, federal agencies ranged from the global to the specific. Some had handfuls of decision units; some had hundreds. Some drove the ZBB process down to discrete cost centers; some lumped them into board categories equivalent to their appropriation accounts.

After identifying their decision units, agencies went through the motions of preparing decision packages, beginning (for most agencies) at a level below current spending and (for most) including at least some packages with proposed increases in expenditures. OMB guidelines, however, drained these packages of genuine decisional utility. In a (largely successful) effort to avoid a predicted paper deluge, OMB cautioned agencies to restrict each decision package to no more than two pages, permitting, however, backup material in supplementary documents. The two-page limit, however, signaled agencies that they didn't have to stuff their packages with analytic content. Bereft of program and performance data associated with alternative levels of expenditure, the decision packages merely indicated that spending can be set at various levels. Only when one compares the prospective outputs of the different levels can one have an *informed* basis for deciding an agency's budget. Otherwise, decision packaging becomes a mechanical exercise or a new routine for budgetary gamesmen.

After the packages have been filled with budgetary data, they must be ranked in numerical order by program managers and agency officials. Unfortunately, more ingenuity has been invested in ranking schemes than in any other ZBB activity. Psychological scaling, weighted voting rules, survey techniques, delphi, just about every voting method devised for human use has been deployed in the service of ZBB. But ranking itself makes little sense, though it affords a wonderful opportunity to wrap budget outcomes in the pseudo-objectivity of numbers. It conveys an appearance of rationality, but it is much less rational than budgetary practices in which priorities are veiled. Under ranking requirements, agencies are compelled to establish preferences independent of sure knowledge as to the funds that will be forthcoming. I doubt that a single fiscal 1979 decision was made by blind fidelity to the rankings on a ZBB list.

ZBB as Managerial Budgeting

If it does not change either the data or the structure of budgeting, how does ZBB expect to alter budgetary outcomes? The answer has less to do with budgeting below the base than with the involvement of program managers in the annual budget process. If all ZBB tried to do was to get agencies to submit budgets below the current level, the technical apparatus would not be needed. All that would be necessary would be a firm rule that each budget be accompanied by a set of estimates below current spending.

Virtually all of the writing on ZBB has focused on its techniques, as if ZBB was nothing more than a different way of preparing budgets. The literature is predominantly "how to do it," taking the bewildered reader step-by-step through the ZBB ropes. There is hardly a word about the purposes or theoretical roots of this new system.

Conceptual silence has been a boon in the implementation of ZBB. Precisely because it appears to exhaust itself in technique, ZBB can be engineered to suit any budgetary approach. As noted, the decision units can be arranged along program or organizational lines without worrying whether the purposes of ZBB are being advanced or impaired. ZBB is predicated on the notion that managers should be involved in preparing budgets for their programs. The very first objective attributed to ZBB in the 1977 guidelines was to "involve program managers at all levels in the budget process." By this test, OMB declared in the 1979 budget, "the results of the first year effort have been encouraging. Program managers were more directly involved in preparing initial budget requests. In ZBB, managerial participation is a self-sufficient measure of success, independent of the substantive results which flow from it."

The drive to engage program officials in budgeting runs counter to the trend of federal administration since the arrival of executive budgeting more than half a century ago. There has been a progressive withdrawal of program officials from all phases of budget work. Most of the busywork of budget preparation and execution now is performed by specialized staffs, especially in large governments and agencies. Even though agency officials review and have formal responsibility for their budgets, they normally are not engaged in the details of preparation.

There are two main reasons for ZBB's strong insistence on managerial participation. The first arises out of the conviction that managers cannot genuinely take responsibility for programs unless they make financial decisions. In order for a manager really to be in charge of a program and its finances, he must invest time and attention in making the budget decisions for it. Only managers truly can express a program's priorities. Secondly, ZBB is grounded on the assumption that if managers behave inefficiently it is because they have not been given adequate incentives and opportunities to opt for more efficient operations. The budget process conventionally confronts managers with the uncomfortable risk of a loss of funds if they try to purge inefficiencies from their agencies. By taking the incremental way out, that is, by according preferred treatment to expenditures decided in past budgets, managers can pursue program objectives by seeking budget increases without eliminating wasteful practices. ZBB aims to overcome this predicament by compelling managers to submit non-incremental budgets and enabling them to propose the terms under which their budgets are reviewed at all stages of administrative consideration. In pure ZBB, that is, in ZBB strictly oriented to managerial efficiency, the budget as submitted by the manager—a person in the bowels of the organization responsible for getting a job done and spending public funds—retains its identity throughout the budget process. The manager decides which should be packaged at each level of decision, and his basic priority cannot be overriden by program superiors. If a manager's minimal decision package calls for replacing an existing activity with a new one, the proposed expenditure must be accorded priority over the older one. That is, the budget can provide funds for the existing activity only if it also funds the new expenditure.

This was the version of ZBB used in Georgia, but it led to the production of thousands of decision packages. The scale and sprawl of the federal government precludes a pure managerial approach; the number of such packages surely would run into the tens of thousands if they were prepared for each "cost" or "responsibility" center in the federal government. Accordingly, OMB permitted agencies to submit "consolidated" decision packages which obliterate program identities and the priorities of lower-level managers:

. . . higher level management's decision-making needs may better be met by recasting all or some of the initial decision packages into a lesser number of consolidated decision packages. The consolidated packages would be used upon the more detailed information in the initial packages, but the information would be recast or reinterpreted in a broader frame of reference to focus on significant program alternatives or issues. The objectives may be redefined to reflect the higher-level manager's program perspective.

This statement is nothing less than license to abandon the managerial purposes of ZBB. But rather than bemoan this deviation from ZBB's original concept, it offers some hope that this system might yet be applied to significant program issues. Evidence from state and local ZBB experiences suggest that the managerial system does generate expenditure shifts within budgets, but it does not lead to any basic reexamination of programs. In other words, ZBB can facilitate the search for more efficient operational methods; it is not likely, however, to encourage agencies to reexamine their programs and objectives. But by tolerating "anything goes" adaptations, the federal guidelines have permitted agencies to devise programmatic ZBB systems in which managerial efficiency is subordinated by PPB-type issues.

The Limits of ZBB

There can be little doubt that ZBB has generated worthwhile managerial efficiencies in federal agencies. For outsiders, these are apt to be unexciting matters, not reflected in the overall trend lines of the budget. But for persons affected by the changes, they can be as momentous and disruptive as the budget innovations which make the headlines. Without dismissing the value of these efficiency improvements—in a budget the size of the federal government's, they can add up to billions of dollars in savings—one must question whether that is the most productive use to which the federal budget process can be applied. A preoccupation with the routines of operation drives out a consideration of program objectives and effectiveness. As much as one might want a budget process which equally attends to the diverse objectives of budgeting, choices have to be made. An agency cannot devote itself to the managerial routines of ZBB while deploying its budget process for program planning and analysis.

Nor can an agency productively search for significant efficiencies each year. The 1979 budget looks for "greater benefits next year as the federal government realizes the full potential of zero-base budgeting." Judging from state experiences, however, one may question whether a recurring search for efficiency will be of much value. After a couple of years of preparing minimum packages, the ZBB process itself becomes routinized. While it might be possible to "cream off" savings in the first year or two, ultimately ZBB will have to move to more fundamental program issues if it is to have much staying power.

The President's 1979 budget offers perhaps the most telling indication of ZBB's limitations. It announces a major effort to stretch the time horizon of federal budgeting to a multi-year framework, arguing that with one-year-at-a-time budgeting, "the budget was difficult to control and changes in the allocation of resources difficult to make." These difficulties cannot be mitigated by dedication to the principles and techniques of zero-base budgeting. No matter how thoroughly program managers scour their operations for savings, the year-to-year changes in the budget are driven by policies over which control can be secured only through non-budgetary actions. With ZBB, upwards of 75% of the budget will continue to be uncontrollable under existing law; upwards of 95% will continue to be de facto uncontrollable. The budget sensibly recognizes the need for a long-range budget process in order to cope with these fundamental issues. Although it does not abandon ZBB, it seems to give priority to an earlier type of budget reform. For budget watchers who have seen a parade of innovations and fashions over the past thirty years, the road from ZBB might lead back to PPB.

Appendixes

Appendix 1:
Example of a Functional Budget
[in billions of dollars]

Outlays	1978	1979	1980	1981
National defense	112.9	121.5	132.3	142.8
International affairs	7.8	7.8	8.1	8.0
General science space and technology	4.6	4.5	4.4	4.1
Natural resources, environment and energy	14.4	15.1	14.9	14.5
Agriculture	2.6	2.6	2.8	2.8
Commerce and transportation	19.4	19.1	18.7	18.7
Community and regional development	6.0	6.2	6.0	6.1
Education, training, employment and social services	15.3	15.3	15.3	15.3
Health	37.7	40.3	43.4	47.0
Income security	147.1	158.3	170.1	182.9
Veterans benefits and services	17.2	16.7	16.3	15.7
Law enforcement and justice	3.3	3.3	3.3	3.3
General government	3.9	3.6	3.6	3.7
Revenue sharing and general purpose fiscal assistance	7.7	7.9	8.0	8.2
Interest	44.8	46.5	46.9	46.9
Allowances	5.6	8.1	10.5	12.8
Undistributed offsetting receipts	−20.7	−21.4	−22.1	−22.9
Total	429.5	455.7	482.5	509.9

Source: "Projected Outlays by Function, 1977–1982," *The United States Budget in Brief, Fiscal Year 1977* (Washington, D.C.: U.S. Government Printing Office, 1976), p. 20.

Appendix 2:
Example of an Object Classification Budget, Federal Agency X

	Previous Fiscal Year	Current Fiscal Year	Future Fiscal Year
Direct obligations			
Personnel compensation:			
11.1 Permanent positions	188,453	203,377	204,982
11.3 Positions other than permanent	12,188	12,990	13,227
11.5 Other personnel compensation	11,405	12,156	12,426
Total personnel compensation	212,046	228,523	230,635
12.1 Personnel benefits: Civilian	22,959	25,325	26,800
13.0 Benefits for former personnel	1,989	2,403	2,668
21.0 Travel and transportation of persons	7,438	8.103	9,723
22.0 Transportation of things	2,721	3,165	3,257
23.0 Rent, communications, and utilities	36,923	41,678	42,794
24.0 Printing and reproduction	1,841	1,787	2,517
25.0 Other services	81,798	104,970	127,535
26.0 Supplies and materials	21,673	24,301	27,351
31.0 Equipment	29,356	42,579	36,809
32.0 Lands and structures	429	438	615
41.0 Grants, subsidies, and contributions	30,257	32,161	31,891
42.0 Insurance claims and indemnities	16	16	16
Subtotal	449,446	515,449	542,611
95.0 Quarters and subsistence	−703	−703	−703
Total direct obligations	448,743	514,746	541,908

Reimbursable obligations:
  Personnel compensation:

11.1 Permanent positions	13,696	14,432	14,316
11.3 Positions other than permanent	1,186	1,488	2,515
11.5 Other personnel compensation	827	640	640
Total personnel compensation	15,709	16,560	17,471
12.1 Personnel benefits: Civilian	1,619	1,452	1,499
13.0 Benefits for former personnel	8	8	8
21.0 Travel and transportation of persons	1,465	2,153	2,153
22.0 Transportation of things	297	866	866
23.0 Rent, communications, and utilities	3,419	3,971	3,971
24.0 Printing and reproduction	187	300	300
25.0 Other services	14,861	28,081	27,123
26.0 Supplies and materials	3,996	5,545	5,545
31.0 Equipment	2,401	1,563	1,563
41.0 Grants, subsidies, and contributions	37	320	320
Total reimbursable obligations	43,999	60,819	60,819
99.0 Total obligations	492,742	575,565	502,727

Source: "National Oceanic and Atmospheric Administration," *The Budget of the United States Government, Fiscal Year 1977, Appendix* (Washington, D.C.: Government Printing Office, 1976), p. 213.

Appendix 3:
Example of an Activity Budget, Federal Agency X

	Previous Fiscal Year	Current Fiscal Year	Future Fiscal Year
Program by activities:			
Direct program:			
Operating costs:			
1. Mapping, charting, and surveying services	32,386	35,082	35,949
2. Ship support services	32,727	39,922	42,596
3. Ocean fisheries and living marine resources	52,794	58,281	62,693
4. Marine ecosystems analysis and ocean dumping	5,929	9,561	7,295
5. Marine technology	3,072	3,981	4,663
6. Sea grant	23,028	23,149	23,214
7. Basic environmental services	104,041	107,779	111,114
8. Environmental satellite services	64,559	66,407	89,669
9. Public forecast and warning services	51,351	60,132	60,333
10. Specialized environmental services	31,704	31,709	32,722
11. Environmental data and information services	12,707	14,710	15,250
12. Global monitoring of climatic change	1,571	1,747	1,826

13. Weather modification	4,468	4,138	4,837
14. International projects	9,672	8,628	8,692
15. Retired pay, commissioned officers	1,781	2,317	2,544
16. Executive direction and administration	21,991	24,190	25,246
17. Construction	—	1,000	970
Total operating costs	453,781	492,733	529,613
Unfunded adjustments to total operating costs: Depreciation included above	−15,705	−16,000	−16,000
Deductions from retired pay	−130	−130	−140
Future cost of retired pay, commissioned officers	−1,160	−1,432	−1,661
Total operating costs, funded	436,786	475,171	511,812
Capital outlay:			
1. Mapping, charting, and surveying services	62	600	600
2. Ship support services	179	198	—
3. Ocean fisheries and living marine resources	165	500	490
7. Basic environmental services	4,096	6,704	6,557
8. Environmental satellite services	2,251	6,724	4,033
9. Public forecast and warning services	791	11,393	14,895
10. Specialized environmental services	13	—	—
12. Global monitoring of climatic change	23	—	—
13. Weather modification	157	5,488	1,528
Total capital outlay, funded	7,737	31,607	28,103
Total direct program	444,523	506,778	539,915
Reimbursable program:			
1. Mapping, charting, and surveying services	8,749	11,549	11,549
2. Ship support services	311	—	—
3. Ocean fisheries and living marine resources	3,066	7,266	7,266
4. Marine ecosystems analysis and ocean dumping	8,091	17,237	17,237

5. Marine technology	131	131	131
7. Basic environmental services	5,703	6,203	6,203
8. Environmental satellite services	3,314	3,314	3,314
9. Public forecast and warning services	3,337	3,550	3,550
10. Specialized environmental services	5,926	6,172	6,172
11. Environmental data and information services	2,584	2,584	2,584
12. Global monitoring of climatic change	398	398	398
13. Weather modification	74	100	100
16. Executive direction and administration	2,315	2,315	2,315
Total reimbursable program	43,999	60,819	60,819
Total program costs, funded	488,522	567,597	600,734
Change in selected resources (spacecraft and launching inventory and undelivered orders; plus other inventory and undelivered orders)	4,220	7,968	1,993
Total obligations	492,742	575,565	602,727

Source: "National Oceanic and Atmospheric Administration," *The Budget of the United States Government, Fiscal Year 1977, Appendix* (Washington, D.C.: U.S. Government Printing Office, 1976), p. 211.